A

Philip E. Lilienthal (signature)

■   ■   ■

B O O K

The Philip E. Lilienthal imprint
honors special books
in commemoration of a man whose work
at University of California Press from 1954 to 1979
was marked by dedication to young authors
and to high standards in the field of Asian Studies.
Friends, family, authors, and foundations have together
endowed the Lilienthal Fund, which enables UC Press
to publish under this imprint selected books
in a way that reflects the taste and judgment
of a great and beloved editor.

*The publisher gratefully acknowledges the
generous contribution to this book provided by the
Philip E. Lilienthal Asian Studies Endowment Fund
of the University of California Press Foundation,
which is supported by a major gift from
Sally Lilienthal.*

Bombay Anna

Bombay Anna

The Real Story and
Remarkable Adventures
of the *King and I* Governess

SUSAN MORGAN

UNIVERSITY OF CALIFORNIA PRESS

BERKELEY   LOS ANGELES   LONDON

University of California Press, one of the most distinguished
university presses in the United States, enriches lives around
the world by advancing scholarship in the humanities, social
sciences, and natural sciences. Its activities are supported by
the UC Press Foundation and by philanthropic contributions
from individuals and institutions. For more information, visit
www.ucpress.edu.

University of California Press
Berkeley and Los Angeles, California

Library of Congress Cataloging-in-Publication Data

Morgan, Susan.
  Bombay Anna : the real story and
remarkable adventures of the *King and I* governess /
Susan Morgan.
      p.   cm.
  Philip E. Lilienthal Asian Studies Endowment Fund
imprint
  Includes bibliographical references and index.
  ISBN: 978-0-520-25226-4 (cloth : alk. paper)
  1. Leonowens, Anna Harriette, 1831-1915.
2. Governesses—Thailand—Biography.
3. British—Thailand—Biography. 4. Thailand—Social life
and customs—19th century. 5. Women authors—
Biography. 6. Women journalists—Biography.
7. Women travelers—Biography. 8. Montréal (Québec)—
Biography. 9. Halifax (N.S.)—Biography.
10. Racially mixed people—India—Biography. I. Title.

DS578.32.L44M67   2008
959.3′034092—dc22   2007044084

Manufactured in the United States of America

17 16 15 14 13 12 11 10 09 08
11 10 9 8 7 6 5 4 3 2 1

For Eric Goodman,
In the transit lounge

I have to cast my lot with those
who age after age, perversely with no
extraordinary power, reconstitute the world.

ADRIENNE RICH

CONTENTS

ILLUSTRATIONS

PREFACE

I first read Anna Leonowens's 1873 *The Romance of the Harem* in 1982, shortly before my first visit to Thailand. I came across the book while browsing through the stacks in the Echols Collection at Cornell University. I remember my astonishment and delight at reading it. It is a preposterous book, a collection of interwoven stories really, extreme in content and style, and wildly sentimental. My tastes are generally quite otherwise; the writer I most admire is Jane Austen. Yet I found *The Romance* full of passion and interest. And, clearly, not quite true. It is not a novel. I can fall back on memoir as its genre, though the narrative's focus is not on Anna but on other women. Is it fictionalized fact or factualized fiction? This unsettling yet stimulating book comes closest to nineteenth-century American "romance."

Eager to bring the book back in print, and thus to encourage other readers to find ways to approach it, in 1991 I edited a paperback edition of *The Romance of the Harem,* published by the University Press of Virginia in its Victorian Literature and Culture series. During the process of preparing that edition, I discovered just how little was known about Anna Leonowens. There were contemporaneous reviews of her three books; those in the United States typically positive (the *New York Times,* in February 14, 1873, found that "this tropical book disarms criticism"), while the English reviews were generally more hostile (the *Athenaeum* found it full of "inexcusable error"). But the reviews did not address her life. Then in 1944 Anna burst onto the stage of twentieth-century American culture as the real-life heroine of Margaret Landon's *Anna and the King of Siam.* The rest, as they say, is media history.

Landon's book and its many adaptations, including one of the major icons of the American musical, *The King and I,* have stood for the past sixty years as a sort of biography of Leonowens. Most of the material that it was based on was invented, in part because so little material was actually available, Anna having done her best to conceal the facts of her life. In particular, Anna's life before taking the position at the Royal Court of Siam was positively mysterious. Landon's laudatory book is full of conversations and private scenes that were made up. Landon was explicit in acknowledging that her narrative of Anna was fictionalized. She also noted that she had done extensive original research but, unfortunately, never specified what was fact and what was fiction, never described what information she had found, and offered no citations. Moreover, as published, Landon's book narrated only Anna's years in Siam.

Landon's representation of Anna stood until 1976, when W. S. Bristowe published his account of Anna's son, Louis Leonowens. Bristowe seconded the "disbelief in [Anna's] historical integrity" (23) expressed by A. B. Griswold in a 1957 article and more fully in his 1961 book, *King Mongkut of Siam*, when he strongly challenged Anna's representations of palace life. Bristowe went further and discredited Anna's representation of her own life. The brief second chapter of *Louis and the King of Siam*, "Anna Unveiled," published for the first time Anna's real maiden name, birthplace, and birthdate (though the rest of his short sketch of her life is mostly inaccurate). Bristowe's handful of facts cast doubt on what we "knew" about Anna and showed that the published versions of her life, including even the *New York Times* obituary, were wrong.

Arguably, there has never been a biography of Anna Leonowens. Since 1976 there have been pieces. A notable contribution was made in 1991 by Leslie Smith Dow, who offered new material about Anna's later years in Canada in *Anna Leonowens: A Life beyond* The King and I. In 1993, Lois Yorke provided a short but useful entry in the *Dictionary of Canadian Biography*. After that I go to Cecilia Holland's 1999 *The Story of Anna and the King*, a beautiful book of photographs of the making of the latest Anna movie, with Jodie Foster and Chow Yun-Fat. The book is worth mentioning because Holland wrote the text accompanying the photographs and contributes some fascinating historical details about army life in India and at the Royal Court of Siam.

During the summer of 1994, I happened to see an obituary of Margaret Landon and through it located her youngest son. I had been wondering about her papers for years, since she claimed in her preface to have based her biography on papers provided by Anna's family. Landon's son told me that all Landon's material, including many nineteenth-century manuscript materials by and about Leonowens, had just been donated to Ken and Margaret Landon's alma mater, Wheaton College. The Margaret and Kenneth Landon Collection (cited as LC in the text) contains more than two dozen boxes, including photographs, Anna's granddaughter's fascinating draft of a biography of her grandmother, complete with letters between Anna and her children and between Anna and the king of Siam, and articles and stories Anna wrote while in the United States and Canada. Its materials include Ken Landon's papers as well as the publication history of *Anna and the King of Siam,* many reviews, and two decades of letters to Margaret Landon after her book had been published, offering additional bits of information.

I had been interested in Anna Leonowens prior to locating the Landon papers, but now I was utterly fascinated. The Landon papers offered an abundance of material, even though they contained little reliable information on Anna's life and family in India—Margaret apparently to a great extent believing Anna's invented autobiography. Still, I owe a major debt to Margaret Landon. The richness of the Landon Collection made this biography possible. I began searching seriously for the facts of Anna's history and life and have now been researching Anna across several continents and for well over a decade. That research project has shaped much of my professional and personal life. And along the way I began to understand just how extraordinary Anna was.

In addition to the Landon materials, I have relied on two other impressively rich sources of primary materials for this biography. The Fields Collection in the Huntington Library in San Marino, California (cited as F in the text), has more than four decades' worth of information about Anna's later life, in the form of original letters from Anna to Annie Fields (the wife of James Fields, the editor of the *Atlantic Monthly* and Anna's first publisher). My other invaluable source has been the British East India Company Collections at the Oriental and India Office Library (recently subsumed under and renamed as the Asia, Pacific, and Africa Collections) in the British Library. It was there that, while searching fruitlessly for some evidence of Anna's ancestors in Bombay (not accepting the "Glasscock" connection offered by Bristowe and others), I became desperate enough to read all the records for several decades of company soldiers who died intestate and stumbled across the response to Reverend Cradock Glascott's inquiry into his deceased son's finances. I had found Anna's British family at last.

Along with these three sources, I have found crucial information about Anna, her family, and her life in many other places. These include Penang, Malaysia; Bangkok and Chiengmai, Thailand; Singapore; Devon, England; Mumbai and Pune, India; Perth, Australia; the McFarland Collection at the University of California, Berkeley; and, of course, the Kroch Library at Cornell University, Ithaca, New York.

Bombay Anna solves many of the mysteries surrounding Anna's life that have eluded searchers for years. It uncovers the history of Anna's immediate ancestors and relatives, as well as many of Anna's own locations and activities. Based a great deal on heretofore unpublished and undiscovered materials, and covering all of Anna's life, it makes a claim to be the first published biography from extensive primary sources of this Victorian woman who has become an icon of American culture. This biography also offers a view of a particularly fascinating and formidable woman, one whose brilliance, unique achievements, and sheer creative daring fashioned a life that looks as rare and admirable today as it must have in the times in which she lived.

ACKNOWLEDGMENTS

I have done research for this biography for more than a decade, and in that time have been helped in significant and often essential ways by many more people than I can name in this space. My first debt must be to the organizations whose financial support made this research possible. My thanks particularly go to the John Simon Guggenheim Foundation for a year of support in which I learned about the British East India Company and wrote a draft of the biography. I am also profoundly grateful to my professional home, Miami University of Ohio, for their generous and continuous financial support. They have been extraordinary in their belief in this project, their commitment to the research, and their willingness over several years to help me fund the costs of searching for Anna's hidden tracks. My support at Miami has come from a variety of sources, most notably the English Department, the Miami University Distinguished Professor research fund, the College of Arts and Sciences Assigned Research Appointment, the College of Arts and Sciences Summer Research Appointment, the International Studies Program, and the Philip and Elaine Hampton Fund.

My second debt is to all the research library staff in so many places who listened to my often vague questions, typically formulated better ones, and then spent hours and often days and weeks lending their superb knowledge of their holdings to the task of guiding my search for evidence that might or might not be there. I am deeply grateful to the staffs of the Record Office in Devon, England, the Elphinstone College newspaper collection in Mumbai, the Hayes Library in Bangkok, the Chulalongkorn University Special Collections in Bangkok, the National Library in Singapore, the National Records Office in Penang, the Kroch Library at Cornell University in Ithaca, New York, and the South/Southeast Asia Collection at the University of California, Berkeley. I am particularly grateful to three librarians. I thank David Malone, head of Archives and Special Collections, and David Osielski, reference archivist, Special Collections, at the Buswell Memorial Library at Wheaton College in Wheaton, Illinois. Last, I thank the incomparable and indefatigable Tim Thomas, reference specialist and researcher extraordinaire, at the Oriental and India Office Library, now the Asia, Pacific, and Africa Collections, at the British Library, London.

My third debt is to the many dear friends and colleagues who encouraged and contributed to this project. My beloved colleagues in Interdisciplinary Nineteenth-Century Studies, Teresa Mangum, Deborah Morse, Anca Vlasopolis, and Richard Stein, have been unfailing in their attentiveness, productive evaluations, and general support. In my own department I have been blessed with the support of Jackie Kearns and the perceptive advice and encouragement of Mary Jean Corbett, Kate Ronald, and Barry Chabot. I am the grateful recipient of genealogical research on the Owens and Wilkinson families, generously provided in private correspondence by Tim Wilkinson and Sue Collins. I particularly thank Fran Dolan, who continually understood the project more insightfully than I and so generously gave me the critical tools to see what she saw. Finally, I offer my gratitude to Ethan and Seneca Goodman, who accepted for most of their growing up that the best vacations were spent in the hotels and libraries of Southeast Asia. My greatest debt is to Eric Goodman, who supported the project before I did and participated in the pursuit of Anna all along the way.

ONE

Introduction

A Life of Passing

ON JUNE 25, 1859, a woman with two young children stepped off a steamship onto the dock of Singapore, island city and British colony at the tip of the Malay Peninsula. The family was arriving from the small island of Penang in the British Straits Settlements, a convenient port up along the northwest coast of the peninsula. The woman was no one important or famous, just a woman, a nobody. She was one minor member of that vast underclass of traveling Victorians outside Britain who are now almost impossible to trace. Their personal histories have vanished because neither their genealogy nor their activities were of high enough status to be more than randomly recorded. But, quite by accident, this particular unimportant woman's arrival in Singapore was recorded in the weekly newspaper shipping news, which listed passenger arrivals at the port of Singapore.

At the moment Anna Leonowens disembarked, she reinvented herself. She simply made up a new "history" of her origins and identity, a new biography. Never discovered, never unmasked, Anna went on to perform that new identity for the rest of her life, actually becoming the character she had made. On the basis of her self-invention, Anna led a wildly adventurous and influential life. A world traveler, she became a well-known travel writer and public lecturer at a time when most women stayed home. She remains the one and only foreigner to spend years inside the royal harem of Siam. She crossed all of Russia on her own just before the revolution. She emigrated to the United States, mingling with the rich and famous, the literary, and political abolitionists in the Northeast, and in her seventies settled down to raise eight children. Hers was a vigorous, intense, and inspiring life.

But Anna's extraordinary achievements are not why most of us know about her. Anna was reinvented not once but twice, the second time by a woman living in the twentieth century. Anna's arrival in Singapore that June day would turn out to be not only the beginning of a new life for her but also an originary moment in American culture and history. Her influence on American culture and international politics has been profound. The second rebirth of this forgotten woman created for American audiences a powerful public myth. Anna's first metamorphosis shaped the personal fates of Anna and her descendants. Her second, at the hands of Margaret Landon and Hollywood, played a part in shaping the fate of nations as well.

Anna's personal history challenges our notions of biography as well as our notions of identity. First, is her life significant to us now only because of the fantasy idol twentieth-century America made of it? Clearly, the very existence of this book suggests that the answer is no. Perhaps my main point in writing this biography is to present to my audience a woman who was extraordinary in her own right. Anna's story is about the always courageous and often downright fabulous experiences of a woman who, whatever her flaws, knew how to live.

Second, how do I tell the life story of a person who stepped off a boat, erased her past, and reinvented herself? Do I simply label that created self a lie and search behind the creation for the "real" person, the "truth," measured by resurrecting the buried facts of an abandoned identity? The problem with that is that Anna's inventions, her lies if you will, were the foundation for her successes. We understand this quite well in America. After all, do we want to claim that the "real" Cary Grant was actually Archibald Leach all along, or that Bob Dylan inevitably remains Bobby Zimmerman? Do we, in other words, raise as sacred the identity narrative that exalts origins, beginnings, the shaping domestic truths of parents, childhood, and domestic life?

Life is too complicated, and identity too often in dynamic motion, to narrate the story of a life as no more than an act of factual revelation. Biography is not exposé; it is more than a journey in search of the facts. Which is not to say that we can simply invent who we are, and that is the story to tell. I do offer the hidden facts of Anna's background and activities. But I use those historical facts in the service of exploring what to make of Anna's tossing facts aside in her reinvention of herself. For the truth is that we all invent and reinvent ourselves, just as we all stand within historical contexts that bind and limit us. As RuPaul put it so unforgettably in 2000, "We are born naked. The rest is drag." In the play between the two poles of a predetermined and a chosen identity, the differences between us may simply be that some lives look more extreme than others. One of those extreme lives was that of Anna Leonowens.

It is hard to know which is the more bizarre, Anna's life or the twentieth-century version of it with which most of us are familiar. It has been even harder to find out how much of her account of her life is factually true. There are some things we can be sure of. Anna Leonowens was a Victorian woman, born in the extensive region of southwest India then known as the British Presidency of Bombay, who became the governess to the children of the royal harem of Siam for more than five years in the 1860s. She then moved to the United States and made her living as a writer and public lecturer, writing about life in Siam and India. When her daughter married a banker in Halifax, Anna moved to Canada to live with them and became a community activist as well as a travel writer.

Although Anna did achieve some fame during her lifetime, her major cultural influence came much later. Anna was reborn when she stepped off that dock in Singapore. She also has the rare and perhaps even unique distinction of being reborn twice, the second time in the United States thirty years after her death. Anna's resurrection in the American media has been phenomenal. Most Americans are familiar with Anna as the genteel lady governess at the Royal Court of Siam in *The King and I*. The play and the musical are one of the touchstones of twentieth-century American cultural life.

Anna was brought back from the dead by another impressive woman, but one who, in terms of her beliefs, could be described as Anna's opposite. Margaret Landon was of Scandinavian origins and a sheltered upbringing in the American Midwest, a woman of unimpeachable moral principles with the Christian rigidity of a missionary, which is what she was. While she and her husband, Kenneth, were serving as missionaries in Siam, Margaret read Anna's books and was entranced by what she saw as the heroic romance of Anna's experiences.

Years later Margaret accidentally came to meet Anna's granddaughter, Avis Fyshe, who persuaded her to take over the job of writing a memoir of her amazing grandmother. Included in the papers that Avis turned over were typed copies of a brief "autobiography" Anna had written. "All that Anna Harriette Crawford Leonowens had to say about her own birth and parentage was written out late in life for her grandchildren on eight small pages of ruled paper," said Margaret. Here was Anna's own version of Anna, written in her very own words:

> I believe that I was born in Wales, in the old homestead of an ancient Welsh family named Edwards, the youngest daughter of which, my mother, accompanied her husband, Thomas Maxwell Crawford, to India, while I was left in charge of an eminent Welsh lady, Mrs. Walpole, a distant relative of my father, to be educated in Wales.

Soon after the arrival of my parents in British India, my father was appointed aide-de-camp to Sir James Macintosh who was then in command of the British troops sent to Lahore, to quell the Sikh rebellion, where, while in the act of performing some military duty, he was cut to pieces by Sikhs who lay in wait for him. My mother married again. Her second husband with Colonel Rutherford Sutherland were my guardians and the executors of my Father's will.

At the age of fifteen I went out to my mother, who was then in Bombay with her husband, who held a prominent position in the Public Works Department. My mother was in very delicate health. Unable to endure the domestic tyranny of my stepfather, and having an independent income of my own, I travelled with some dear friends, the Reverend Mr. and Mrs. George Percy Badger, to Egypt, visited Damascus, Jerusalem, sailed down the Nile, that flows through old, hushed Egypt, and its sands like some grave, mighty thought threading an unravelled dream; ascended the First and Second Cataracts; in fact, I went to visit everything that was worth seeing, —the pyramids, Luxor, Theves, Karnak, etc., etc. On my return to Bombay in 1851 I married Thomas L. Leonowens, a British officer holding a staff appointment in the Commissariat office, which marriage my stepfather opposed with so much rancor that all correspondence between us ceased from that date.

When I was only eighteen, the death of my mother and my first baby came upon me with such terrible force that my life was despaired of, and my husband embarked with me on a sea voyage to England. But the ship 'Alibi' went on some rocks, through the carelessness of the captain, I believe, and we were rescued by another sailing vessel and taken to New South Wales. Here I buried my second baby, an infant son, and still dreadfully ill, we took a steamer for England and finally settled down at St. James's Square, London for nearly three years.

My husband's repeatedly extended leave of absence having expired, we returned with our two children to Singapore, where he was appointed. Here I commenced the study of Oriental languages with my husband under native teachers, but our life was again disturbed by the Indian Mutiny, and we suffered more than ever, not only in the heartrending calamities that befell some of my nearest relatives, and the just retribution that seemed to overtake us as a nation, but in the failure of several India banks, especially the Agra bank, in which the bulk of my fortune was deposited by the executors of my father's will. (LC, VI C, 4)

It was an amazing document, enough to stir the heart of any biographer.

Anna's little narrative was full of public as well as private history, full of those amazing events that, as Walter Cronkite used to say, "alter and illuminate our times." Those events look awfully like the romantic tropes so beloved by many Western readers. There is the dashing British officer who dies in India, "cut to pieces by Sikhs who lay in wait for him," the widow "in very delicate health," the little girl left at boarding school in Wales, not to mention a wicked stepfather, an uplifting tour of the Holy Land, a dead baby, a shipwreck, the Indian Mutiny with its "heartrending calamities," and losing a fortune because of a bank crash. Anna later added to this list of sentimental tropes her husband, another dashing British officer, falling dead at her feet after a tiger hunt.

Who could resist such a tale? Margaret Landon was enchanted by the evocative adventures and trials and courage, perhaps the more easily gulled because Anna's false tale so satisfyingly fulfilled her own fantasies of the exciting and heroic life of a white woman in nineteenth-century Siam. Margaret determined that she would flesh out this brief sketch. Using the materials from Avis, she would research and combine that information with her own extensive knowledge of Thailand and whatever she could glean about Siam in the nineteenth century. Along with Anna's own version and the historical and cultural background information Margaret amassed, she brought two other key elements to the project: her conservative Christian values and the missionary experiences that shaped both her perspective on Siam and her fantasies about the inspirational life Anna led.

The result was a dramatic narrative that recounted the adventures of a proper British lady struggling to civilize the savages in Margaret's Christian version of nineteenth-century Buddhist Siam. Her book was more or less true to the information she had, much of that taken without question from Anna's own published and unpublished writings with some added fictions of her own. Since the book was admittedly fictionalized, Margaret felt free to fill it with invented conversations, actions, and events, none of which she had historical records for; she simply projected them as plausible, given her own attitude toward Siam. The American version of Anna and, at least as important, of Siam and its people sailed unforgettably into American culture.

American audiences do not seem to tire of Margaret's Anna. Since *Anna and the King of Siam* was published in 1944, we have had multiple adaptations, including plays, nonmusical as well as musical, several movies, and even a television show. Margaret's Anna is the one whom American audiences watch and love. She tends to look a lot like Irene Dunne or Deborah Kerr or Jodi Foster. Though the official nationality of the role (but only sometimes of the actress) is "British," this Anna whom Margaret created during the terrible years of World War II is homegrown American. She is a transformed descendant of the version that Anna herself invented and presented to her family and contemporaries, a sort of younger first cousin to that proper British lady. But the two are crucially different. Whereas Anna's "British lady" stands for the most part for tolerance and cosmopolitanism and cultural inclusion, Margaret's stands firmly for Western cultural and religious superiority.

Who was Anna Leonowens? The story Anna invented and passed on through her writings and travel books was immortalized by all the standard dictionaries of biography and even Anna's obituary. This is the Anna Harriette Crawford from Wales, who stayed behind while her parents went to India, where her father died. When at age fifteen she rejoined her mother, she found a wicked stepfather as well, and married a charming officer without that stepfather's consent. Tragically widowed, but with two children born in England, the captain's lady took a job as governess to the children of the king of Siam. Sending Avis, now seven, to a boarding school in England, Anna, along with Louis, now six, sailed to Bangkok in March 1862 and worked there until the summer of 1867. When King Mongkut died unexpectedly, she immigrated to the United States, stopping in England to pick up her daughter and to leave her son in boarding school.

In 1976, W. S. Bristowe challenged Anna's and Margaret's versions, offering for the first time in print a darker version of Anna's biography. In his chapter "The True Story of Anna Leonowens," using East India Company records, Bristowe pointed out that Anna was born in India (not Wales), on November 26, 1831 (not 1834), the second child of a poor private named Edwards (not a major named Crawford), who died three months before she was born. Her mother married another soldier (a corporal, soon demoted to a private) when Anna was two months old. Bristowe claimed that Anna and her sister, Eliza, were sent back to school in England and returned to India in 1845. Anna met the thirty-year-old Rev. Mr. Badger in 1845 upon her return to India at age fourteen and went with him to the Middle East. Their trip together was, at the least, a serious impropriety. Anna then returned to India and married Thomas Owens. He died several years later, leaving her and two children. She sailed to Bangkok in March 1862. After she left Siam, this shady, melodramatic woman who "may have had what was called 'a touch of the tarbrush' in her veins" (Bristowe, 27) came to America. She made her living writing sensational and false stories about her time in Siam, crassly slandering her noble employer.

Margaret Landon's version of Anna has taken its place as the official, if romanticized, re-creation of Anna's personal history. Below it, as it were, as a shadow on its light, is the dark "factual" version that would burst the romantic bubble created by Anna and Margaret and Hollywood. Landon and

Bristowe have what I would call an argument about heroes. Landon (and Hollywood) have picked Anna, while Bristowe and many other American "experts" on Thailand have picked her employer, King Mongkut. But we should notice that each side claims the same achievements. Did Anna bring those great European cultural advances, underwear and forks, to Siam? The anti-Anna position says not so much that Siam had a great Eastern culture as that King Mongkut had already chosen to modernize, which seems always to mean Westernize, his country before Anna came along. The forks and underwear were already in place. Mongkut is the "real" hero because he had the wisdom to see that the way of the future was the way of the West.

There is no sense in being pulled into this debate. It is precisely such reductive polarities between the West as civilized/modern and the East as barbaric/backward that Anna's own life so vividly challenges and overturns. This adventurous woman, neither wholly Western nor wholly Eastern, was a complex embodiment of both East and West. She was a combination of languages, classes, races, and nationalities. Her multiple identity seems to me the defining quality of her life. The ways she understood the world, the things she did, and the perspectives from which she wrote have everything to do with what I might call her unusual biographical comprehensiveness. In fact, most people have some kind of mixed heritage. Few, and Anna is one of those few, have the perceptiveness, the openness, and the strength of imagination to embrace that heritage in all its inclusiveness, even as she lied to the world and her own family about it.

This leads to another reason why Anna's life is so compelling to a biographer: the sheer range of her experiences. Anna lived again and again in what I might call the right place at the right time. Her private history is entwined with the whole public process of the British taking India in the eighteenth and early nineteenth century. She grew up as a poor army brat in the forts of southern India and was living in Western Australia in the 1850s just when it was becoming a major convict destination, and in Singapore while it was becoming the busiest port in the world. She was in Siam during one of the key decades when it fought so successfully to keep its independence from the imperial powers. Anna witnessed slavery in Siam in the very years when the United States was engaged in a historic civil war triggered in part by the question of slavery. She was in the eastern United States during the heyday of American postbellum idealism, part of an upper-class social scene and a literary scene that included Harriet Beecher Stowe and James Fields, the editor of the hugely influential *Atlantic Monthly*. She became a visible and active feminist at the turn of the century in eastern Canada, traveled through

Russia and wrote of the coming revolution, and lived in Germany in the years shortly before World War I.

The point is not that Anna really got around, though that is certainly true. The point is that her life looks like multiple lives, spanning diverse issues, events, continents, and even centuries. From the poor outstations of British India in the early decades of the nineteenth century to the elegant universities of prewar Germany at the beginning of the twentieth is quite a reach. Anna does, with a literalness unimagined by Walt Whitman, "contain multitudes." And Anna's multiple lives mean multiple identities. There is no one Anna. I agree with Thongchai Winichakul's wry comment to Susan Kepner in 1995, that "I have a little trouble with the attempt to find the 'real' Anna" (Kepner, "Anna and the Context of Siam," 28). Appreciating the sheer inclusiveness of Anna's varied life means trading in a narrow view of biography as a matter of individual achievement for a wider vision of the historical and personal range that composes even one individual's history.

One of the most familiar first lines in the history of American musicals was sung by Judy Garland in her 1954 film, *A Star Is Born*. As Judy told it, "I was born in a trunk, in the Princess Theater, in Pocatello, Idaho." The cultural power of this single line has everything to do both with Judy Garland and with what Americans understand about origins and biography.

Much of the pleasure in the lyrics (which, after all, are not that inspired) lies in the audience's delighted awareness that Judy is making it all up even as she claims it is real. Judy Garland was not born in a trunk, in Pocatello, Idaho, or anywhere else. Nor does anyone in the audience imagine she was. Judy's performance encourages us to believe that her identity as a performer includes the power to play with the facts. She can invent the truth about her life, can reach back to define and locate her origin, can even choose where she was born.

Judy's musical medley operates as a sort of fictionalized autobiography, and not a naïve sort, either. This is quite a self-conscious autobiography, one which, however comically, makes its own serious claims for what we are to understand by personal identity. It argues for a beautiful correspondence between origins and fate, between where we come from and what we become. But in Judy's version it is the fate that determines the origins, and not the other way around. Judy's performance argues for the insignificance of mere facts, for the irrelevance and even distortedness of those pesky details of birth and family circumstance that exist on the mundane level of fact.

Much as American audiences can be counted on to accept origins as determinants of who we are, we also love to believe that we do not have to be stuck with those origins, that, to borrow Katharine Hepburn's magnificent declaration to Humphrey Bogart in *The African Queen,* "Nature, Mr. Ornot, is what we are put on this earth to rise above." The power of natal origins is only one popular narrative of American subject formation. The opposing narrative is another, equally dominant and equally mythic. As Humphrey Bogart happily discovers at the hands of Katharine Hepburn, this second myth offers a thrilling and, if possible, even more dangerous ride.

This second narrative emphasizes the possibilities of movement and change, and of identity as transformation. In it, social class, that most "un-American" of categories, is reduced to no more than a fluid indicator that we fill to the level we choose. This narrative carries the promise of upward mobility, of the correspondence between talent and effort and achievement, of the self-made man. It is, finally, the promise that, unlike those tradition-bound Europeans (or Asians, or Africans), an American's origin does not determine identity, that heredity does not predict status, that—and here is the wildest dream of all—we can create a future that can rewrite the past.

Judy Garland could sing compellingly of being born in that trunk in the Princess Theater because, through her own talent and the power of her performance, she had made herself into a person with the power to choose. Is identity driven by the circumstances of one's birth or by one's flexibility and talent to transmute those circumstances or by some combination of the two? Americans still have a hard time choosing. The contents of that trunk in Idaho include not only the infant Judy (note the absence of her mother, who, in spite of the claims of biology—those mere facts again—presumably would not fit in) but also the two major and yet conflicting narratives of identity so dear to American culture.

Judy Garland inventing and recalling the Princess Theater is only one of many moments when American art has called upon notions of performance in order to take its place in the ongoing debate about the making of identity. And the debate is expanding. In the late twentieth and early twenty-first centuries, autobiography and biography, as the *New York Review of Books* frequently announces, form a pastime amounting to a national obsession. Americans seem to have a profound interest, whether as cold curiosity or as warm sympathy, in the process of tracing people's lives.

But something more than just interest is involved. Trying to understand the movement of a life, whether someone else's or our own, includes trying to understand such basic and frightening questions as where we came from and how much that origin matters, how much birth and family shape who we are and limit who we may become. Is identity destiny or performance? Is who we are inevitably determined, or a matter of choice? And when we choose, are we simply lying, deceiving ourselves and everyone else, or are we in some sense reborn?

Beyond these questions lie others. To what extent can we—and, just as important, should we—choose to become other than what we have been? If people could freely choose to shed identities that according to a culture's unspoken (and often spoken) rules mark them as less than other members of the culture, why shouldn't they? And why wouldn't they? If it were possible, if you could get away with it, why not make a better place for yourself in the hierarchy of your culture, rewrite your origins, and create a different you?

This biography of Anna Leonowens is the story of a woman who did just that. Hers was an admirable life, filled with lies but also filled with extraordinary and sometimes breathtaking accomplishments. And not the least wonder of Anna's inventions is how the lies she told and the image she dreamed up and made come true would have their influence on American policies and people a century later. Thailand became a location for American military bases and a rest and recreation center for American soldiers fighting in Vietnam in the 1960s and 1970s for many reasons. At least one of those reasons is to be found far in the past, in an Indian Army brat's deceptions and achievements, including her magical years at the Royal Court of Siam. How did such a rare as well as admirable woman come to be? To begin to answer that finally unanswerable question, I turn first not to her story but to the story that would become the groundwork of hers, to Anna's factual origins, and to the real ancestors from whom she came.

TWO

Ancestors

A Methodist, a Soldier,
and a "Lady Not Entirely White"

ON A STEAMING JULY DAY IN 1810, the air still wet after the morning rain, a young Englishman leaned on the railing of an East India Company frigate at anchor in the Bay of Bombay. He was of medium height, with the brown eyes and even darker brown hair that bespoke his Welsh heritage. William Vawdrey Glascott, named after a family friend in Cornwall, William Vawdrey, who in turn gave two of his sons the middle name of Glascott, answered to the name of Billy or Will. He was to become Anna's grandfather. But at the moment he was twenty-one and just beginning the great adventure of his life. Billy had joined up with the Indian Army, the private army of the British East India Company, as a cadet and now strained eagerly on the crowded deck for his first sight of the foreign city where he planned to spend his life.

The *Sir Steven Lushington* was a big Indiaman, with a weight of 608 tons (Sutton, 155), making its last voyage to the East. The voyages from England in the East India Company's Indiamen were full of horrors. "There were courts-martials innumerable amongst the recruits" (Hervey, *A Soldier of the Company,* 9). One traveler related that "the cat o' nine tails was constantly at work" during his voyage in 1809, and "so many of the soldiers on board were flogged" that at last the captain intervened "and informed the senior military officer that he 'would not have his quarter-deck turned into a slaughter-house'" (Cotton, 60). But the greatest danger was disease, and the decks were filled with sick and often dying men.

The trip had taken four months because it was made before the development of the Overland Route, when passengers from Europe could travel by land to Suez and there pick up a regular steamer on to India. The first scheduled steamer east from Suez did not sail for another twenty years, and it would be sixty years before the Suez Canal opened in 1869, allowing ships to sail due east from the ports of Europe. The 1810s was still an age when travelers to India took the long route. Billy's ship left Portsmouth on March 14, 1810, and sailed south, down the west coast of the African continent, around the stormy Cape of Good Hope, then north, up the east coast. Turning east at last, on its port side the ship passed the Persian Empire and crossed the Arabian Sea to the western coast of the Indian subcontinent.

Billy's first sight was an enormous semicircular bay lined with waving coconut palms, just visible along the low hills. The air had changed and now carried the strong smells of rotting fish and dank shallow waters. There were seabirds screeching everywhere. Small boats swarmed around the ship, the people in them holding up their wares to the foreigners. There was an air of celebration, making it easy to forget the ugly truth that these new soldiers, most without any training, had come to strengthen an army of occupation, that they were reinforcements of the foreigners who held these lands by force against the wish of most of its Indian peoples.

The Company did have a military academy, known officially as the East India Company's Artillery and Engineer Seminary, unofficially as Addiscombe. It took boys from ages fourteen to eighteen to train them for the artillery or as engineers, considered the more elite branches of the Company's military. Admission required that a boy "have a fair knowledge of Arithmetic, write a good hand, and possess a competent knowledge of English and Latin Grammar" (Vibart, 15). The fee was sixty pounds for two years, high enough to keep out most would-be cadets, who joined the infantry instead. The boys who joined the Company's army were typically impoverished second and third sons or bastards (since the class structure and sexual mores of Great Britain created a seemingly endless supply), from country families all over England, Scotland, and Ireland.

William Hickey, a cadet a few years before Billy, left us a vivid account of the emptiness of the testing process:

> I attended before a Committee of Directors to undergo the usual examination as a Cadet. Being called into the Committee room . . . I saw three old Dons sitting close to the fire, having by them a large table, with pens, ink, paper, and a number of books lying upon it. Having surveyed me, . . . one of them . . . said:
> "Well young gentleman, what is your age?" Having answered
> "Nineteen," he continued:
> "Have you ever served, I mean been in the army? Though I presume from your age and appearance you cannot."

I replied, "I had not."

"Can you go through the manual exercise?"

"No, sir."

"Then you must take care and learn it." I bowed.

"You know the terms upon which you enter our service?"

"Yes, sir."

"Are you satisfied therewith?"

"Yes, sir."

A clerk who was writing at the table then told me I might withdraw, . . . I went to Mr. Coggin's office, who . . . presented me with my appointment as a cadet. (Callahan, 18)

Here was an examination that was hard to fail. Billy had "Passed the Court" on January 24, 1810.

Billy was a cadet of the lowest status. First, he was in the infantry, the worst paid of the East India Company's three military branches. John Low, who served in and around Bombay during the second decade of the nineteenth century, wrote home vigorously warning mothers against letting their sons join the infantry. As Ursula Low (34) put it, "the lot of the Infantry Officer in the pay of John Company at this date appears to have been deplorable." Second, even in the infantry, there were better and worse assignments. Billy got a worse, a Native Infantry regiment, meaning all native troops with only the officers European. Third, Billy had been sent to Bombay, the lone company center on the west coast of India, rather than to Madras or Calcutta on the east coast. Bombay had a reputation throughout Britain and its colonies as "the last choice of all ambitious young writers and cadets" (Furber, *John Company at Work*, 212).

In the early nineteenth century, huge sections of the Indian subcontinent were not controlled by the British. Three major British territories had been carved out in different regions, which the English, with typical arrogance, had named the presidencies. Each had a port city, with a fort from which the East India Company would send out its armies. Bombay was a much less active military center than the two east coast presidencies, but it was the busiest port.

Soldiers assigned to the two east coast presidencies had much better financial opportunities. The battle pay, called *batta*, was not for being in battles at all. It was a bonus received whenever a soldier was sent outside the boundaries of company territory, and paid to him as long as he was stationed there. The beautiful and alluring fact was that from the moment a battalion marched out of company territory, every man received this bonus. The Company's *batta* policy, which the directors in London were always trying to eliminate and the soldiers were always clamoring to increase, was the major financial mistake that from the late eighteenth century on kept the Company in bankruptcy while its army flourished. And it was why so many senior officers in the field used extremely dubious arguments (an "insult" had been given, spies spoke of gathering arms) as excuses to invade a prince's territory and stay. It is hard to overestimate the importance of the *batta* policy in the history of the British takeover of India.

In Bombay, where "allowances were low, pickings slim, and expenses higher than anywhere else in India" (Callahan, 27), soldiers almost never received *batta* or prize money. In terms of daily business opportunities, the commonest being to get a percentage on the food sold to the regiments at the bazaars, Bombay soldiers made the least extra money. They also waited the longest for their promotions, and they still died by the thousands of disease. All these details marked Billy Glascott as one of those "doomed to Bombay" (Furber, *John Company at Work,* 212).

In the British Army, officers joined with a commission, which was expensive and required a recommendation by a gentleman. The notion was straightforward: officers were "gentlemen," well born, well connected, and having money or relatives with money. This simple system ensured for generations that the officers in the Crown's service, those responsible as leaders for the military protection and the advance of Britain, all came from the same elite social class.

The startling fact is that from the seventeenth through the middle of the nineteenth century there were two different armies in England. One was the Crown's; the other was the private military arm of the East India Company. The Company's army had its own system for officers. They did receive commissions and needed a sponsor. But there the similarity to the Crown's system ended. Men joined the Indian Army precisely because they did not have the social status, connections, or money to join the Royal Army. The directors were explicitly "opposed to the appointment of well-born men as officers for fear that they would resent being ordered about by merchants and become quarrelsome" (Bryant, 204). The Company wanted its officers to be subservient, socially and professionally, to the merchants they served. It wanted, in Warren Hastings's words, to "afford employment and support to the middle-class of the subjects of Great Britain" (Bryant, 220).

Still, recruitment was a permanent problem. Company officers had a bad reputation, as "base born adventurers" and "people of very low education" (Cadell, 45). The Duke of York dismissed the Company's officers as "young men who have ruined themselves and are obliged to fly the Country or very low people who are sent to make their fortunes." Until the nineteenth century, "the quality of men attracted to the service was poor: a band of political renegades, runaway debtors, ne'er-do-wells, illiterates and ancients." Indeed, "a certain degree of financial and social desperation had been required for a man to become an officer in the Company's army" (Bryant, 203–5). With "their heterogeneous social background" (Bryant, 219) and their typical dream of having a small business in India, these men lived lives that were a far cry from the world of the British Army's "officer and a gentleman."

So what could have led Anna's grandfather to join this disreputable army? Billy was minor gentry, but still gentry, the second son of an obscure country parson. But Reverend Cradock Glascott was a "very remarkable man" (Martin, 357), part of a revivalist movement called Methodism within the Church of England, which swept the countryside and the industrial cities in the eighteenth century. Calling themselves the "Bible Christians," these serious young men were dedicated to serving the poor, whom they saw (somewhat accurately) as abandoned by the church. In 1767, Cradock Glascott joined a famous group of ministers who worked as itinerant preachers, known because of their patron as "Lady Huntingdon's Connexion." He described in his diary a sermon he gave in 1768, when he was twenty-six: "last Sunday after a Volley of Eggs and huzzas, which obliged us to preach some distance from the Tree, I preached to two or three hundred in the highway, who for the [most] part were very serious and attentive [and] entreated me to come again" (Welch, 100). By 1781 he was still riding all over England ("I am engaged to preach this week at Darleston, Walsal, Dudley, Bromwich and Birmingham . . . if the weather is favourable a table will be my pulpit, the Canopy of Heavens my Sounding board"), and the response was phenomenal. "At Darleston we had at least fifteen hundred poor Colliers and Nailors," and at Nottingham "at eight in the morning we had at least two thousand and in the evening at the Market cross at a moderate computation there were not less than Five thousand" (Martin, 358).

Rev. Glascott was a traveling preacher for an astounding fourteen years. In December 1781, he accepted a poorly paid position as vicar in the little town of Hatherleigh in Devon, in the west of England. His traveling days were over. He and his beloved wife, Mary, the daughter of William Edmonds, spent the next five decades never moving from the solid square parsonage. (See figure 1.) The Glascotts had five children. Mary Ann was born in March 1785. A year and a half later came the first son, Cradock John, baptized on November 20, 1786. Then came Billy (William Vawdrey), baptized on July 26, 1789. Three years later a third son, Thomas, was baptized, on August 29,

FIGURE 1. Hatherleigh Parsonage, as it looked in 2001. Photo: Susan Morgan.

1792. And finally, in 1794 there was the fifth and youngest, named Selina in honor of the reverend's beloved patroness, the Countess of Huntingdon, but she died before the age of two. Billy carried the warm memory of these siblings with him throughout his life in India. Their names echo throughout this narrative, reincarnated as his descendants. Billy named his first daughter Mary Anne, Anna named her first child Selina, and Williams and Vawdreys abound.

Rev. Glascott served with great success as vicar of Hatherleigh for fifty years, the lone Methodist in the region, much admired by his fellow Methodists as "the one solitary clergyman shining as a light in a district which embraced a large number of parishes" (Bourne, 3). He died, at age eighty-nine, on August 11, 1831. His half century of dedicated service to the small town in Devon is memorialized by a plaque on the south wall inside the church. It pays tribute to the spirit and the achievement of the man Hatherleigh Parish considers its greatest spiritual leader.

Billy was the only one of the children to leave. The other three stayed home, two right in Devon and the other in Gloucester. Mary Ann married Samuel Walkey, a surgeon, on July 6, 1811. The couple lived in Exeter until Mary Ann died on Christmas Day, 1857. Cradock John followed in his father's footsteps. He took a B.A. from Trinity College, Dublin, in 1807 and was ordained. He did not have a prosperous career. He started as a curate (below the vicar) at Exmouth, on the Devon coast, marrying Georgiana Goodin Bourke in June 1814. For years he boarded pupils in Exmouth to make ends meet. Finally in 1838 he received his own living, as the vicar of Seaton-cum-Beer, Exeter Diocese, with an annual income of 265 pounds and a house. He and Georgiana had six children (Edmund, Ann Jane, a baby who died, Georgina Charlotte, Editha Mary Ann, and Mary Ann Letitia). The couple died within three weeks of each other in 1867, after a half century of married life.

Thomas also followed his father's career, and he too spent decades in poverty. After attending Balliol College, Oxford, he was ordained and got a small curacy, at Stockleigh Pomeroy, in 1815, and then in 1818 became curate of Rodborough, in Gloucester. Thomas married his Devon sweetheart, Caroline August Morris, in 1819. He remained a curate in Rodborough for twenty-two long years. Finally, in 1840 Thomas became the vicar of Rodborough, with an impressive annual income of 310 pounds and a house. Thomas and Caroline had at least one son, who also grew up to be a curate and later spent almost twenty years as the chaplain at Versailles.

Rev. Glascott's radical Methodist position had put him and his children outside the sphere of social influence and mentoring. Cradock John's and Thomas's long years in genteel poverty were an inevitable cost of their father's religious actions, which deprived his children as well as himself of the social and professional connections so necessary for advancement among the English gentry. Billy's response to his lack of prospects in England was not to settle for a poorly paid curacy but to sail away and take his chances in India.

Billy Glascott's peaceful childhood in rural Devon was in stark contrast to the life he lived in Bombay. The city had been British since 1660, when the monarchy was restored to the throne after Cromwell's Puritan Revolution, with its distaste of many things, including theaters and all things foreign, had failed. Charles II married Catherine of Braganza, daughter of the king of Portugal, whose dowry included the island of Bombay. The problem was that the Portuguese had controlled Bombay for two centuries, had married locals for generations, and rejected the notion that Bombay was now British. When a British Army force of five ships and more than four hundred soldiers sailed into the bay in 1662, the Portuguese governor refused to allow them to land. The stalemate went on for three years, by which time out of the original "force of 400 just 97 emaciated castaways finally . . . scrambled ashore at Bombay" (Keay, 133). They were the unprepossessing beginning of the Army of Bombay. In 1668, "heartily glad to be rid of the place," Charles ceded the island to the East India Company (Keay, 131).

By 1810, Bombay was a bustling place, dotted with low wooden buildings called factories, where the Company stored its goods. The famous crescent-shaped harbor was a forest of masts, full of ships loading and unloading at the docks or anchored farther out and waiting their turn for a spot. When Eliza Fay landed in 1784, "the many fine ships building and repairing with the number of Europeans walking about, almost persuaded me I was at home, till the dress and dark complexion of the workmen destroyed the pleasing illusion" (Fay, 233). Commercial shipping was what nourished and sustained Bombay.

Behind the docks stretched the town, with a population of more than one hundred thousand, the islands joined by the land reclamation projects of the eighteenth century. Behind the town were the Deccan Mountains, rising four to five thousand feet. In 1810 there were several hundred stone buildings, wide avenues, and an extensive grassy area in front of the bay, called "Bombay Green." Many travelers were moved by the first sight of Bombay, with "the foothills very green after the monsoon, the sea very blue, the buildings mostly white and looking very gorgeous from the sea, and altogether a feeling of opulence and luxuriance" (Allen, 37).

Travelers emphasized the city's cosmopolitan character. Captain Hall, a British naval officer, wrote in 1812 that "in twenty minutes walk through the bazaar of Bombay my ears have been struck by the sounds of every language that I have heard in any other part of the world, uttered not in corners and by chance as it were, but in a tone and manner which implied that the speakers felt at home" (Albuquerque, xiv). Only Singapore would have a similar reputation for an international population. But in 1810 Singapore had yet to be dreamed of, let alone built.

As one of the few European-controlled ports in India, and the major port on the west coast, Bombay was a center for craftsmen, a place where one could buy anything.

> Ports in the Persian Gulph furnished its merchants with pearls, raw-silk, Carmenia wool, dates, dried fruits, rose water, ottar of roses. . . . Arabia supplied them with coffee, gold, drugs, and honey. . . . China [supplied] tea, sugar, porcelain, wrought silks, nankeens. . . . From . . . the eastern islands they brought spices, ambergris, perfumes, arrack, and sugar; the cargoes from . . . Africa consisted chiefly of ivory, slaves, and drugs; while the different parts of India produce cotton, silk, muslin, pearls, diamonds, and every precious gem. (Forbes, 97)

But the single most important product in Bombay was ships. The harbor boasted an enormous dockyard, center of a major international shipbuilding business that played a key role in the history of Bombay, of Europe, and of the Americas. In 1736, the Company brought in a group of Parsi carpenters from Surat. This extraordinary family took the surname Wadia, meaning "shipbuilder." They were about to revolutionize shipping throughout the world.

The ships were teak, built at a time when the great oak forests of southern England were being depleted. Bombay ships not only cost far less, handled better, and were stronger, they also lasted "thirty years against an English vessel's average of twelve." By 1810, the Company had a superb supply of Bombay-built ships, including the famous Indiamen, and so did the Royal Navy. The Wadias were the first family of Bombay, an international business dynasty. Their status was so high that an English lady in 1809 who met the brothers assured her readers that "I should never guess they were not Englishmen, if I did not see their dark faces and foreign dress, or read their unusual names at the end of a letter" (Asiatic Society of Bombay, n.p.). One Wadia mansion has been taken over by Bollywood. It is owned by a major film studio, Raj Kamal.

For all Bombay's commercial bustle, daily life was somewhat quiet. The Chinese, the Hindus, the Muslims, the Europeans, the Parsis, the Armenians, and many others banded together in their own neighborhoods. The British living in the fine neighborhoods of Byculla and Mazagaon included "a few very wealthy merchants, some talented civilians, and a number of military officers" (Asiatic Society of Bombay, n.p.), all company employees. In England the richest were called nabobs, men who had made enough money in India to be thought of virtually as princes. The other group of Europeans in Bombay were the soldiers. They lived in the military cantonment, the "Fort," on the right side when facing the city from the water, balancing the softly rolling Malabar Hills on the left. There were crowded barracks, long "single-storied buildings with thatched roofs," for the European regiments (Bancroft, 9). The buildings were far apart, to pick up breezes, with open areas where the sepoys slept, no buildings being provided for them.

And then there were the tents, thousands of tents, an entire city of tents. They belonged to both the sepoys and the European regiments. Those living outside kept their gear in these semipermanent tents, although all cooking throughout the cantonment was done outside. The tents not only kept out the fierce rains, they also conveniently solved the expanding needs of a diverse and ever-changing military population. For the fact was that the Fort was not a world of soldiers. It was a city, housing all the people and animals connected to the soldiers: the water haulers, cooks, barbers, washerwomen, food vendors, and buffaloes and chickens. Soldiers in the canton, European and Indian, typically lived with their families, their ladies (legal or illegal), their children, and a variety of relatives. There were tens of thousands of camp followers connected in some way to the Bombay Army who lived in the tents.

When the army went on marches, the camp followers went too, loading hundreds of bullock carts with tents and necessities, including their children, for life on the road. The women who followed the army were known as "heavy baggage." When they camped, one area was for the soldiers and another for the families. "This assemblage of tents, *pals* and hovels, of a variety of forms and sizes, presents a striking contrast to the regular encampment. . . . Tis only the poverty-stricken married soldiery who are so miserably provided for" (Hervey, *A Soldier of the Company*, 132).

Billy Glascott was quick to learn canton life. He began his military career in India as an ensign in the Fourth Regiment of Native Infantry as of July 2, 1810. The Native Infantry, or N.I., reflected the Company's recruitment problems. Given the absence of willing Europeans, it turned to the "topas" (or "topaz"), a military term for the local descendants of Portuguese/Indian intermingling, and after them to the non-Christian natives, the sepoys. Billy was an officer to sepoys. What Billy, and everyone else, actually did while on duty was simple. In 1810 the Company's military strategy for training and exercising infantry was to have them form orderly lines and practice marching in step, turning, and stopping on command. One kneeled or stood, depending on which line one was in. And one fired. Training for battle meant virtually nothing more than drilling: learning by endless repetition the commands for moving in a group. So Billy drilled. Off duty, he grew to know and love Bombay.

Billy was a lowly ensign for more than four years. But if you did not think too much about promotion, then life in Bombay was grand. Billy would have agreed with another ensign's reminiscences of those times, that "all that one has ever heard, or read, or conceived of India, falls infinitely short of the reality; and so lively, so novel, so animated, and so interesting is that picture which presents itself, that the effect has a much greater resemblance to enchantment, than to fact" (Welsh, 1–2). Billy lived in the officers' barracks, set up his "cot" from the ship, with his boxes under it, and enjoyed the noisy company. It did not take him long to learn that the best place to sleep, and the best place to live as well, was outside.

After finishing the day's drills, this country boy spent much of his time exploring the city. He learned that "*here* no European uses his own legs; but that all ranks and ages must bend to the custom of the place, and be carried" (Welsh, 3). And carried he was, in a palanquin, a conveyance that used, on average, twelve people to carry one European. Radically changed from that July morning when he first saw Bombay, Billy was no longer a sheltered Englishman of pious upbringing from Devon. He could never go back to being simply an Englishman again. Part of what defined him as a nationality had melted in the heat and the intense smell for which Bombay was notorious. It featured a putrid combination of the sea and the low marshes and the garbage and the effluvia of so many thousands of people, and only the monsoons were strong enough to blow it away. A century earlier, Dr. Fryer, a company surgeon, had noted rather pompously that "the people of Bombay walk in a Charnal house, the climate being extremely unhealthy, at first thought to be caused by *bukshor* or rotten fish but though that is prohibited, yet it continues mortal. [There is] an infecundity of the earth, and a putridness in the air" (Rodrigues, 115).

But the sea breezes and the rains could refresh this city of low marshy islands, and Bombay soon enough began to smell comfortingly familiar. Like many others, Billy realized that "as I shall probably never more visit England, [I] will make everything as agreeable for myself as possible." The Englishmen in the Company's army shared a "sense of exile in an alien land" (Callahan, 25), but most also shared a sense that India was now home. Billy became comfortable with ways of thinking and living that were incomprehensible to his family back on that other, colder island.

Life in "an European regiment was not, at that time, the best school for either industry, morals, or sobriety" (Welsh, 9). But Billy had learned from his father a deep concern for the lives of local peoples, a sense of equality with the poor, and a respect for the views and opinions of those whose experiences were far from his own. Growing up in a family that had itself been marked as different, and that prized the inner life over the externals of rank and wealth, Billy brought to Bombay neither the typical snobbery nor the ignorant fear of foreigners that characterized too many of his fellow cadets and officers in India. His Methodist faith had prepared him well. It had taught him tolerance and humility, a respect for spirituality rather than its trappings, and that poverty was not a sign of spiritual paucity and was, in fact, nothing to fear.

Sepoy and European alike, brought together in this strange and in so many ways unethical military enterprise known as the Honourable Company's Army, shared basic qualities of the military life. The days, filled with "drills of all kinds, morning, noon, and afternoon" (Bancroft, 21), were repetitious and deadening. Billy's lack of cultural arrogance probably helped to save him from the demons that destroyed so many unhappy Englishmen in India: drinking, debts, duels, and gambling (Ram, 63, 74). He became acquainted with the sepoys in the Fourth N.I., many of whom were of a higher class and generally more cosmopolitan than he. Billy and some of the other Europeans spent many of their evenings talking and drinking with their men, particularly the group leaders known as the subedars. He learned the views of Muslims and the Hindu castes, so similar in their rigidity to the military rules of rank, and knew better than to pass food around carelessly or ask someone to touch someone else's drinking bowl. But these were the simplest lessons. The talk ranged from basic information to questions of cultural and religious comparisons, to regional and international politics and the British role in India.

The Company's economic purpose became increasingly dubious as it sank into debt. In 1813 the news spread rapidly to everyone in the Company's army, down to the drummer boys, that the monopoly status of the Company was over. Parliament's 1813 Charter Renewal Act not only canceled the Honourable Company's trade monopoly but, after a bitter fight on the floor of Parliament, forced the Company for the first time to allow Christian missionaries into India. European and Indian soldiers alike rightly feared that the days of easy camaraderie would be replaced by the pressure to blend together less. The British presence was clearly no longer about trade. What it was about instead—the cultural, economic, and political domination of the subcontinent by the Company's Indian Army—was increasingly visible to all.

What sustained the troops, Europeans and natives, at this uncomfortable historic moment was probably not any noble cause or national pride but rather their friendly sense that they were all in this together and their dreams of promotions and *batta*. When that was not enough, "the bazaars sold spirits and opium, the former the solace of the European infantry, the latter of the sepoys" (Callahan, 31). On November 24, 1814, a small piece of Billy's dreams came true. He received his appointment as a lieutenant in the First Battalion of the Fourth Regiment N.I. But Billy's job did not change much. He stayed with his battalion, joining the leaders of the drills on Bombay Green, but now as an officer and with a raise. The latter was crucial, not least because "Bombay had long been noted as a very dear place to live in, and in 1814 it was a hundred per cent. dearer than any place in Hindustan" (Douglas, 187). The moneylenders who lived in the cantonment smiled benignly on Billy as he moved out of the barracks into a bungalow.

It was time to think of a wife. The senior officers sometimes had parties, particularly on the rare occasions when a few single ladies arrived from England on the ships that poured into the harbor. But there were so few girls from Great Britain in the early years of the century (the ratio of British women to men was estimated as an astounding one to fifty, including wives) that none would dance with a mere lieutenant. They had come on serious business. Even the most tenderhearted and least materialistic of English girls in India were in the marriage market. An ensign's salary supported no one, including the ensign. A lieutenant's salary could support a wife and family in only the meanest way. Everyone knew that between the Company's two categories of servants (employees), the civil (meaning the merchants) and the military, only the civil servants made enough money to pay for a domestic life. The senior officers were all right too, though not as desirable as a merchant. No lieutenant had a prayer of marrying an English girl.

Billy Glascott did have a family in India. But who were they? This question is remarkably difficult to answer. Because British records focused on the upper class, the facts of Billy's family's existence either were not recorded or have long vanished, leaving only the fewest of tracks. But there are tracks. Billy had a wife in Bombay and at least three children, a boy and two girls. Though there are no baptism records, there are references to the children in a few places in the official documents. Billy's oldest child was Mary Anne, named after his oldest sister, and his second daughter was Elizabeth (Eliza). Billy's youngest child was William Frederick, named after his father.

Local women who were connected to company men in India were often called "sleeping dictionaries," and "hard facts about these women are frustratingly elusive" (Baron, 29). Billy's wife, Anna's grandmother, was a local woman. She remains a mystery, standing completely in the shadows of history. In the big ledgers kept by the civil servants of the East India Company, with their black leather covers, pink and then blue ruled lines, and handwritten lists of marriage and baptism records, this woman and her children simply do not appear.

Their very absence from the company registers highlights an important piece of historical information. The one certain fact about Anna's grandmother is that she could not have been European. The most likely possibility is that Billy's wife was an Anglo-Indian (of mixed race), born in India. Even with no company record of a marriage, I assume that Billy married his lady. He could not afford a mistress of good family. Nor, I believe, would this parson's son from a large and happy family have wanted one. And given the Company's rules for its soldiers at the time, we can draw no moral conclusions from the fact that there is no record of Billy's marriage or his children's christening. A marriage to a local was completely acceptable among the lower officer and civil levels of company employees during his time. It was understood that officers lived with locals (Ram, 24). Billy's commanding officer was almost certainly at the wedding and knew the family well. Although by the late eighteenth century the company rules sent from faraway London generally forbade the immigration of European women and condemned marriages with locals, the reality was that a soldier's hopes for a home and family lay with the Eurasian girls of the Anglo-Indian community in Bombay.

The pool of available women for a lower officer consisted of mixed-race Christians, typically with Portuguese ancestry and family links to the Company, the daughters or granddaughters of other soldiers. In the society of British Bombay, these women formed a respectable middle class, definitely not the sort to accept relations outside marriage. As they, and their families, were perfectly aware, the acute shortage of eligible women who were Christian and whose language was English gave them a special cachet as rare and invaluable participants in the social scene. And it worked both ways. For these Anglo-Indians, the one available pool of eligible men was the Company's soldiers.

Billy Glascott and his shadowy lady were destined to begin an extensive Anglo-Indian family. Their many descendants would be personally successful and often publicly distinguished. But their own lives were relatively simple and, economically at least, quite poor. They lived in one of the numerous small bungalows, usually a room or two along with a wide front verandah, for rent in the cantonment. Billy's lady would not have been referred to as a wife, because no one was. The polite term among the British for one's spouse was "lady" until the 1840s. Only then did it become acceptable in society to refer to her as "wife" (Kincaid, 150). The lady's family and Billy's military buddies with their families provided the couple's social life.

Made lieutenant almost four and a half years after his arrival, with a ranking date of November 24, 1814, Billy married sometime in 1815, after he received his commission. Once in their bungalow, the Glascotts settled down to start a family. First came Mary Anne, born sometime in late 1815 or early 1816, probably within a year of the wedding. We have her age listed at the time of her recorded death. Billy's merit appointment as adjutant came after Mary Anne's birth, proof of his commander's approval of his family and high opinion of him. Within a year of Mary Anne's birth, in late 1816 or early 1817, came a second daughter, Eliza. Billy's children are listed as Christians, meaning that they had been baptized.

The girls were raised in the Fort with the rest of the army children, daughters of an officer, though a junior and impoverished one, and a Eurasian mother not "on the strength." But mother and daughters were British by language and religion, like almost all the wives and families of lower officers among whom the Glascotts lived. One of the things we can learn from Billy's story is that in that time and place the very definition of "British" was a highly malleable notion. Did the couple have more children who died? There can be little doubt that there were more pregnancies. If there were more babies before William, they must have been girls, in view of the custom of naming first sons after the father. In the historical records of British India, lower- and middle-class girls, losing their surnames so quickly, are even more invisible than boys. If Mary Anne and Eliza Glascott had sisters, I have not found them.

During the next three or four years, the Fourth N.I., including its junior officer from Devon, saw no military action. But in 1817 there was a great stirring. The Maratha princes around Bombay, who had for many decades hated the British invaders and waited for an opportunity to drive back these oppressors, decided the moment had come at last. One of the Maratha princes, the peshwa (the chief minister) of Poona, ninety miles east of Bombay, was particularly determined on war, incensed by the humiliating terms of a treaty the British had forced on him.

The British response was nothing short of enormous. The Company amassed two huge armies to cover most of central India. One moved down from the north (the Grand Army of Bengal) with troops from Calcutta, and the other moved up from the south (the Army of the Deccan) with troops from Madras and Bombay, destroying all opposition in their way. Their goal was not only to rout localized adversaries such as the peshwa of Poona but also to destroy what remained of the Moghul rulers in India. John Shipp, the baggage master of the Left Division of the Grand Army, recorded that the Left Division had 8,000 soldiers. They were accompanied by "80,000 men, women, and children, 50 elephants, 600 camels, 11,000 bullocks, horses, mules and pack ponies, 500 goats, sheep and dogs, 250 palanquins, and vehicles of every kind and description" (Ram, 35). Such ratios were standard.

The Maratha Wars of 1817 and 1818 were momentous events in the history of the British takeover of India, and especially in the presidency of Bombay. The peshwa of Poona "attacked and burnt the British residency, only to see his army defeated by the Bombay troops" (Heathcote, *The Military in British India,* 67). The pervasive British blindness about and condescension to the peoples it conquered can be seen in Maria Graham Callcott's memoir of visiting Poona. She casually remarks of the peshwa, who would soon lead a courageous revolution, that though she would like to get a look at a native prince, "I am told that he is a man of little or no ability, a great sensualist, and very superstitious" (Callcott, 77). The official English view of the Maratha Wars and the British presence in India generally was an exercise in ethical inversion. It held that "victory was due to the moral ascendancy of the British troops" (Cadell, 151).

After the peshwa fell, the rest of the princes in this fight for independence were similarly beaten. By 1818, the British had annexed Poona and various other dominions around Bombay. The defeat of the Maratha princes was the death knell of the power of the Moghul emperor in India. "Although until 1835 the Company would continue to strike currency bearing his cipher, India was now subject to a new empire, and a new military system" (Heathcote, *The Military in British India*, 67). The invaders from the West had conclusively defeated the remaining descendants of the long-ago invaders from the East. India was theirs.

The Maratha Wars brought military action, and *batta* bonuses, to most of the Bombay Army regiments. The Fourth N.I. was not one of them. A flank company, it spent the war in reserve in Ahmednuggar, a town far east of Bombay, on alert and ready to move, but the call never came. Yet the Maratha Wars were a turning point for Billy, the beginning of fateful changes. The first and best of those changes was that on July 1, 1818, Billy was appointed to be the adjutant to the First Battalion of his regiment. This new job was not a promotion in rank, but it brought more responsibilities and more pay. Although there is no written account of the personality of this lowly obscure lieutenant who lived almost two hundred years ago, his merit appointment as battalion adjutant tells us how the men who worked with Billy evaluated him. A strong sense of fairness, being well liked and sociable, and an easy familiarity with and respect for local ways were the crucial requirements for this important and much-coveted job.

The adjutant was in charge of battalion enlistments and in charge of understanding and solving problems for and about the men. Billy had a semiofficial bungalow, where he and his family lived. From there, usually on the verandah, he made the recruiting decisions and the judgment calls that helped the battalion to run smoothly. When an Indian wanted to join the regiment or when one of the battalion's sepoys brought a relative to join, they went to see Adjutant Glascott. When they needed to settle a dispute or ask for special treatment, or needed a go-between to the battalion commander, they would head for the adjutant's verandah. In an army where not everything was set by rules, Billy was a kind of semiofficial judge. He determined not only recruiting but also such matters as who needed to move his tent, who was getting too much duty and who was slacking off, and who could go on personal leave and for how long.

Billy kept his lovely appointment as adjutant for the 1st/4th N.I. for only two years. In 1820, the Company yet again decided it needed more soldiers, and Billy, as an experienced officer, was transferred to the newly created Twelfth Regiment N.I. It turned out to be a bad move. He was sent into action at last. In 1821, his new battalion, the 2nd/12th, was shipped out of India, west to Kishme, a tiny island just off the Persian mainland in the Persian Gulf. Kishme (now Qishm) was considered strategically located along shipping routes, since it lay on the northern side along the route of ships from Europe heading for India. The Company, continuing the "disastrous British obsession with offshore properties" (Keay, 333), directed the Bombay Army to "quell the piracy of the Arabs in this region" (Cadell, 169). Piracy was conveniently defined as any native person seen as an obstacle to British business and political interests and having a boat. Billy's regiment, as well as some others, was sent on the pointless little task of flushing out and battling the "rebel" Arabs on Kishme, with the goal of "the complete subjugation of the whole of the tribe" (Mainwaring, 233), particularly the infamous Arab pirate tribe known as the Beni Boo Ali.

It was an action of many months. In the first assault, one of the tribe's many forts was taken, but the British force was then successfully attacked. The 12th, along with Billy's old 1st/4th, was sent as part of a second force, on January 10, 1821, to fill a role Billy knew quite well: the backup troops. The big battle took place on March 2, 1821, with the Arabs being defeated. But a few months later, on October 31, 1821, Lieutenant William Glascott of the Twelfth Regiment N.I. died in Kishme, of unlisted causes. Since no battle injury is listed, and his name is not among those in the casualty lists, the likely cause of death was disease. He was thirty-two.

Judging only by his army records, the young Methodist from Devon who went for a soldier led an uneventful life. Billy's public role, hardly a noble one, was as a foreign soldier in an occupying army. But his private role was as an accommodating young man who made a distant and vastly different world his home. Billy was mourned by the Glascotts of Devon. But for all their love of the son and brother who sailed to India, when he died more than a decade later they no longer knew the man for whom they grieved, the man he had come to be. Perhaps the greater grief was felt by the family he left financially as well as emotionally bereft, the Glascotts of Bombay.

Billy never saw his son. When he was shipped off to the Persian Gulf in late December 1820 or early January 1821, he left a pregnant wife behind.

Given William Frederick's age recorded at his death, he was born after February 5, 1821.

When Billy died, he and his lady had been married for six years. She was left with at least three children to support: Mary Anne, age five; Eliza, age four; and a newborn. From the perspective of the British upper class, such women did not even exist. Mrs. Fenton, writing seven years later about the widow of a captain, commented that "the situation of these native born young women . . . is most often pitiable under *such* [impecunious] circumstances." Mrs. Fenton's sympathy was, of course, limited. She concluded that surely these "dark Ladye[s]" are "generally unfitted by their birth and education to retain a place in their husband's class of life? These marriages are unfortunate for both parties, and seldom turn out otherwise" (Steuart, 97).

When Billy died intestate, Rev. Glascott hired the Bombay Agency of Messrs. Shotton Malcolm and Company to discover the state of Billy's finances. The news was long delayed, quite typical, and not good. In July 1824, two and a half years after Billy's death, the Company's Bombay Court concluded that, although the Company owed Billy 8,000 rupees, he owed the Company double that, 16,000 rupees, from his lieutenant's bond. Presumably, giving up his life was considered sufficient to erase his debt.

We have no way of knowing how Billy's lady managed. There is no sign that she had any contact with the Glascotts of Devon, or that the reverend and his lady even knew that she and the children existed. But we do know her options. She and the children would have been evicted almost immediately from the Glascott bungalow, not by the army but by the moneylenders. Her husband's debts, come due in the event of his death, could be paid by losing the bungalow and furniture. Mary Anne lost her chance to attend the regimental school, which at five years old she would have just begun. Billy's company friends, themselves always broke, chipped in a little, as was the custom. The Company would not have turned them out destitute. There was a small pension for families of deceased officers, lasting three to six months, from the Clive Fund. After that there was nothing.

Billy Glascott's widow, a "lady not entirely white" (Sherwood, 396), had only two real choices: move back to her family or remarry. Much depended on the lady's age, her looks, and her relatives. Perhaps she and her three children were able to move into her family's home. But the more likely choice, and absolutely the solution she would have tried for, given the continuing acute shortage of available women for British soldiers at the time, was to remarry, to someone else in the Company's employ. I hope this is what happened. Even though I look back unable even to have discovered her name, I wish her well.

THREE

A Company Childhood

You know I think the tendency of one's life is to harden
into commonplace living. We ought to struggle against
it, for surely the world about us is a living poem, and
every one has the power to make life a living poem or
else a dead letter.

ANNA
letter to Avis, June 2, 1880

ANNA LEONOWENS WAS BORN ON NOVEMBER 26, 1831, in the presidency her grandfather had loved so well. She was christened Anna Harriett Emma Edwards. Her mother, Billy's eldest child, was still mostly a child when she married in 1829, eight years after her father died in the Persian Gulf. She was just thirteen years old. Life in Bombay Fort required that British, and particularly Anglo-Indian, children not stay a financial burden on their parents. For the orphan children of company men who were lower officers or in the ranks, the situation was extreme. It was common to talk of the "destitute condition of the offspring of European soldiers [living as well as dead], who if they fortunately escaped the dangers of infancy, were notwithstanding exposed to the corrupting influence of scenes of profligacy" (Carey, 169). The children who stayed alive grew up fast. The boys joined the army and the girls married soldiers.

There were plenty of young men waiting impatiently to snap up the small pool of female children that the Anglo-Indian community produced, as soon as these girls reached puberty. On March 15, 1829, Mary Anne married Thomas Edwards at St. James Church, Tannah (a neighborhood of Bombay). The two witnesses, Robert and Sarah Earle, were illiterate (as, most likely, were the bride and the groom). Tom was twice Mary Anne's age, twenty-six, quite old for a soldier in India. He had enlisted at Westminster in the spring of 1825 and arrived in Bombay on the company ship *Lady Kennaway* on October 12, 1825. Tom was born in St. George Parish in Middlesex, but was listed in the company registers as from Hereford, where he had spent his childhood. In other words, Anna's father was a country boy, one of those young, almost always uneducated men from poor families in rural England during the early decades of the nineteenth century. Like so many other rural boys in that era of industrial expansion, he had no future in the countryside.

One of the rank and file, Tom had enlisted in the infantry, the inevitable place for men with no skills, training, or promise. Many observers, often the soldiers themselves, wrote of the low reputation of the rank and file, still controlled in Tom's time by the reliable discipline of flogging. Tom's occupation was recorded in the Company's recruitment ledger as "cabinetmaker," a much-used designation that allowed recruiters to fill in the slot labeled "occupation" with something that sounded significant. The truth was that most of the Company's common soldiers were farm boys. "Cabinetmaker" sounded like skilled labor, and the listing was not a lie since, in those times when all country people made their own furniture, it basically meant that the young man knew how to wield a hammer.

Tom enlisted in the infantry but he did not stay there. In Bombay he was placed in the one category of even lower status, the "Sappers and Miners." This was the Company's work crew, the laborers who went first, ahead of the marching infantry, to clear the land and hack paths through rough terrain. These were the men who actually built and maintained the roads, the trenches, the barracks, and whatever else needed building or repairing in the Company's ever-expanding territories. It was a "period of almost continuous activity for the Sappers and Miners" (Sandes, viii). When Tom landed in Bombay in the fall of 1825, the Bombay Sappers and Miners already had a fifty-year history. Poona, which became their headquarters in 1837, would later play an important role in Anna's life in India. In late 1820, the Sappers and Miners were shipped out to a hot spot far west of India, on the Persian Gulf. They were sent to the island of Kishme to clear a path through difficult terrain for company infantry troops and back them up in the attack on the inland fort of the Arab "pirate" tribes of Beni Boo Ali.

With this small historical fact we are suddenly looking at the wonderful serendipity of Billy's regiment being on the same tiny island in 1821 as was the corps of laborers from which would come the man who eight years later married Billy's daughter. The Sappers and Miners were sent to Kishme on January 5, 1821, and Billy's regiment followed five days later, on January 10. Since both Billy's regiment and the corps were mostly native troops, there were probably no more than twenty Englishmen on Kishme, together for several months. Billy's death on Kishme allows me to imagine that someone who was with him there from the Sappers and Miners contacted Billy's widow on returning to Bombay, perhaps to console her and the children or to tell them of his last days. Starting at least with that someone, soldiers in the corps would have kept up the acquaintance between the Glascott family and corps members, a connection that led eight years later to one of their own marrying Billy's daughter, Mary Anne.

Anna's parents were not an outwardly impressive couple. The twenty-six-year-old farm boy/soldier and the Indian orphan, the mixed-race army brat, probably descended from an earlier union between a native and a soldier, did not seem bound for success. Yet the descendants of this couple would make history, including American media history. Tom and Mary Anne's union produced two children, both girls. In different ways both children proved exceptional. The elder, Eliza, had a daughter, also Eliza, whose nine children included a judge, a diplomat, and an actor who went to America and made movie history under the stage name of Boris Karloff. The younger, Anna Harriett, became the governess to the royal children in Bangkok and wrote the only published account in any language of life inside the royal harem of Siam. Her unique experiences became the basis for a book and one of America's most famous musicals, *The King and I.* But on that March day in Tannah in 1829, no one would have predicted such fruit from the union of this obscure and unprepossessing couple.

Tom and Mary Anne settled down in Ahmednuggar, where Billy had sat out the Maratha War. Ahmednuggar (variously spelled by the British as Ahmednagar or Ahmnuggar) was 150 miles inland of Bombay. Tom had been assigned there because in 1829 it was the headquarters of the Bombay Sappers and Miners Corps, relocated from Bombay Fort. From Ahmednuggar, the Sappers and Miners began building the road west toward the sea, through Sirur and then through Poona, and on through the mountains down from the Deccan Plateau to the marshy coast and Bombay. Anna's childhood is partly marked by the direction and progress of this road.

By the 1850s, Ahmednuggar was "the established depot of the British artillery belonging to the Bombay presidency, and is consequently provided with a noble barracks" (Anon., *Life in Bombay,* 329). But in the late 1820s, the "noble" barracks, like the good road west to the coast and Bombay, had yet to be built. Private Edwards and his bride lived in the simple barrack huts. The two ends of each barracks were where the married men set up their family's cots and hammocks, with sacking hung up to screen them off from the single men in the rest of the room. These accommodations seemed to horrify those from England. A lady visitor in the 1830s, Mrs. Postans, thought the barracks unspeakable. It is unlikely that she ever even entered them, though perhaps she peered into one. She was almost as appalled by the officers' bungalows, describing them as large "mud huts" (Postans, 140). Mrs. Postans pointed out to her British readers that the rank-and-file European soldiers in India were "dissolute" and their women "immoral," the wives often as drunk and prone to fisticuffs as the men, and "heartless" besides (160–62).

There are many accounts of the horrors of life for rank-and-file European soldiers in the Indian Army. A common theme was the smell. The stench in the barracks "was simply awful. Rubbish accumulated from the adjacent bazaars and what was too noisome to be eaten by scavenging dogs or carrion, simply rotted—vermin and clouds of flies flourished throughout the bazaars and barracks, contaminating food. Inside the barracks, the whiff of lice and flea-ridden unwashed soldiery was leavened by the smell of their pets— usually monkeys or parrots—and powered up by temperatures which customarily reached a minimum of circa 90 degrees F. in the hot season and no punkahs" (Putkowski, pers. comm., 12/20/1999).

Along with the smell, the memoirs of soldiers and visitors speak again and again of the one pervasive and terrible habit that destroyed the lives of so many of the Company's European staff: drunkenness. To live in the barracks was to be surrounded daily by "habitual drunkenness." A recruit in the British Army to India in the 1840s reported that the barracks was a "den of living abomination," the recruits full of "vice and ruffianism" (MacMullen, 14), everyone "desperate for liquor" (137). One sergeant found it "absolutely astonishing to see the eagerness with which the mass of European soldiers in India endeavour to procure liquor, no matter of what description so that it produces insensibility, the sole result sought for" (MacMullen, 137). The only people considered to be worse than the British soldiers were the Indian Army troops, who were described as always "even drunker" (MacMullen, 140).

In 1829, at just thirteen years old, Mary Anne Edwards took up a life that even company soldiers themselves alternately described as a hell of alcoholic violence and a "dull stultifying existence" (Ram, xxvi). In the barracks everybody drank and everybody who could afford it, which meant the officers, gambled. There was no privacy, a severe shortage of women, and plenty of fights, as well as other kinds of dissolution. The women in the barracks, in part because widows remarried so quickly, were besieged by admirers "while the tears which decency demands are still coursing . . . down [their] cheeks" (MacMullen, 164). But Mary Anne had spent her childhood around the barracks and knew it as home. In this raucous, putrid, and violent environment the young couple proceeded to do what all young couples in British India did: they made love at the end of the room behind their curtains of sacking and started a family.

Within four months of the wedding Mary Anne was pregnant, and on April 26, 1830, now only fourteen, she gave birth. On June 20, the Reverend Ambrose Goode baptized Eliza Julia Edwards. Her father is duly recorded at the baptism as Sergeant Edwards. Young Tom had clearly managed to obtain a little promotion. Eliza Julia was not even a year old when Mary Anne became pregnant again. She gave birth on November 26, 1831, to another girl. Mary Anne named her second child Anna Harriett Emma and called her Harriett. But this time Tom Edwards was not at the baptism. He never saw his second daughter. Instead, he met the fate of so many of the soldiers of the Honourable Company. Tom died young in Ahmednuggar. There is no mention of cause of death. All the India Office record offers is that Thomas Edwards, a sergeant, was "deceased July 31, 1831" (L/MIL/12/155, p. 195). He was twenty-eight years old, or maybe just twenty-nine. Mary Anne's father, we recall, had managed to stay alive until the age of thirty-two.

Tom left his family not a cent. Like Billy Glascott, Tom owed the Company more than it owed him. Now sixteen, Mary Anne found herself in almost the identical position her mother had been in barely more than a decade earlier: a destitute widow with young children. With Eliza Julia younger than two and Anna a newborn, Mary Anne quickly resolved her situation by finding another man. Remarrying was no problem, any more than I believe it would have been for her mother. Even in the 1840s, when many more British women and families had emigrated to India, an infantry sergeant assured his readers that persons from Britain "can form no idea of the scarcity of white women in India" and it was almost as hard to find "half-caste wives" (MacMullen, 163).

Mary Anne Edwards, widow, married Patrick Donahue (usually spelled Donohoe, sometimes Donahoe, but Donahue on the marriage record) on January 9, 1832, only six weeks after Anna Harriette was born. Neither Mary Anne, who had babies to feed, nor Patrick, who was not about to risk losing his prospective bride to some other all-too-eager soldier, saw the point of wasting much time. The groom's military rank is recorded at the wedding as that of a second corporal in the Corps of Engineers. Patrick stayed a noncommissioned officer in the Engineer Corps, becoming a sergeant, the highest level of promotion for a rank-and-file soldier.

Patrick Donohoe had been born in Limerick. He was on the infantry list as a private, as these farm boys always were, and sailed to India on the *Edinburgh* in the fall of 1828, three years after Tom Edwards. In the corps he met Tom and his young wife. As a member of the same regiment, he probably even danced at the couple's wedding the March after he arrived. Mary Anne also had another tie to Patrick. He was a friend of her sister's husband. On July 3, 1831, when Mary Anne was four months pregnant with Anna, Eliza Glascott, after whom Mary Anne had named her first child, got married in Seroor. The pattern of Eliza's choices was very similar to Mary Anne's. Eliza was fourteen years old. Her groom was Tobias Butler, an Irishman from Kilkenny who was in the Sappers and Miners. He had enlisted in Liverpool and sailed to Bombay on the *Edinburgh* along with Patrick.

If Mary Anne had been unlucky with her first husband, she would be extremely lucky with her second. First, and best of all, he would live. Also, when Mary Anne and Patrick married, she was sixteen and he was about twenty-three. For the bride this second time around, the difference between sixteen and twenty-three must have seemed notably less gaping than that between thirteen and twenty-six. Whatever the reasons, the couple seemed to have a compatibility that enabled them to enjoy a long life together. Patrick proved a loyal husband and good provider and the family prospered.

Life for Mary Anne and her young daughters did not change much in the beginning of this second marriage. Patrick simply moved down to the end of the barracks to join the recent widow and her baby girls behind the curtain. They had a ceremony to make it all legal. The first step in this second marriage was more children. Their first living child was a son, John Donohoe. Given how soon Mary Anne's next pregnancy followed, John was probably born in the middle of 1833, since the wedding was January 1832, and Mary Anne needed a little time to recover from the birth of Anna Harriett at the end of the previous November.

The couple's second child and Mary Anne's fourth was Charlotte Mary Anne. Charlotte was born April 1, 1835, when Eliza was four, Anna Harriett three, and John at least one. By the middle of 1835, Mary Anne Donohoe, now nineteen, had four children under the age of five. Since her wedding Eliza had produced two children of her own as well, Anna's first cousins, Henrietta on June 9, 1833, in Sevoor and Louisa Ellen on July 11, 1835. By 1835, Toby had been reassigned and the Butler family had moved to Bergaum.

Soon after Charlotte's birth, Sergeant Donohoe was also assigned to Sevoor (or Sirur), about thirty miles west of Ahmednuggar and halfway to Poona. The corps' move from Ahmednuggar to Sevoor and then to Poona reflects its progress of road building, with each city a step west, closer to Bombay. With the fifth child, Ellen, baptized on December 6, 1836, Mary Anne now had four daughters and one son. Luckily, the seven of them did not have to fit in at the end of the barracks behind a curtain. In the new barracks the corps was putting up in the Company's military outposts, there were now real accommodations for wives and children. By the second half of the 1830s, barracks were equipped with small rooms, one to a family, known as the married men's quarters.

The first real tragedy for the growing Donohoe family was Charlotte's death, when Anna Harriett was a little over six. At this point the Donohoes had moved south to Bergaum, where Toby Butler was stationed. It was a delight for the two Glascott sisters to be living with their respective families in the same cantonment. Mary Anne had Eliza to console her when Charlotte was buried on February 13, 1838, age "two years, ten months, twelve days" (N/3/13/378). But Toby was reassigned to Surat, a port up the coast from Bombay. There Eliza Butler, Mary Anne's younger sister, died of an illness on September 7, 1839. She was twenty-three. Even in grief, Mary Anne was giving birth to her sixth child and second son, William Arthur (named for her father), born sometime in 1839. Then came another girl in October 1841, when Anna Harriett was almost ten, bringing Mary Anne's total number of children to seven, with six alive. By then the family was living well in a cantonment to the north, Deesa. I suspect that Mary Frederica did not live long since there is no record of her aside from her birth.

There were at least two more children, many years later. The next baptism for the Donohoes listed in the ecclesiastical records is not until December 20, 1853. It was a girl, Blanche, parents Patrick and Mary, the right family because the father was listed as a supervisor with the Department of Public Works in Poona. Mary Anne was thirty-seven. There surely must have been other pregnancies in the twelve years between Mary and Blanche, perhaps of infants who did not survive, perhaps simply unrecorded. The final baptism record for this incredibly fertile woman was another son, Vandry Glascott Donohoe, born in 1858 when his mother was forty-one or forty-two.

Naming the youngest child in memory of Mary Anne's father was certainly a loving act. But it is also an indicator of the ways Anglo-Indian families in the nineteenth century were committed to carrying on the traditions that would demonstrate their British and upper-class heritage. Mary Anne's brother had changed his name as an adult from William Frederick to William Vaudrey, in tribute to his English father. When her brother died in 1856, Mary Anne and Patrick took the first opportunity to make sure Mary Anne's precious English inheritance was carried on in the family, through the name of her youngest son.

One of Mary Anne's grandchildren, Ellen's son with her first husband, Sam Phillips, recalled Mary Anne in a letter dated July 8, 1898, which offers the only extant remarks about her. Ellen had followed the path of her mother, her aunt Eliza, and her oldest sister, Eliza Julia. She married a sergeant in the Sappers and Miners on May 24, 1852, in Poona, when she was fifteen. They had one son. After Sam died at only twenty-five, Ellen married Henry Savage, a subconductor, and had six more children with him before dying herself of rheumatic fever in 1872 at age thirty-five. Thomas Phillips Savage, her eldest child and the principal of Cathedral High School in Bombay, wrote in 1898 that his grandmother Mary Anne had "numerous children" by a second marriage and that "all but one died out" (LC, VI C). The claim is more or less accurate. Of Patrick's and Mary Anne's seven children that I know of, most were dead by 1898.

But in the 1830s and 1840s, all that was still to come. The Donohoe family when Anna Harriett was a child, apart from the brief time when Charlotte and Mary were alive, was a fine family of seven, the parents and five children. Eliza Julia was the oldest. Then came Anna Harriett, two years younger, then her younger half-brother John, followed by Ellen and then William, the baby. Blanche and Vandry would not appear until Eliza and Anna were married and gone.

Before she was ten, Anna Harriett had moved several times, in a half moon around Bombay. Since Patrick was one of the lowest-level bosses of a construction and road crew, the multiple moves reflected the piecework that characterized his military career. The family was living in Ahmednuggar in 1832, in Sevoor in 1836, in Bergaum in 1838, in Deesa in 1841, and finally settled permanently in Poona in the 1840s. But the life was not as transient as it sounds. This was an army family, moving from cantonment to cantonment, from barracks to barracks, all the housing choices looking pretty much the same. In the early years, most of the family's housing was standard barrack accommodations or, depending on the season and the available facilities, the tents. These were desirable not only because they could be cooler than the barracks but because they allowed for an expanding family by simply expanding the space.

Nor were the moves that wrenching. The Donohoes moved not in isolation but as a social group, with Patrick's whole regiment reassigned. The family was part of a floating but fairly constant community. At each different place the same people, soldiers and their families, would appear. And the buildings looked, or soon would look, pretty much the same. Much of what Patrick and his crew were doing during the 1830s and early 1840s with all these moves was building those barracks, to accommodate the rapidly expanding number of soldiers in the Indian Army. The first decade of Anna's childhood, for all its mobility, was socially stable as well.

Patrick Donohoe was the only father Anna ever knew, her parent since she was six weeks old. What the family's life and Anna's early childhood were like in those years of moving about depended in part on what sort of provider Patrick was. There are some clues to suggest that he was a good one. First, he was a sergeant, up from his enlistment level as a private. He was selected as a leader. His success had to counteract the deep prejudice against the Irish in the Company's army, including the belief that the Irish were the worst drunkards and the perpetrators of virtually all army murders, and that "the Irish are more vindictive and vengeful than either the English or Scotch" (Mac-Mullen, 169).

Most tellingly, Patrick kept his noncommissioned officer leadership position for the length of his army service. This meant not only that Patrick was not one of the many soldiers addicted to drinking and brawling but also that he could get along with the men he gave orders to and took orders from. It also tells us that he knew something about building. With an occupation listed as "smith," a little more unusual than the ubiquitous "cabinetmaker," Patrick probably entered the army with some specific skills.

Moreover, this was, of course, not the Crown's but the Company's army, founded on the principles of private enterprise and kept going for most of its existence by the canniness of the men in its service. It was perfectly acceptable, even encouraged, for men to make their own deals. As a sergeant, and with a "country-born" wife and relatives, including possibly a mother-in-law and certainly a brother-in-law, Patrick was in an excellent position to do a little business on the side. He had many opportunities to acquire building materials, and there is evidence that he did take advantage of these opportunities. He was able to hire himself out for private jobs between work assignments in the corps. Patrick also had friends among his army company who could help him with his outside construction projects, as he helped them with theirs.

The Sappers and Miners typically dealt with the fears and the dreams of their lives of poverty in British India by sharing their skills as laborers to help one another get ahead. The corps was held in some contempt at the time, many arguing that "in a country where the peasant's labour is cheaper than that of the soldier, to give military organization to a body of men who are merely to make roads and break stones" (Sandes, 110) was idiotic. In ways strikingly similar to the Irish immigrants in America, these devalued men saw

India as a new world and a land of opportunity. And many of them, including Patrick Donohoe, made the most of it.

In spite of the fact that the rank and file of this corps of laborers were of the lowest status in the Company's army, in practical ways they were better off than the infantry soldiers. Perhaps the single greatest enemy of the Company's soldiers, the enemy that drunkenness was embraced in order to ward off, was boredom. But unlike the infantry regiments, as laborers the Sappers and Miners worked hard. When there was fighting, they "hacked their ways through miles of jungle, prepared siege material and built batteries, carried ladders in every assault, and after the fighting was over, destroyed the enemy's fortifications and buried the dead" (Sandes, 111). When there was peace, they built roads and buildings and faced long hours of physical labor in the heat and dust. They faced exhaustion. But they did not face endless drills.

Well before the move to Poona at the beginning of the 1840s, Patrick had managed to provide some sort of housing for his increasing family. At each reassignment during the 1830s, from Ahmednuggar to Sirur (then Sevoor) to Bergaum to Deesa, he was able to increase the family's financial base, first living in the barracks and being paid on the side for extra building, then probably sharing the building of a bungalow, then selling the share and participating in building a little better one at the next site, until he had his own. And after a while Patrick had more than one, becoming a landlord himself.

Life for the Donohoe family in the 1830s and 1840s is a story of upward mobility, of progressing slowly into the lower middle class. By the 1850s, there is evidence that Patrick Donohoe and his family were living comfortably in a house they actually owned in Poona. They reached a level of economic stability that was extraordinarily rare in British India for rank-and-file soldiers. Even for the soldiers in the Sappers and Miners, such success was extraordinary. The general wisdom was that "their status was humble, their rewards were few" (Sandes, 111). Patrick and Mary Anne were an exceptional couple. Just being among the lucky few who were able to stay alive through their thirties and even beyond was a major factor in their success. And promotion came to Patrick in part through sheer longevity.

There never would have been any consideration of "going home" to Britain. The very phrase is a misnomer. The couple was home, and saw themselves as belonging there—though the century to come would see violent (and nonviolent) demonstrations challenging their right to be in India at all. But at the time, it seemed obvious that India was their country. Mary Anne and her whole side of the family were natives of India, as were Anna and the other children. And Patrick had, by joining the Indian

Army, permanently left the poverty of his native Ireland. To join the Company's army meant not so much to be stationed somewhere foreign as to immigrate to India. For husband, wife, and children, the Bombay presidency was their true home.

In the mid-1850s, Patrick had served his twenty-plus years in the Company's military and chose not to reenlist. Unlike most of the Company's soldiers, he could afford to have a choice. Only in his forties, he took what was apparently a civilian job, but wasn't. Although Patrick was officially out of the military, he now worked for the British government. He was what was called a "conductor," the government version of a sergeant, or construction crew boss, in the Public Works Department, known as the PWD, in Poona. Patrick had worked himself and his family up to a solid middle-class life.

A clear measure of the family's upward mobility is that, from 1852 (first mentioned in 1853) on, Patrick made the list in the British-published *Bombay Calendar and General Directory* as one of the European "residents" of Poona, a gigantic step for the uneducated country boy from Ireland who enlisted as a private. Patrick and Mary Anne had a long (for that time and place) and good life together. They kept their health. They slowly worked toward financial stability, and all of their living children found jobs and marriages. The farm laborer from Ireland and the sixteen-year-old, uneducated, half-caste widow from Bombay had started, with some early input from Tom Edwards, a little dynasty of their own. And the meager evidence suggests that they were a contented couple.

The Donohoes' financial and social achievement is conveniently measured by turning to an annual volume published by the Bombay Educational Society Press. Called the *Bombay Government Gazette,* it was a kind of almanac of yearly information about the city and the presidency. One of its many lists was the "List of Persons Qualified to Serve as Jurors." This was a list of European men outside the Company. But it was also a list of economic status. The other criterion besides racial ancestry and gender for appearing on the list was that the person reside in a house having a value of at least three hundred rupees. The jury list was effectively a measure of a man's standing as a member of at least the middle class.

Patrick Donohoe died October 30, 1864, in Poona, age fifty-five years and seven months, of an unlisted cause. He had done well enough in the Public Works Department to have been promoted, and at the time of his death his title was officially listed as deputy commissary and sub engineer in the PWD of Poona. Patrick died in much better financial standing than either Billy

Glascott or Tom Edwards. He left a will, actually having property to leave. And it is an impressive will. Patrick's property was extensively described as "my houses and Household furniture, linen and wearing apparel, Books, plate, Pictures, China, Horses and Carts and also all and every Sum or Sums of Money which I may have in any of the Banks or with Merchants and about my person or due to me at the time of my decease." Also notable is the emphatic warmth of his description of the single recipient of all of his property. Patrick left "all and every" bit of it to "Mary Anne Donohoe my dear wife for her own use and benefit absolutely."

The impressive list of Patrick's property in the will is a legal formula. But that Patrick really was a man of property can be concluded from a special provision. This was that Mary Anne not sell "the houses with appurtenances situated in the Conductors lines and bearing register #2 on the Books of the Poona Brigade Office" without the permission of the two witnesses to the will. Patrick owned houses as rental properties in the NCO housing section of the cantonment. Selling them would be appropriate only when they did not have tenants.

Mary Anne (Edwards) Donohoe, née Glascott, lived even longer than her husband, reaching very old age by the standards of British India. She was a widow with financial security. Soon after Patrick's death, Mary Anne did sell those houses "in the Conductors lines." She moved back to Bombay, a major international city and much expanded from when she had been born to Billy Glascott and his lady at Bombay Fort. It had been thirty-five years since the thirteen-year-old girl had married and left Bombay.

Mary Anne moved back to the city of her childhood for quite the usual reasons, to be near her family, her children, and her many grandchildren. Mary Anne died on August 19, 1873, fifty-seven years old, of carditis, or heart failure, and was buried at Nusseerabad, in the archdiocese of Bombay. She had outlived many of the people she loved. Both her husbands were dead. Her brother, William, and her sister, Eliza, were dead. At least four of her daughters were dead, two dying in childhood, her eldest, Eliza, in 1864, and Ellen in 1872. Her son William was long dead. He had married Emilie Trott in 1862 and lived until July 21, 1866. Blanche and John may have been still living, though I have not been able to confirm this. John McCarthy Donohoe had married Emma Dewey in 1859. He was listed as a Bombay inhabitant up to 1866. Then nothing.

Vandry, Mary Anne's youngest, was still alive in 1873. He would marry Rosalina Thomas in 1877 in Poona. John, William, and Vandry spent part of their professional lives working as clerks and ticket takers for the railways, an indisputable proof that they (and, therefore, their mother) were Anglo-Indian. Jobs on the railway were officially reserved for Anglo-Indians. Vandry did not die until October 8, 1903. He is buried near his brother, William, at the Sevree Cemetery in Bombay. And finally, when Mary Anne died in August 1873, her second child, Anna Harriett, who had been gone from India for twenty years, was alive and well on the east coast of the United States and just publishing her second book. She would outlive them all.

FOUR

Daughter of the Deccan

THERE IS ALMOST NO INFORMATION about Anna Harriett Edwards's early years. Without public records, a biographer can usually turn to personal records. But Anna herself has been the greatest obstacle to discovering anything of her personal history. She threw away or destroyed any records, family letters, or souvenirs and replaced them with lies. When she was quite old in Canada, and pressed by her grandchildren to provide them with a record of her adventurous life, Anna did write that infamous narrative about her earlier times. This brief story included the claim that she and her older sister, Eliza, were born and grew up in Wales, educated there when their parents sailed away to India, and sent to Bombay when Anna was fifteen and Eliza was sixteen, to live with their mother and stepfather, whom they had never met. The portrait is of two genteelly educated white British sisters who arrived in India only when they had completed their schooling and reached marriageable age.

It was all fake, of course. Just as were Anna's follow-up claims that her father was a Major Crawford, aide-de-camp to Sir James Macintosh, and that he died nobly outside Lahore, "cut to pieces by Sikhs who lay in wait for him," and that her mother was from a notable Welsh family with the distinctively English name of Edwards. These are "facts" that the official East India Company records disprove. The same records also disprove the crucial centerpiece of Anna's narrative, the single most important "fact," which Anna's inventions did not explicitly say but were all designed to claim, that Anna and Eliza Julia were of fully British descent and born in Britain.

What was Anna Harriett Edwards's childhood really like? The children in the Donohoe household, Eliza, Anna Harriett, John, Ellen, and William, though considered by British visitors to be "not of a colour to introduce to the world" (Sherwood, 309), enjoyed a fine life. They grew up in an extensive social—virtually a communal—world. From the moment that the two girls were born behind the sacking at one end of a barracks, their lives were spent among large numbers of people. Among the lower social levels of the people connected to the Company in British India, there was little sense of a nuclear family as we understand it today. Most families were what we now call blended, because one spouse or another died all the time and the remaining spouse usually remarried, and often the maternal relatives were there as well.

Fort children ran around in packs. They played together, watched drills together, and, when suppertime came, ate at their fire or at someone else's. When it was time to sleep, they often lay down with a wrap or a ground cloth in piles like puppies. Often near the tents were the animals as well, "camels, together with elephants or buffaloes" (Waterfield, 25). The privacy we strive for so relentlessly today would have been considered a sign of dementia in the cantonments of the Bombay presidency. In camp life, people lived together in that crowded noisy world with an ease we can no longer understand.

Anna and her family belonged to the army community and also to the closely knit community of mixed-race Anglo-Indians. The community consisted of natives of the Bombay presidency, but with a communal pride in their cultural inclusiveness and rich heritage, combining ancestors of many races but with a predominance of Indian, British, and Portuguese. Visiting British, ignorant of the ways of the Company, frequently referred to them with scorn as "half-castes" or sometimes used the somewhat more respectful term "Eurasians." But in the Bombay presidency, the Anglo-Indians were a mutually supportive and politically active community. They were proud of their mixed heritage, regarding themselves as a superior combination of different peoples and cultures. The Donohoe family was a welcome addition.

In many a family like the Donohoes, the two groups, the soldiers and the Anglo-Indians, intertwined. Anna was raised in a multicultural community of extraordinary richness and integration, full of peoples of many and mixed races, and many languages. The living quarters and sanitary conditions were poor. But the social conditions were not. Anna played with the children of Christians and Muslims and Hindus; kids whose fathers her father worked with, or whose mothers her mother shopped the bazaar stalls with, and visited with, and made a few rupees doing officers' laundry with; kids whose parents or grandparents or great-grandparents came from all over Europe and not only all over India but the rest of the East as well. To be young and belong in the Bombay presidency in the boom times of the 1830s, to be mixed race in a place where (except among the foreign elite, and sometimes even there) it was socially accepted, to be part of the Company but not part of the constrained upper classes of its officers and civil servants, was very heaven.

As a child of a company family, Anna lived in a protected world, with a way of life both mobile and stable. During that first decade of her life and the Donohoe marriage, the family was frequently on the move. When Anna was about four, they shifted from her original home in the barracks at Ahmednuggar to the cantonment in Sevoor for about three years, and then they spent two or three more years first in Bergaum and then in Deesa. Patrick was building barracks and other buildings and roads in each of these places and the family lived the camp life. Somehow, in this process Eliza and Anna and the younger children began to get an education. Mary Anne's second daughter must have shown signs even at this young age of the unusual intellectual curiosity and ability that would shape her future.

Schooling in the cantonments, though limited, was far superior to anything the rural and urban poor had in England. There were regimental schools, typically a room of company children of all ages. The schools used "the Madras system," meaning that the older children taught the younger reading, writing, and arithmetic, or the job went to a sergeant. Mrs. Sherwood had a school with a sergeant on her verandah for barracks children. She was particularly proud that she refused none, "even when the children were coloured" (Sherwood, 276). She was one of those teachers full of the sense "that many of my pupils were extremely wicked—in short, to use a vulgar phrase, that there was nothing that some of them were not up to" (Sherwood, 276–77). The Company not only set up schools in their cantons but in 1821 set up garrison libraries as well (White, 30). Literacy was a marketable attribute.

Anna and her siblings received a far better education than they could ever have hoped for in Britain, where they would have spent their days in farm labor. Anna's days had many pleasures. She spent two to four hours in the morning at her books, then she and the other children enjoyed a glorious freedom. There were many chores, but even these had a kind of freedom. They had to look after their siblings, run errands to the bazaar for the night's dinner, haul water, gather firewood and tend the fire, carry messages, and help Mary Anne with the laundry at the river.

The best aspect of camp life was to be had outside of school. Anna belonged to a community where at least 80 percent of the soldiers were natives and probably 95 percent of the families were as well, a community of many kinds of Muslims and Hindus and Armenians and Portuguese mixes. To an outsider like Mrs. Sherwood, in India temporarily, rank and file were "men of an inferior grade," and the children "of white men and coloured mothers" (397) were even more inferior. But in the regional cantonments, even the few white children, unless they were upper class, mingled with everyone else.

For little Anna, the peoples of the canton provided an education richer than anything to be had in the finest schools in England or Bombay. She became fluent in Hindi as well as English and learned to read and write in Sanskrit as well as learning her ABCs. She was fascinated enough by, and learned enough details about the culture and beliefs of, the Rajputs and Mussalmans and native Christians to put them in one of her books when she lived far away in America. And she never forgot the lessons of equality among the races that she learned as an army child in the tent camps and soldiers' barracks of the Company's Indian Army.

Anna Harriett's first identity was as the daughter of an illiterate teenage Anglo-Indian widow and an already deceased "rank-and-file" English soldier. Her second identity, starting when she was six weeks old, was as the stepdaughter of a penniless lower-class Irishman who moved from place to place for almost a decade, working at construction sites in provincial India in the early nineteenth century. For Anna Harriett, there would be several other identities to come. This child of poverty and ignorance somehow metamorphosed into the highly literate and polylingual Anna Leonowens, genteel widow in Singapore, governess to royalty in Siam, musical duenna and Sanskrit scholar in Germany, traveling journalist in Russia, and international author and public lecturer in the United States and Canada. It was a phenomenal, even dazzling, feat. The question is: how did she do it?

The metamorphosis is, first of all, an indication of Anna's remarkable intelligence. What a brilliant child she must have been to learn so much, although with few formal educational opportunities, and being a girl at that. Marriage, at fourteen and at the latest by fifteen or sixteen, was the recognized path for lower-class Eurasian girls. It was the path Anna's sister, Eliza Julia, took quite happily. Intelligent and intensely curious, Anna not only studied her books but also learned some of the various languages, religious beliefs, and social customs that her friends, their parents, and her stepfather's diverse fellow workers called their own. She had a facility for languages. Through her camp experiences she also learned to be at home, or at least to make herself comfortable, in unfamiliar cultures with customs far different from her own. Best of all, she learned tolerance, a sense of the value and the rights of all kinds of people. It was the kind of education that allowed her future to take its many interesting shapes.

Perhaps what most characterizes the long life of Anna Harriett Emma Edwards Leonowens is the range of different cultures in which she lived and thrived, and perhaps even belonged. And for that she has to thank not only her own character but also the Indian Army camp life she was born into. Anna was not a chameleon. That is too pat an analysis. She was not self-effacing. But her life must surely challenge our conventional notions of what the "self" means. For she did have what I would call a highly flexible subjectivity, an ability to shape herself into a person who could fit with whatever culture she found herself living in, and at the same time keep a strong sense of self, whoever at the moment that self happened to be. The Anglo-Indian child running free in the camp, the studious teenager, the young wife and mother in Bombay, the British governess in the royal palace in Siam, the antislavery professional lecturer in Philadelphia and New York, the musical doyenne in Germany, the liberated woman and patron of the arts in Canada: Anna Harriett was every one of these characters and at home in them all.

Born with more than one identity as a result of her mixed heritage, Anna was comfortable with the notion that it was not only possible but pleasant and even highly desirable to have more than one identity. She accepted that a person could have several identities, and not just those provided by one's parents, no matter how diverse their backgrounds. She grasped more than the content of her multiple situations. She grasped the principle as well. Anna Harriett would come to realize not only that she was more than one category of person—a fact constantly impressed on her by her double (at the very least) heritage and the complex and changing cultural meaning of Anglo-Indians in British India. She would also come to see that she had some control over the process, that she could become other categories, other kinds of people. And she could do it not as a matter of cultural history or an accident of birth. She could do it by choice.

Anna did have exceptional intellectual and personal gifts. She grew up to be self-disciplined and strong-willed. But her family heritage and her special abilities, along with the social contexts of her early childhood, though key factors, are not the whole explanation for her later achievements. Another crucial factor was a matter of location. Anna was particularly blessed in that she lived in Poona, the city known as the "Queen of the Deccan," for her teenage years. Anna stayed in Poona from 1842, when the Donohoes moved there, to Christmas Day, 1849, when she married a young man in Bombay.

Sergeant Donohoe had been transferred to Poona (now Pune), about ninety miles east of Bombay, when Anna was a little more than ten. Poona had been the regimental headquarters of the Bombay Sappers and Miners since

1837. Before moving to Poona, the Donohoes had really covered the territory of the western presidency, living in the east, the south, and the north. Distances, road conditions, and travel methods all meant that the Donohoes were cut off from the big-city amenities of Bombay. They were an outstation family. Poona was reached by traveling inland and up into a range of steep hills known as the Western Ghats. Once across them, the traveler entered a vast area of higher, drier ground, a treeless plain subject to occasional drought because it lay in the rain shadow of the Ghats. This extensive plain with its "flat-topped hills" (Diddee and Gupta, 21), to which Poona was a gateway city, was called the Deccan Plateau, or just the Deccan, or even the "Desh."

The road between Bombay and Poona in the early nineteenth century was barely a track. It took four days to cover the ninety miles, though with some road improvements the time was shortened to two days. But it remained a rugged trip. The road included a well-known spot in the Western Ghats, the Bhor Pass. "Carriages could not be driven over the steep gradient. Passengers had to leave their coach at the top of the *ghat* and be carried down in palanquins and then get on to another coach for the rest of the journey. Private carriages had to be carried up and down the *ghat* swinging from poles carried by workmen" (Diddee and Gupta, 140).

Though hard to get to from the coast, Poona had a lot of charm and even more history. The two major conquering peoples of India before the British had been the Moghuls (Muslims) and the Marathas (Hindus). Leaders of both groups had fought over Poona, this city on the Deccan at the confluence of three rivers. Poona was a vibrant city, "set amidst cypress groves, mango orchards, and gardens" (Diddee and Gupta, 79), with elegant mansions and elaborate temples. Colonel Welsh described it in the early years of the nineteenth century. "The streets, as in most native towns, are extremely narrow, and full of bazaars, which contain an innumerable quantity of articles of merchandize, the produce not only of India but of China and Europe" (Welsh, 152). He reached the happy conclusion that "it appeared to us a place of great wealth, and to concentrate all the trade of the empire" (155).

Poona was the capital of the Maratha Empire and home of the peshwa of the Marathas, who were the last best hope of the subjugated peoples of the Indian subcontinent against the British. Poona was "considered the most influential city in India" (Diddee and Gupta, 12). H. D. Robertson, the first collector (British governor) of Poona, commented that the city "is looked upon with a respect that is quite surprising, and it has been considered by the lower classes (nor can I drive the belief from their heads) that he who rules in Poona governs the world" (Diddee and Gupta, 53).

The British won the city at the Battle of Khadki in November 1817, "the saddest event in Maratha history" (Diddee and Gupta, 74), and captured the peshwa in 1818, the two events symbolizing the moment when the British finally conquered all of India. After the victory and the flight of the peshwa and virtually everyone else of public consequence, the city that had sparkled with pomp and riches lost its sheen. The Maratha court and all its members and visitors were gone. "Since that time the city has not been so flourishing" (Urwick, 212). Even Mountstuart Elphinstone noticed that "the absence of the Hindu government occasions a void that alters the effect of everything. Our respect for the place is gone, and the change is melancholy." Showing unusual sensitivity for a conqueror, he went on to comment, "How must the natives feel this when even we feel it" (Diddee and Gupta, 133).

The thriving bazaars, famous for their luxury goods from far-flung places, lost their customers and closed. The "Kashmiri shawls, inlaid stoneware from Agra, bidri-ware from the south, ivory, gold and silver," everything was gone. Poona as a luxury market was no more. Instead of the former bustle and purpose, the city "presented the tameness of poverty." The shining Queen of the Deccan had been irretrievably dulled. At the crisis moment of 1825, seven years after the British occupation had begun, the city looked very bleak. When grain prices rose and there was famine in the city, "scarcely a horse passed along the listless streets which were empty except for starving tailors and better fed butter dealers" (Diddee and Gupta, 133).

Poona as "a conquered City" (Moledina, 1) seemed to have turned into just another British backwater cantonment. But there was one special difference that distinguished this fallen paradise: its glorious past was quite recent. Poona's still highly diverse inhabitants remained full of memories of the grandeur they had seen and known in their own lifetimes. They were actively and loudly regretting, dreaming of, and reminiscing to curious children about the glory days just behind them.

The 1820s to 1840s in Poona were a time of economic depression, though by the 1840s the city was coming back to life. The British, with some wisdom, decided not just to move in and take over. They established a military cantonment outside Poona, to the east. The cantonment had three sections. We might translate them as the business district, the suburbs, and the mall. The cantonment was on a large plot of land bounded by two rivers, essential for providing a water supply. All public and military institutions, such as "Jail, Police Chawls; Dispensary; Hospital; Market; Burial Ground; Gibbet [hanging place] etc.," were located within the canton (Moledina, 52).

The second part of the cantonment was the Civil Lines. This was the kind of place where our present-day fantasies about British life in India come from. The Civil Lines were the bungalow area, sort of a suburb for high-ranking officers and the Company's civil servants. The Lines consisted of "wide tree-lined roads flanked by riding paths and the typical secluded cottage-like bungalows in neat plots" (Diddee and Gupta, 141). The bungalows had long drives and large "English"-looking gardens, but with flower beds producing a riot of color all year round. "The size of the plot as well as the house was in accordance with the strict hierarchical ranking system of the army." The bungalows were large and high ceilinged, with a deep verandah that "ran all around the house. In the rainy season it afforded an after-dinner walk, and it was also the place where afternoon tea was taken or morning visitors entertained" (Diddee and Gupta, 145).

But neither the main cantonment nor the Civil Lines had anything to do with the Donohoe family. The lives and experiences of the upper class were a world away from the lives and experiences of the "other ranks." The Donohoes did not live in the main Poona Cantonment with the rest of the army. Instead, they lived in a smaller, second cantonment for the construction crews, across a river and more than a mile to the north and west. The Company had set it up "near the village of Khadki on the small flat plain within the meandering curve of the Mula river to the north" (Diddee and Gupta, 141). So they called it the Khadki or, more usually, the Kirkee Cantonment.

The Kirkee Cantonment was the site of the Gunpowder and Small Arms and Ammunition Factory. Also, in 1835 the governor of the Bombay presidency decided that for strategic and climatic reasons it would be well for the governor and council to spend the hot months up in the dry air of Poona. The practical effect of these two factors was a greatly increased need for large construction crews for all the new buildings. Before there were barrack accommodations "the troops were placed in huts outside the towns and lived a camp life" (Moledina, 32). In 1837, the Bombay Sappers and Miners relocated their regimental headquarters to the Kirkee Cantonment and got to work. Patrick Donohoe and his company of laborers arrived at the beginning of the 1840s, and Kirkee Cantonment became their permanent home.

The family began its residence in Poona familiarly enough, in a tent, and camp life was as ever for Anna and her family. The children went each day to the Mula River bounding the camp to haul buckets of water back to their outdoor kitchen area for food and drink. Mary Anne made a few rupees doing some laundry for officers' families. The Kirkee bazaar carried the necessaries for curries and rice, as well as mangos and bananas and many other fruits. There were new friends to be made and old friends to be rediscovered, as the familiar rhythm of life for the Donohoes was established once again.

But Poona in the 1840s was getting back some of its old vitality and glow. It would never reach its former glory, but the Queen of the Deccan was coming alive again. It was in the middle of a building boom, and the Donohoes soon changed from the tents to what the soldiers so aptly named hutments, "temporary low, single-storey structures with tile roofs" (Diddee and Gupta, 142). Patrick Donohoe was building barracks, though not at first for himself and his own family. The first barracks building, finished in 1842, was for the European troops. Still, by the middle of the 1840s there were even barracks in Kirkee, and Anna's family had at last a closed-off room of their own.

During the 1840s, life in the Indian Army for the rank and file was changing rapidly, in keeping with the great changes in relations between the British and India. Permanent barracks were one sign of the changing times. The old camp life, with its easy mixing of religions, cultures, and races, was being displaced as more and more the daily lives of Indian Army soldiers, and the daily lives of their families, were being improved but also segregated and controlled. After the British takeover of 1818, the Company had moved fairly quickly to establish in Poona many of the structures of British culture. The Company had a small regimental school and a regimental library as early as 1825.

Anna and her siblings attended school through their early teens. Macaulay's 1835 Minute on Education guaranteed that what was taught in the regimental schools included more than just the rudiments of reading and writing and arithmetic in English. Along with grammar, the students, both boys and girls, were expected to learn something of the culture of the "mother country," to read some Spenser and Shakespeare, and also some Dryden and Johnson and even Wordsworth; to know the geography of Great Britain and continental Europe; and to have at least a little familiarity with English history, including the Magna Carta and the Spanish Armada. Much like the standard education in the "humanities" that our children receive to this day, which is a modified version of the educational ideas evolved in British India, the curriculum aimed to teach the historical greatness and general superiority of the English people.

Anna Harriett did well in the regimental school. The educational opportunities that the Company had not provided to Mary Anne in the earlier decades of the century were now available to this next generation of company children. But Anna's sister, Eliza, though she may have done well enough at her studies, does not seem to have been an unusual child. She took the path that was typical of her class and sex in the Anglo-Indian community in

British India. She finished school at around fourteen and, just two days before her fifteenth birthday, like her mother and grandmother before her, married a company soldier. This one was James Millard (sometimes recorded as Milliard), whom she had met in Deesa. James was from County Buckingham and had landed in Bombay on June 5, 1836, disembarking from the *Duchess Atholl.* Nine years later, on April 24, 1845, he married Eliza in Bombay. The two official witnesses at the ceremony are recorded as P. Donohoe and A. Edwards, Patrick and Anna.

The most significant fact about James was that his military career was from the beginning at a higher level than that of Eliza and Anna's father or stepfather. Though still rank and file, James enlisted in a horse artillery regiment, not the catchall infantry, and as a corporal. When he married Eliza Julia, James was a sergeant major. Eliza had married slightly "up." Anna's family's fortunes were definitely improving, from what must have been their low point, when Billy Glascott died in debt leaving his lady with at least three small children, and his daughter Mary Anne's best option had been to marry a construction crew private when she was just thirteen.

Eliza had two children with James. The first was James Edward, born May 25, 1846. Anna had become an aunt. Their second was Eliza Sarah, born June 25, 1848, when they were still living in Poona. In 1852, James left the army and took a government job as inspector of roads, first at Girgaum and then at Cowasjee. He appeared regularly in the *Bombay Almanac and Directory* in the list of European residents. Sometime in the late 1850s or early 1860s, the couple moved to Bombay and James became superintendent of the reformatory. It would prove to be a bad move for Eliza Julia. Anna's sister died on June 13, 1864, only thirty-four years old, the cause of death listed as "Inflamation of the Peritonitis." Eliza left a son just turned eighteen and a daughter one week shy of sixteen. Her stepfather, Patrick, died just four and a half months later. The year 1864 was terrible for Mary Anne, who outlived her first child as well as her husband by nine years. When Eliza died, Anna had already been working for two years as a governess to the royal children in Bangkok.

Eliza Sarah, known as Lizzie, did well for herself, though her mother missed seeing it. In 1864, a little more than four months after her mother died and six days before her grandfather Donohoe died, Lizzie married. She was just sixteen and the groom was in his late thirties, and already twice a widower. But he had impressive professional credentials. Edward John Pratt was the son of Edward Pratt, a lieutenant in the Native Infantry regiment, the same rank as Lizzie's great-grandfather, Billy Glascott. Just like the first generation of Glascott children in India, Edward John was born in Bombay to a lower-level officer in the Indian Army and a mixed-race lady. Like so many Anglo-Indian men, once real advancement in the East India Company had been denied them by the exclusionary directives of the late eighteenth century, Edward began professionally as a government clerk. He worked his way up to be head assistant in the Judiciary Department of the Secretariat in Bombay.

The widower married Eliza Sarah on October 24, 1864. The couple had a long successful life, eventually moving to England from India. Their eight sons were also quite successful. The eldest, Edward, became a judge. The sixth son, Sir John Thomas, was part of the British legation to Peking and wrote books on China. The eighth son, Anna's great-nephew, her niece Lizzie's ninth and youngest child, was William Henry. He was born in England and attended King's College, London, and then moved to the west coast of Canada in 1909. At that time, unknown to him, his great aunt Anna was still a public figure in Montreal. William took up acting and gave himself the Russian-sounding name Boris Karloff. Ultimately, he moved to Los Angeles and had a hugely successful screen career.

Eliza Julia helped to recoup the family fortunes of her paternal line through marriage and through her children and grandchildren. Anna took a different path. She was determined to make her own success, and in her own lifetime. She too finished the regimental school when she was about fourteen. But whatever she did then, it was not look for a husband. It would be four years before Anna got married. In her little autobiography, that beautiful but fictitious document, Anna claimed that after finishing her formal schooling she spent three years touring the Holy Land under the tutelage of an East India Company chaplain and Persian/Arabic scholar, Rev. Percy Badger, and his wife. I am certain she did no such thing.

Anna enjoyed acquiring languages. Teaching at a boys school (the Berkeley) on Madison Avenue in New York in 1880–81, she boarded with a German family who did "not speak one word of English," so as to develop her German (LC, VI C). As a child she spoke not only English but at least two of the major languages of the subcontinent, Hindi and Marathi, the language of the Muslim population of southern India, including Poona. Hindi and Marathi were both based in Sanskrit, the "Latin" of the East, no longer spoken but the language of ancient Hindu sacred literature. The written language of the Muslim empire and the official language of the administration of India at the Moghul courts was Persian, until it was banned by the Company in 1835 and replaced by English, the language of the new conquerors (Bayly, 154).

As an older woman Anna knew Sanskrit well. She taught a six-week introductory summer course in it at Amherst in 1878. This is perfectly credible, at least because she was a gifted linguist but also because, as far as I have been able to determine, Anna made no false claims about her achievements (only about her background). She wrote to her daughter Avis, on her honeymoon in England and Scotland that summer of 1878, that Professor Boucher of Harvard had commented that Anna's "manner of teaching Sanskrit" was better "than that of the great Bopp and that my pupils had made more progress in three weeks than he had done in six months under that of Bopp, the great German and Sanskrit scholar in Berlin" (LC, VI C).

Anna's excellent knowledge of Sanskrit was also evident during her three-year stay in Leipzig, Germany, at the end of the century. Anna was there as guardian of one of her granddaughters, who was studying music. Writing to her son-in-law in September 28, 1898, Anna commented on her upcoming birthday, which "will find me far into the sixties, sixty-four—I do not feel old at all." In fact, Anna would be sixty-seven. But why even point out such discrepancies about a woman who could go on to say:

> I am no longer young; but mentally and physically I find very little change in myself. In the Harz I walked for miles, climbed the highest mountains, not as rapidly as the young people, but better than any other German woman or man my age could in the whole place. I took up the study again, of Sanskrit in the University here and find myself quite equal to the young and old German and American students in the class, in unraveling the intricacies of the Sandhi rules—and the difficulties of the idiom. (LC, VI C)

Even in her older years, Anna was mentally and physically a dynamic phenomenon.

She wrote again to a friend in 1899 about her experiences at the University of Leipzig in Professor Ernst Hindrich's advanced Sanskrit class:

> In the Maha Bharata [*Mahabharata,* a classic Hindu epic] Class, where there are only German students, I was at first regarded as a half witted old body, who *thought* she knew Sanskrit, but since the Dr. has called me up to the black board to read or rather *intone* some of the high sounding verse, and translate them into German there is a marked change in their attitude toward me; althogh I am still of the opinion they think women have no right to venture beyond the *Kitchen,* the *Nursery* and the *Church.* I am glad to have it in my power to give them a substantial object lesson. (LC, VI C)

Anna took more than one class in Sanskrit texts at Leipzig. She wrote to her grandson on July 31, 1899, about her Rig-Veda (the earliest of the Vedas) class and a fellow student who was a twenty-two-year-old American from Harvard. Arthur Ryder went home to become an instructor and assistant professor of Sanskrit at Harvard and then moved to California as a professor of Sanskrit.

So where did Anna learn fluency in Sanskrit and Persian? Anna's own mythmaking account is found in her third book, *Life and Travel in India*. In it she claims that when she and her British officer husband set up house in the elegant suburb of Malabar Hill in Bombay, "my husband and I took up the study of the Sanskrit and Hindostanee languages" (39). Combining Anna's various claims, her narrative is that the Persian she learned from Rev. Badger and the Sanskrit she learned from a tutor on her staff in Bombay.

But, of course, Anna never lived on Malabar Hill, had no "staff," and never traveled with the Badgers. And she had no formal schooling in Sanskrit or Persian. Then where could her fine knowledge of Sanskrit have come from? A likely answer can be found back in Poona. In the 1820s, "the earliest educational institution to be set up by the British in Pune" was Poona Sanskrit College (Diddee and Gupta, 185). It was housed in one of the old mansions, known as *wadas*, left from the time of the peshwas, until it moved to a new building in 1868 and was renamed Deccan College. Because of her facility with languages and her fascination with learning them, Anna most likely found a way to study Sanskrit in Poona, probably with a local friend connected to the Sanskrit College.

As for Persian, that brings me back to George Percy Badger. Rev. and Mrs. Badger (he did have a wife; the record lists "the Rev. G. P. Badger and Lady") arrived in Bombay on May 9, 1845, from Aden. He had come out from England to be an assistant chaplain in the Bombay presidency. Born in England in 1815 but raised in Malta, Rev. Badger knew Persian and Arabic and became a well-known scholar, writing many books on Arabia and an English-Arabic lexicon. The Badgers stayed in Kolapoor, far south of Bombay, for about a year, and then on October 1, 1847, "Mrs. Badger, Rev. G. P. Badger" sailed back west on the *Semiramus* to Aden. But did Anna know him? They could have met in his travels between Bombay and Kolapoor, since the route was east to Poona and then south to Kolapoor. But he would never have taken this half-caste sergeant's daughter on a tour of the Holy Land. More probably, she knew of him and she read his books.

There is a simple explanation for Anna's learning Persian. The written language of Poona, headquarters of the Maratha government, as of all Moghul India, was Persian. Up through the 1840s, the public documents in South India were in Persian, except for those of the colonial government.

Even though in the 1840s the language of official documents was English, the written language of so much else of the business of living was still Persian. There were Persian newspapers, and the bazaars of Poona were full of scribes sitting cross-legged under umbrellas, their inkpots covered as protection from the dust. They were no longer employed by officials, but they still had a wealth of local customers who, in this world of extensive illiteracy, hired them to write their business and personal letters. The language of commerce, both economic and social, in the vibrant world of Poona, was Persian. Anna learned Persian in the homes and bazaars of Poona, where she learned so much else.

FIVE

Love and Bombay, at Last

ANNA HARRIETT HAD ONLY ONE ROMANTIC LOVE in her life. His name was Thomas Louis Leon Owens. He was from a middle-class Protestant family, literate but not well-off. John Owens and Mary Lean, Tom's parents, had married in 1810 in the diocese of Ossory, Ireland. Their son was one of thousands who emigrated to escape the economic blight caused by the potato famine that swept Ireland from 1845 to 1850. Most of these young men went west, flooding into America. But some went east, to the Company's India, hoping to find a career and a life. Tom Owens immigrated to India sometime in the second half of the 1840s, in late 1847 or possibly 1848. For the first time in this Glascott family history in India, the young man in question had not come to India by the path of becoming a soldier for the almighty East India Company. By 1849, young Tom Owens was living in the district of Bombay City known as the Fort.

In the middle of the nineteenth century, Bombay was a major international and commercial center, far different from the city that had greeted the young cadet's eyes when Billy Glascott landed there forty years earlier, in 1810. British Bombay had grown into a grand urban metropolis, much of it modeled after the architecture and the infrastructure of London. There were grand boulevards and a wealth of those gigantic stone buildings so loved by nineteenth-century Englishmen. The centerpiece of British Bombay was probably its Town Hall, finished in 1830, an enormous stone edifice complete with Doric columns, built on the site of what had been Bombay Green. "The steps and colonnade of that imposing structure provided a dramatic backdrop for the public reading of the Queen's Proclamation in 1858" (Asiatic Society of Bombay, n.p.). There had been an active chamber of commerce since 1836, and the Bank of Bombay opened in 1840. The Bhor Ghat Road to Poona, which opened in 1830, was the rough beginning of what became a major commercial route for goods to come into Bombay from the Indian interior.

The boundaries of the city had expanded enormously in forty years, as the various little islands were connected by causeways and their marshy lands drained. The big public buildings, the churches, and the bigger merchant houses were concentrated in the Fort area, jostled by cheap housing. By the end of the 1830s, there were "only a few Europeans who continue to inhabit the Fort" (Roberts, 238). By 1850, the Fort was so crowded that it was like a "large basket so full of goods that they threatened to tumble out of it." Along with the urban center of the Fort, there was a range of crowded adjacent districts, including Girgaum and Parell (now Parel), which made up what the British upper classes referred to as "Black Town" or "Native Town" (Roberts, 299). This was where most of the Indian residents, the "country-born" mixed races, and the lower- and middle-class Europeans lived. The richer Europeans, merchants and upper-level officers, lived apart, in early suburbs, building so-called bungalows on the outskirts of the city, on Malabar Hill and Mazgaon. Many of these bungalows were actually enormous stone villas, in the Gothic or Renaissance style, set among charming gardens complete with statues and fountains.

The expanding infrastructure of the British presence in Bombay created a modest but flourishing job market of salaried positions outside the Honourable Company, particularly at the lower levels of clerks and copyists, for those men who could speak and write English. These were of two groups: the mixed-race Anglo-Indian community born in India (such as the male children in the Glascott/Donohoe family) and the many middle-class British people without prospects at home who had immigrated to India looking for work. Tom Owens found a job, and by 1849 he was working as a clerk in the Commissary General's Office and living in the Fort area. He was twenty-one years old.

A clerk's salary was not much. But one of the compensations for Tom was that he found many other young men in similar circumstances. Among the society of hardworking clerks in Bombay, Tom got to know a young Anglo-Indian named William Glascott. In 1849, William, Mary Anne's younger brother, was twenty-eight years old. He had been a clerk in the Military Board Office in Bombay for five years. At some point in 1848 or in the first half of 1849, Anna and her family had come for a visit to Bombay. In the fall of 1848, Anna was still sixteen, not turning seventeen until November 26.

There are two reasons for believing that Anna Harriett and her mother made the four-day journey to Bombay from Poona in the fall of 1848, perhaps as late as the Christmas holidays or January 1849. In June 1848, Anna Harriett's sister, Eliza Julia, and her husband, Sergeant Major James Millard, an NCO with the Fourth Troop, Horse Artillery, had their second child, a daughter, Eliza Sarah. Sergeant Millard was stationed in Bombay, but Eliza had gone home to her mother for the birth, and the baby was born in Poona. Since Sergeant Millard would not have been released from duty to get his wife and baby, Anna Harriett and Mary Anne brought Eliza and her new daughter to Bombay.

The women also brought Mary Anne's son Johnny Donohoe (and probably Ellen and little William as well). In the winter season of 1848–49, Johnny was fourteen years old. He had finished the regimental school at Poona and it was time to think of his future. Johnny was apparently somewhat of a problem child and Mary Anne brought him to her younger brother to see what William could do with him as well as for him. She and the children, including her grown-up daughter, Anna, met William's friend, Tom Owens. Mary Anne left Johnny in Bombay, watched over by his Uncle William and put in lodgings either with or near Tom.

We do not know what William thought of taking on this responsibility. But it is clear that he had serious doubts about Johnny. Tom, who addressed his letters to "Annie" (he always called her Annie) and signed them "Leon," wrote to Anna on November 14, 1849, about the situation.

> From a conversation I had with him some time ago when he attempted to persuade me that Johnny was irreclaimable, I am induced to think Glascott has not Johnny's interest at heart, and that in everything that concerns him he is actuated more by caprice, and other feelings not at all more amiable. For a length of time before Glascott left me he took no notice of nor did he speak to Johnny because the boy had some time before offended him about some trifling matter, and after that when Johnny went near him he was ordered to "go away from there." That is by no means the way to treat a boy and such treatment cannot mend or benefit him. (LC, VI C)

Clearly, by 1849, Johnny, now fifteen, had a reputation as a boy who had already given his family some difficulty.

Tom had more patience with a teenage boy than William did. But before reading too much into the situation or into their respective characters, particularly William's, we should remember that at this moment Tom was only twenty-one himself, while William was almost twenty-nine. Tom was a good deal closer to remembering "how to treat a boy" than William was. By the time of this letter, Johnny had been lodging with either William or Tom for a while. In one of Tom's previous letters to Annie, almost a month earlier on October 20, he closed by saying, "remember me most kindly to Mamma and all. Johnny and Glascott are well."

There are points about this letter that tell us something about Tom and why Anna was attracted to him. First is the high degree of literacy. The young man who, at twenty-one, could write phrases such as "induced to think" and "actuated more by caprice" was well spoken and intelligent. Moreover, apart from his ability to judge accurately the relations between Johnny and his uncle, about which we lack enough information to evaluate, Tom's account does show concern and sympathy. He was also capable of discretion, suggesting in his postscript that Annie "mention this matter to your mother but do not go into particulars."

Also, it is indisputable that young Tom Owens was on good terms, and committed to being on good terms, with Anna's family. In another letter written that fall of 1849 before their marriage, Tom responds to Annie's news that there has been a little illness at home: "I was sorry to hear that you have not all been well particularly your sister Mrs. M. [Eliza Millard] to whom I beg you will present my kind regards and say that it will afford me much pleasure to renew (I wonder if she ever knew me at all) my acquaintance with her, at Poona." This note, referring to the fact that Tom has met Eliza before, and in circumstances that suggest that she would not remember him, implicitly confirms that he met her when her family brought her back to Bombay after she gave birth. At that time she might not have been in a state of mind and health to attend to the new acquaintance. Tom will renew the acquaintance when they all meet again at his wedding in Poona.

Tom continues his attentiveness to Anna's family in this letter, asking her to "remember me most kindly to your mother who is, I trust, much better." Nor does he forget the youngest girl of the family, humorously reminding Anna to remember him also "to dear Ellen whom I beg you will kiss for me, provided she will not pout." Moreover, Tom has financial arrangements with Patrick Donohoe. He is sending Patrick money, perhaps having to do with Johnny's salary or perhaps with Patrick being their banker in the sense of investing or looking after part of their salaries. In the same letter he asks Anna, "Did Mr. D. get the Bill on England and was he satisfied with it? You have not said a word on the subject, and he has not acknowledged its receipt, so that for all I know it has miscarried, and heaven knows what may be the consequences, to poor me and Johnny." It is clear that Tom Owens was deeply entwined with the Donohoe family. He was engaged to Anna, fond of Ellen, eager to be better acquainted with Eliza, doing business with Patrick, and in Bombay spending his time with Mary Anne's brother and son.

What is most remarkable about Tom's letters to Anna during that fall of 1849 before their Christmas marriage, when he was twenty-one and she was still, until November 26, seventeen, is how incredibly romantic they are. Here is what he has to say in October, having waited for a letter from her from Poona and feeling "greatly disappointed," not having received one for "the last three days": "Oh Annie, how much how fervently, and truly, do I love you, by day you constantly occupy my thoughts and by night I dream of you. At present I have no abiding place, no home, nor can I ever have until you become mine. Do you, Annie, love me, continue to love me as of yore? But why ask you! Knowing as I do, how constant and true the heart is that has blessed me with its pure and true affections!" Tom talks in this letter of how hard he has been working "to ensure your being as comfortable as you could possibly desire when you become my own darling wife." He explains that "the possibility of my failing to do so fills me with the utmost annoyance, occasioning me a feeling of care that I cannot dispossess myself of."

Tom expands on this theme, to explain in one impressively extended sentence why she means so much to him.

> You pursue the even tenor of your way exposed to but few annoyances, but you know how much a man that mixes in the world, is continually subjected to, particularly those who are far away from home without relations or friends (in the true sense of the word, acquaintances are very numerous) to sympathize and cheer with them, they are in fact strangers in a strange land, and it is they who truly know the blessing, and appreciate the value of the affection and love of Woman for without anything else that can deeply interest them under such circumstances, a man so situated, if he is a man, and has the feelings of one, looks only to the woman he loves for sympathy and affection, who is to him all in all, the solitary sharer of his griefs, and she only can be a participator in the true joys of his heart.

We hear in this Tom's loneliness and his homesickness, but also the depth of his passion for Anna. Tom closes this letter with a dream of the intimacy of their future together. He hopes that "hereafter Annie, when spending our evening together perhaps alone we can lay bare, the passing thoughts of our minds, and the knowledge of those alone, will be of itself happiness."

Tom writes again in a November letter, one of many, that "my affection and love for you makes your happiness of the first and greatest importance to me. To ensure that I have laboured hard and will ever do so." Tom was an eager suitor. He goes on to say that "now that the period of our union is drawing nigh, with what pleasure am I filled, at the thought of making you my darling, my beloved Annie, all my own."

We do not have Anna's responses to this outpouring of passion. But there is every reason to believe that her letters expressed the same deeply romantic feelings as did his, and that she wrote more letters than he did. Tom frequently apologizes for being remiss in his letter writing, for not replying often enough to her letters. He explains that he has been "harassed to death" in his attempts to make everything perfect for their life after the wedding. At the same time, Tom refers frequently to Anna's love for him and to his certainty as to her joy in the coming marriage, for "surely you dearest look forward to that event with the same pleasure." His letters express a sense of security in mutual affection that makes it clear that theirs was a love match. In fact, Tom Owens would be the one true love of Anna's very long life.

Tom describes his efforts to arrange their married life in a November 20 letter to Anna. The arrangements were impressive:

> I have taken a large airy house in an excellent healthy situation near Government. It is a long way from the Fort [where Tom worked], but that is of no consequence compared to the advantage of a splendid house on reasonable terms and a good situation with pure air. I have also purchased a Shijram and horse and completed the furniture as far as I shall be able to go. . . . Our house will be neatly furnished, but not very amply, as it would take an awful lot of money to furnish a house in a complete style. As it is I have expended about eleven hundred rupees, from which you can judge that setting up house is no joke. (LC, VI C, 4:2, 28)

With the exchange rate at about ten rupees per pound sterling, Tom was saying that he had spent about 110 pounds on his arrangements. This was a huge sum for a middle-class clerk in India. Tom had gone significantly into debt in making these arrangements. His loving enthusiasm outstripped his good sense.

In another letter that fall, probably written in early December (though the beginning is lost), Tom says that he has made the move to the new house. He describes it to Anna in these terms: "Johnny is with me in the country, and delighted with it. He has a beautiful airy bedroom, with wind enough to blow him out of bed, very different from the dirty hole he was smothered in at the fort." But Tom is clearly worried about money. He points out that "the charge for [marriage] licenses is heavy, and we can be 'Called' (I believe that is the term) at the Poona Church. We had better perhaps avoid an unnecessary expense." Banns took longer, but had nowhere near the cost of a special license. It is clear that Tom wanted to be married by banns. Though he made the generous statement that "as for myself I am too happy to care much whether it is by banns or license," his worry was obvious. He ended the paragraph with the exhortation, "do not fail to write early on the subject."

"Thomas Leon Owens," son of John Leon Owens, and "Harriette Edwards," daughter of Thomas Edwards, were married, by banns, at St. Mary's Church, Poona, on Christmas Day, December 25, 1849. Rev. Allen, the senior chaplain, officiated. Though Anna Harriett had turned eighteen just a month before, on November 26, she was still listed as a minor. Selecting December 25 for the ceremony was a romantic and spiritual gesture. More to the point, it also was a practical one. As a lowly Bombay clerk on a limited salary, Tom could not afford to take extra days off from work. And the trip to Poona took two days each way. Scheduling the service on Christmas Day meant that he could use already established holiday leave rather than asking, and perhaps being turned down, for unscheduled days off.

All of Anna Harriett's family seems to have been there. The official witnesses at the ceremony, those who signed the register, were Patrick Donohoe, John Donohoe, William Glascott, and James and Eliza Millard (who had already been married for three and a half years). I am sure that along with these guests who signed as witnesses—her stepfather, stepbrother, uncle, brother-in-law, and sister—her mother and the rest of the Donohoe children were also present, and probably her nephew and infant niece as well.

After the wedding it was off to Bombay at last. The newlyweds moved to the new house in the Parell district of Bombay. It was a thrilling change for the girl from the distant outstation. The city once described as the backwater of the Company's holdings was now an economic boom town. The overland route from Europe to India opened in 1830, with the arrival of the first steamer from Suez to Bombay. This regularized route greatly expanded trade possibilities with the Indian subcontinent, all goods moving through Bombay. One of the most rapidly expanding businesses in Bombay was cotton, popularly nicknamed "White Gold." Starting in the early 1830s, when Americans raised the price of raw cotton that they shipped to Britain, sales to England from Bombay had gone up and up. The cotton boom continued until the end of the American Civil War. In the 1850s, Bombay was one of the most active ports in the world.

In her 1884 "memoir," *Life and Travel in India,* Anna, playing the upper-class British young lady, new to India, wrote of her visits to the markets of Bombay: "It was my first initiation to the commerce of the world to visit this spot. Previous to this day I had hardly purchased a ribbon for myself, and could not conceive what trade really meant" (23). However far from the truth this preposterously artificial self-portrait of Anna as a traveling British ingénue might be, her delight in the move to Bombay and her admiration for its impressive bazaars were real.

Accounts of Bombay toward the middle of the nineteenth century present it as a kind of commercial wonderland, utterly international and endlessly fascinating. Mrs. Postans was one of many visitors who rhapsodized about the shopping in Bombay. She remarked that "auctions at the Fort are of daily occurrence, and damaged goods of every description are sold for a mere trifle," including "horses and carriages" (Postans, 24). She was particularly eloquent on the China satins, the teas, "superb dinner and breakfast services, glass ware," not to mention "bijouterie, gold lace, sauces, brandied fruits, riding whips, and other European superfluities" (25, 23).

Tom may have admiringly described her quiet life in Poona as pursuing "the even tenor of your way," but Anna, at eighteen, like so many young women, had had enough of even tenors and was ready for the dazzling displays and cosmopolitan joys of life in the big city. One of the qualities that make Anna's story unusual is that her move to Bombay became only the first of many exciting steps. It was an important move for Anna, not least because it was the beginning of what would be a lifelong pattern for her. Starting with this move, the rest of Anna's life was a series of choices directed to leading her to greater adventures and larger worlds. Those choices would take her a very long way from Poona and the cantonment at Kirkee.

In January 1850, Tom and Anna settled into their new home and immediately proceeded to begin a family. To the delight of the newlyweds, in just a little more than two months Anna was pregnant. Sometime in the summer or early fall, Anna went back to Poona to stay with her mother during her pregnancy and for the birth, just as her sister Eliza had done with her two pregnancies. The exciting time in the big city had lasted barely more than six months. Anna found herself back in her childhood home again. She settled back into life in Kirkee, that "small but pretty" (Postans, 260) cantonment, surrounded by good roads.

Once at home again, missing Tom and missing Bombay, Anna picked up her old habits of quiet reading and studying, taking up her Sanskrit again. As a Halifax resident would comment after Anna died, "what a passion that woman had for education" (LC, VI C). That passion sustained Anna during the lonely months of the fall, surrounded by her family but longing for her young husband. Anna did what she would do again and again for the rest of her life. She threw herself into her books, finding not just consolation for Tom's absence but real delight in learning about other places, other languages, other cultures and times.

An English visitor to Poona in 1857 scorned the place, commenting that it was "very rare for any Sahib, more especially a lady, to enter the city, and we did not see a single European in traversing the city from end to end" (Paget, 94). But Mrs. Paget was too culturally blind to see either the actual inhabitants or the cultural life of Poona. It had a thriving theatrical community. Sometimes in the evenings Anna attended the performances in the little theater in Kirkee or walked the two miles along the broad military road through the city to the main cantonment. There she saw the more elaborate theatricals, complete with a good orchestra, because "on the occasions of a dress rehearsal, soldiers and their families [had] an entrée" (Postans, 245).

Alone in Bombay, Tom was relieved to give up the "large airy house" in Parell, and the horse and Shijram as well. He settled into simple bachelor lodgings again, this time in the very crowded section of Girgaum. His change of accommodation helped lower the debts he had foolishly contracted in the enthusiasm of his engagement the previous fall. In fact, the goal of lowering the couple's debts was a significant factor in the plan to have Anna return to live at home with her parents during the pregnancy, allowing Tom a face-saving way to move into cheap rooms. It was an effective cost-saving measure for the young couple, who had overextended themselves.

On December 10, 1850, Tom and Anna's first child was born in Poona. They named her Selina, thus honoring Billy Glascott's long-dead youngest sister, who was herself named to honor Billy's father's beloved patroness, the Countess of Huntingdon. Tom had a Selina in his family too, a Wilkinson niece. Tom was not there for the birth, since he was at work in Bombay. He had tried to make it. He had taken some vacation days for a trip out to Poona for a little while in November, which was when the baby was probably due. But as is so often the case with first pregnancies, Anna could well have been late in the delivery. Certainly, Tom was in Poona too soon and had to tear himself away and go back to Bombay with his wife still on the verge of giving birth. He missed the great event.

When the doctor wrote him of her "safe delivery of a little girl," Tom was ecstatic: "With what anxiety have I ever since I left Poona, looked for this intelligence, and oh, my darling my beloved Annie what feelings of delight and deep gratitude to God did I experience when I learned that our long and ardently expected baby had come home, and that you were both doing well. The consciousness of your deep love for me and my own affection for you always afforded me delightful employment for my thoughts, and it only wanted this intelligence to complete my happiness." With the rapture of a first-time father, Tom goes on and on: "I trust my love you did not suffer much, and that you are now all right; be careful of yourself and our darling baby. How I long to see you dearest to press you in my arms once again and to imprint my first kiss on the virgin brow of my child." Surely this is the kind of letter any new mother would thrill to receive.

The loving and considerate young father next turns to the question of the child's sex. In an age when it was generally considered preferable to have a son he wishes to reassure Annie of his perfect happiness in a daughter. As he put it, "we thought we should have a boy, we shall however be none the less happy or love our child the less that it is a girl. Oh no." Nor does Tom forget his mother-in law's role in attending the birth, telling Annie that "I shall always be most deeply grateful to your mother for her kindness to you." And he once again urges her to "mind my beloved your health, for now the happiness of your child as well as your husband depends on you."

Tom turns again to his regret in being absent for the birth, and his recent visit to Poona: "I long to see you both and would give almost anything to be but for a few moments by your side. How delightful it would have been if this had taken place when I was in Poona when I could have tended on you and soothed and consoled you in suffering." Clearly Anna had said to Tom either when he left Poona or in a letter that this separation was too hard, too horrible, for his next point is to agree with her. "You say truly my beloved we must never part again." He goes on to assure her that "in future whatever either of us may have to endure it will be together when we can support and comfort each other." It is a loving sentiment, made particularly poignant by its revelation of how deeply they loved each other, along with our knowledge of how short their future together would be.

Tom closes this joyous letter by repeating "how supremely happy and grateful I feel." As he says himself, "in fact, I can scarcely write coherently." He ends with a plea: "May God bless you my beloved wife. And may he bless and smile on our darling daughter I can almost picture you both. As soon as you are able to sit up write me a line as I long to hear from you." And he signs off "your own devoted and ever affectionate husband Leon."

Tom went to Poona to see his new daughter for the first time and to see his beloved wife as soon as he could manage it. But for most of 1851, Anna and Selina continued to live in the Donohoe home in Poona while Tom worked in Bombay, doing his best to get his finances in shape and living frugally in Girgaum. Tom had managed to get Johnny a job where he worked, also as a clerk at the Military Pay Office, also called the Commissary General's Office, in Girgaum. Johnny would work there for the next two to three years. His employment was a relief to everyone.

Much as the couple hated to be apart, their separation was a practical necessity. As a new mother, Anna had been weakened by the birth. In Poona she was not left all alone for long hours with her baby, as she would have been in Bombay. She had the practical support, the advice as well as the help, made possible by living in a household with her mother, stepfather, and younger half-sister, Ellen. There were always other hands to take the baby when she needed a rest, or to suggest the right treatment for the croup or the pains of teething. This is yet one more detail in the history of the young couple's ongoing relations with the Donohoes that gives the lie to Anna's melodramatic rewrite a half century later that her "marriage my stepfather opposed with so much rancor that all correspondence between us ceased from that date" (LC, VI C, 4:2). Conveniently, the fantasy version kept anyone from wondering why she was not in touch with her relatives.

On November 11, 1851, Anna had been back in Poona for almost a year and a half and Selina had just turned eleven months. It had been a very long time for this deeply loving couple to live apart. And their separation was still painfully felt. Tom sent one of his usual chatty and loving letters. He had just returned from the wedding breakfast of a Miss Howell and Mr. Henderson. Tom described how, while he talked and laughed, "I had not a thought or feeling in common with any one of them, that my thoughts were far way, with you beloved of my heart, and of you." Tom used this account of a Bombay social occasion as a way to distinguish generally between "higher and holier feeling" and common sentiment: "The more I know of these people of Bombay the greater my contempt for them, they are a dull, stupid, inert race without a sentiment above the Commonest occurrences of everyday life, and as unable as higher and purer minds are, to extract a higher and holier feeling out of these mere daily occurrences to which other are able to add such charms."

This distinction led Tom into discussing how he saw Anna and himself as separate from the rest of the world:

> I never contrast you with others my beloved, because it would be absurd, my love is yours, is fixed unalterably on you, and I never for a moment think how I could associate with such people in such intimate relations of domestic life because it would be *impossible*. But I often feel when I look around and form an estimate of actual worth of those I meet with, that had I not known you, I *never would have married*. You, my darling, are after my own heart. You realize all my earliest and brightest dreams of what I would wish my wife to be.

We can hear the youthful naïve arrogance in this. But the deeper note is Tom's loneliness, frustrated passion, and longing. Sitting at that wedding breakfast with the happy couple, how he missed Anna, how he appreciated her fine qualities, and how he longed for his own domestic bliss.

The rest of this letter to Anna turns on how much he wished to be with her, as she had written that she wished to be with him. It was an outpouring of passionate love and erotic longing:

> As I peruse your dear letter of Sunday night how full of happiness I feel. Yes darling the days are long and the times hang heavy to us, loving ardently and passionately as we do, and longing to fly to each others arms, oh my beloved, my own sweet wife, brightest and sweetest treasure of my heart, how I long to hold you to my heart, to drink the bliss the highest bliss from your dear lips and then realize the highest the most exalted and most passionate delight in your arms—How inadequate are all the expressions of fondness and affection I can command to describe my love, my devotion to you darling—as I write I lack words to tell you how ardently and passionately I love: I worship and adore you my own darling, and my very feelings of the fondest love and adoration are to me happiness because I know how worthy, how more than worthy you are of that love and adoration.

Tom here seems overwhelmed by how much he loves and misses his wife.

For the separated couple these letters provided a kind of substitute for being together. Tom's passionate statements were a response to Anna's, and he looked forward to reciprocity in her response: "In the letters I wrote to you on Friday & Saturday I laid bare my soul to you and told you why I loved you and why I shall always love you, read those letters over again dearest in your room and *then* write me *all* your thoughts, all your feelings, all your wishes—." We hear in this request the erotic as well as the passionate, the tones of a young man too long deprived of his wife.

Just when Tom's account of his love seems too endlessly romantic, he tempers it with a note of realism: "It is strange dearest that you accuse yourself of omissions to me while I accuse myself of many faults and want of foresight for your happiness—We have doubtless our faults Annie, but love gilds them, and we will live on trying with unswerving efforts to increase each others happiness, seeing no fault in each other." And in the same paragraph he offers a purely practical point. Referring to Anna's having been weakened, probably from giving birth, he asks if she is "getting strength now dearest? Use cold water frequently, but always dry yourself carefully afterwards."

At the end of this letter Tom turns to his efforts to be reunited, to having "you my cherished wife again by my side." He tells her, "I have not yet got a house." Girgaum district in "Black Town," where he is staying, will not do because "I detest Girgaum and cannot bear the idea that you and Selina should always have to breathe such a foul murky atmosphere, for myself I don't care." Tom said nothing of costs, but finances were clearly implied when he acknowledged that Girgaum was a strong possibility, though "it will be much against my will if I take a house in that locality—I will however first try and get one elsewhere." He assures her that distance from his job is not a priority, that "even if it is a mile or two further, it will be better than that you should night and day have to live in such a place."

Tom wrote that letter about two weeks before Anna's twentieth birthday. In a little earlier letter (date unavailable) he tells of the present he is sending her because she has often "expressed a wish to have a black satin dress." He found the material for it, "only 2½ or ¾ yards in the piece which will perhaps be enough." At that point he says that he will miss her birthday and, "I only regret that I cannot on that day clasp you to my heart." Yet when he wrote again, on November 11, Tom did plan to get to Poona a little after her birthday, for "I hope to go for you by the end of this month, have your dress made up to receive me in it."

Tom did come to Poona and pick up his beloved wife and daughter, "dear Pussy" as he called Selina, either at the beginning of December 1851, in time for Selina's first birthday, or, more likely in terms of when he could get days off, around Christmas. In any case, by the beginning of the new year in 1852 the family was together at last and living in Bombay. Tom had gotten a new job, probably at a little better pay. He was still a clerk but this time at a merchant firm, an auctioneer house called Robert Frith and Company, on Marine Street in Bombay.

There was no airy house. Tom had, indeed, ended up having to take lodgings in the much detested Girgaum district. Money continued to be a problem. But they were happy times, full of life, of family, of hope. In early 1852, not only William Glascott and Johnny Donohoe but also Anna's well-loved sister Eliza Julia, with her husband, Jim, and their two little children, were living in the Girgaum neighborhood. Little Jimmy was five and a half and Eliza Sarah was three and a half. It was a sociable life for them all.

We catch a glimpse of Anna's household from an account offered in a letter in 1899 by Anna's great-nephew (her sister's daughter's sixth child), John Pratt, recording what his mother, Eliza Sarah, had written to him: "I was a great pet of hers (Mrs. Leonowens) and often went over and spent a week at a time with her and my little cousin Selina. . . . I wonder if she has as vivid a recollection of her little niece Lizzie as I have of my kind and beautiful Aunt Annie who then was an accomplished pianiste" (LC, VI C, 4:2). Although we may wonder how well Lizzie (Eliza Sarah), at three and a half, could judge the level of her aunt's looks or her accomplishments as a pianist, what she could judge was the pleasantness of the household. Tom and Anna Owens were young and deeply in love. They were together, their child was a joy, their family was around them, and the future was theirs.

SIX

Metamorphosis

"A Life Sublimated above the Ordinary"

ON JUNE 25, 1859, a woman got off a boat in Singapore. She was nobody special, part of that vast underclass of travelers in the far reaches of the British Empire in the mid-nineteenth century, and just a woman at that. There is no reason for us to know she existed, much less to know that she arrived in Singapore that June of 1859. But passenger arrivals in that port were recorded, I am happy to say. The boat was the *Hooghly,* coming from Penang, and the arrival notice in the following Saturday's edition of the *Singapore Straits Times* announced the arrival of "Mrs. Leonowens and (2) children."

Anna stepped off that boat with a brand-new identity and began a new life. She had chosen her new biography with care. It had to be a story that would account for her having no money, no available family, and no ties to her past, and—at the same time—would render plausible that she was a gentlewoman, entitled by birth to be part of the higher social classes, and also educated enough to qualify for work as a teacher. The story Anna came up with was, in fact, a very clever choice. It explained how she came to be in Singapore on her own with no recourse to relatives or friends. It explained how she was both of good family and without access to family support. This was a crucial ingredient of the lie because Anna could not afford any links to her real past, which would open her up to exposure. She had to cut all ties to her true history. Successfully passing as white, British, and gentry required that no one ever find out about her mixed-race, lower-class origins. Her story also explained why, even without being able to produce any visible family, connections, or means of support, Anna's supposed history would give her a claim on the goodwill of the upper-class British society in Singapore at that time. In inventing the story of her life, Anna could not have done better.

She was, she said, Mrs. Leonowens, born in Wales and daughter of Captain Crawford, who died heroically in the Sikh rebellion, widow of Major

FIGURE 2. Singapore—from an original sketch (ca. 1857). Culver Photos.

Thomas Leonowens, with two children born in England. She was, regret-
tably, without family or income. Her grief-stricken mother, widowed in
Bombay, had remarried a crude and materialistic man, and brought her
teenage daughters out there from England. The crass stepfather disapproved
of Anna's marriage choice and all intercourse between them had ceased.
Anna's first child had died in Bombay, Anna's mother died at virtually the
same moment, and a second baby had died in New South Wales after their
ship returning to England foundered there. She and her husband, after
spending time back in England where they produced two children who
lived—bless that English climate!—had returned east when he was reassigned to the Straits Settlements. But all her fortune had been lost in the
bank failures after the terrible Indian Mutiny, and her beloved husband was
dead, prostrated by heat after a tiger hunt. She found herself, alas, alone, un-
protected, with little money, and with two children to raise. But she had
come to Singapore full of determination. She was, after all, a British lady,
well born and well brought up, well educated and firm of character, quite
the right sort of person to earn a genteel living for herself and her dear children by educating the young.

And so the new Anna was born. It was an excellent role, suited both to her
passionate nature, so nourished by Tom's love, and to her deep intelligence.

It was a role both highly romantic and requiring great strength of character. It disposed of her family in India, thus allowing the Indian Army "barracks rat" from Poona to cross the virtually uncrossable social divide of Victorian society, and have a chance to make something of her intellectual and personal potential. It allowed her to live in a world where her achievements had the possibility of matching her large talents and her at-least-as-large dreams. And just as important, on the simplest practical level it allowed her a means of earning a living to support her children and herself.

The beauty of Anna's story, her virtually uncheckable story, was that all it required was that she be able to act the part. Everything depended on how well Anna could play the role, could put across her new identity as a lady. And it is a tribute to her extraordinary intelligence and the extent of her knowledge and skill that Anna was able to play the part. She definitely rose to the occasion. She met the challenge of accent, that immediate giveaway of race and class in India. She was able to speak in the tones of the British upper class and even provided herself and her accent with a little leeway by locating her birthplace in Wales. And she knew how to behave like a lady as well.

After all, what was the truth? Anna was highly gifted. She was also well educated, I might even say exceptionally well educated, though not in the formal ways those phrases imply. This daring young widow, twenty-seven and a half years old when she landed in Singapore, was already an impressive linguist. She could speak English, Hindi, and Marathi, as well as read and write Sanskrit and some Persian Arabic and Pali. She was familiar with many cultures from her life in India and was by taste as well as ability scholarly and well read. She was musical as well as literary and loved to play the piano. She already had an extensive knowledge of the world, both academic and experiential, that was rare enough in anyone's life. And her maternal grandfather was of the English gentry. Surely, she deserved to present herself as both educated and a lady.

Anna's looks made her passable as well. She was never spoken of as particularly pretty, but people frequently commented on her intense gaze and classically simple form of dress. She was tall, with notably large yet elegant hands. Her granddaughter's letter to Margaret Landon in 1943 quoted her as saying that "it was necessary to have big hands, in order to have a firm grasp on life." Louisa Dresel, who used to see Anna in New York in the 1870s, described her as having "very intense dark eyes, and a dark complexion which I somehow connected with Siam." In 1868, the people in the little town in the Catskills of New York where she was living accounted for her coloring by believing her "to be the ex-queen of Syria, come to live among them." Her granddaughter simply described her as "burned dark from the sun" (LC, VI C). Clearly, Anna was notably dark complexioned, with dark brown eyes and almost black hair. But in Singapore she passed for fully white, in part because she said so, and in the accents of the British upper class. But she also explained her coloring quite cleverly to the Europeans of Singapore by giving her origin as Welsh. Many of the Welsh were quite dark.

After all, why should Anna have gone along with the British racial and social categories that would have permanently relegated her, and her children, to an inferior social place? We need to remember that she was creating a new future for them as well as for herself. She merely and, it could be argued, quite appropriately, revised the pesky facts to fit the deeper truth. Giving herself and her children new identities when she stepped off that boat was an act of imagination and courage, and also of practical sense.

I can imagine Anna, after Tom's burial, full of grief and thinking about her options. Even apart from the terrible pain of a life without Tom, how was she to support the children, how was she to go on? In her late twenties, with two dependents and impressively self-educated, Anna had long since become too fond of her years of independence in the larger world to run back to her semi-literate mother in Poona. And she was probably too old for the standard solution of widows in that time, not to mention that she was still in love with Tom and could not bear the thought of remarriage. What Anna really wanted was to be self-sufficient. But without an independent income, how was that to be done? It was a dilemma many a Victorian woman suddenly widowed had faced with a pervading sense of despair.

At some point after the funeral, probably when she was still in Penang, it came to Anna that if she were to make a future for herself and her children, if she were actually to try to make a living on her own, she would have to find some way to widen her options. And to accomplish that, she would have to change who she was. British officers did not give mixed-race women their children to educate. She realized that this was an imaginative opportunity not to be missed. But Anna needed a change of location for the story and her plans of being employed to succeed. She got on the boat to Singapore and perhaps on board tried out the new identity on her fellow passengers, perhaps worked out more of the details, certainly going over them on the trip south. But her major emotional focus would have been on her children and her grief.

When the Leonowens family disembarked in Singapore, Tom Leonowens (a surname he had preferred) had been dead for just six weeks. He died in Penang, also called Prince of Wales Island, of apoplexy and was buried

May 8, 1859, in the Protestant graveyard there. His profession at the time was listed as hotel master, an unclear designation that perhaps indicated a kind of hotel manager rather than simply a general clerk. His tombstone (since *The King and I* become a rather massive tomb) says that he "departed this life on the 7th of May 1859" and was "aged 31 years and 5 days."

How had the widow come to appear in Singapore with two children? What had she been doing all these years? The answers are sketchy. What we do know is that Anna and little Selina were reunited with their loving husband and father at the beginning of 1852, when the three settled down to live happily ever after in the Girgaum district of Bombay. It is perfectly possible that Johnny, who was now seventeen or eighteen, was living with them as well. If not actually sharing lodgings, he was certainly living very close, since his residency at that time was listed in the *Bombay Calendar and General Directory* as Girgaum. Maybe he was now sharing digs with William Glascott, since William was also listed as living in Girgaum, as was Anna's sister Eliza and her family. Moreover, Johnny and William now worked as clerks in the Military Board Office, the very office where Tom had worked with them until he took the position at the auction house sometime in late 1851.

In the spring of 1852, the branch of the family in Bombay and the branch of the family in Poona were both doing well. Three of Mary Anne's children, Anna, Eliza, and Johnny, and her brother William all lived near one another in the same neighborhood in Bombay. Back in Poona, Ellen, Mary Anne and Patrick's youngest child, had turned fifteen in December 1851. In the spring she became attached to one of the men in her father's regiment, a twenty-three-year-old sergeant in the Poona Sappers and Miners. The wedding was set for May 24.

But the general good fortune of the Edwards/Donohoe family did not last. Anna and Tom did not make it to the wedding ceremony. Ellen Donohoe, minor, married Samuel George Phillips on May 24, 1852, at St. Mary's Church, Poona. On that very same day, by one of those horrors that can sometimes occur in our lives, Anna and Tom found themselves attending a funeral instead. They were in Bombay, at Colaba, on May 24, 1852, burying their daughter, Selina. She was seventeen months old.

Selina's sudden illness and death were devastating to the young parents. Anna and Tom felt that their world had collapsed. Through it all the couple received special sympathy and support from William. Their grief was mitigated by the fact that Anna was advanced in pregnancy when Selina died. She gave birth to her second child, almost certainly a boy, in late July or early August 1852. Years later, Anna wrote to Avis from Siam on October 21, 1866, just before Avis's twelfth birthday, to say that she was sending her "an old and very valuable locket" as a birthday present. She told Avis that Mamma "shall put dear Papa's hair in it; also the golden locks of your little brother and sister in Heaven—with that of dear Louis and mine" (LC, VI C, 4:2, 29). Whatever Anna's powers of deception about the facts of her history, and they were quite breathtakingly impressive, she was not speaking falsely to her living daughter of a brother as well as a sister in heaven. Yet I do wonder about those "golden locks." Are they meant to be a metaphor for an angel or yet another detail claiming whiteness? Louis, Avis, and Anna had dark brown hair.

That fall of 1852 this second great grief was yet to come. Perhaps encouraged by William, the couple began to make plans for a new life and decided that they had to leave India. It was probably during this autumn that they made their arrangements to move to Australia. Their decision was motivated almost entirely by the determination to keep this second precious child alive. But it was also true that Anna longed to see new places, and Tom may well have hoped for a more interesting job than clerk/copyist. Both may well have been eager for adventure and not wanted to stay permanently in India.

On November 16, the couple and their new baby left Bombay. They took passage on the Peninsular and Oriental Company ship *Ganges,* under Capt. Purchase, going from Bombay to Calle (Ceylon) to Penang and on to Singapore. Mr. and Mrs. Leonowens disembarked in Singapore on December 4, 1852. They were not alone. With them was a Mr. Glascott. William, supportive and kind in this terrible period of their lives, and perhaps himself interested in a new future, away from his government's strictures against Anglo-Indians, had accompanied his friend and his niece. But considered from the perspective of those left at home, particularly Mary Anne Donohoe, I doubt that the departure looked like a new beginning. All at once she lost her brother, her daughter and son-in-law, and her grandchild. This group exodus could well have been one cause of the rift between Anna and her family in India.

Of the six and a half years from December 4, 1852, when Anna is recorded as disembarking in Singapore, to June 25, 1859, when she is once more recorded as disembarking in Singapore, having lost her husband and with two children in tow, we know little. Anna's version of those years we may recall from her fantasy autobiography. Once again, it is a charmingly romantic story, complete with a shipwreck and rescue, all aimed at establishing her and her children's racial and social claims to being British, white, and upper class.

When I was only eighteen, the death of my mother and my first baby came upon me with such terrible force that my life was despaired of, and my husband embarked with me on a sea voyage to England. But the ship 'Alibi' went on some rocks, through the carelessness of the captain, I believe, and we were rescued by another sailing vessel and taken to New South Wales. Here I buried my second baby, an infant son, and still dreadfully ill, we took a steamer for England and finally settled down in St. James's Square, London for nearly three years.

Here she produced English children, Avis Connybeare, born October 25, 1854, and Louis Thomas Gunnis, October 25, 1856 (his birth certificate lists October 22, though in a letter in the Ford Collection dated October 25, 1880, Anna congratulates him on being twenty-four). Then the major was reassigned and they went to Singapore and Penang. The tiger hunt detail, with the brave young major dropping dead at the feet of his horrified wife, appears in the story as Anna told it to her grandchildren in Canada.

In 1852 and also in 1859, Anna's mother was, of course, alive and well in Poona. And Anna and Tom never went to England. But neither did they stay in Singapore. Anna's choice of Singapore in 1859 as the place to try on her new identity indicates that she felt secure in being quite unknown there. She knew Singapore very little, and the European society of Singapore did not know her. She could hardly step off a boat in 1859 and claim to be the widow of Major Leonowens if she were at risk of running into people who had met Tom the clerk in 1852, along with his "country-born" wife and her uncle.

The three adults and baby were in Singapore very briefly in December, in transit just a few days before continuing their journey on the ship *Alibi,* bound for Melbourne, Australia. At this point reality matches Anna's fantasy autobiography. There really was something of a shipwreck. The *Alibi* got stuck on a reef off the western coast of Australia while heading into the port of Freemantle for what was supposed to be a short stop to replenish its water and provisions. The ship sat for eight days on that reef, sixty miles north of Freemantle. Finally, it was brought in on March 18, 1853, after being 102 days out to sea. In the court hearing to determine if hitting the reef was the second officer's error, one of the passengers, a Mr. Glascott, is recorded as testifying (*Inquirer,* 3/23/1853).

The passengers all had to disembark at Freemantle and probably went on to the main settlement at Swan River, now Perth. The repairs on the *Alibi* went slowly. By late April the captain still could not get the ropes or horses needed to shift the ship in order to begin the repairs (Colonial Secretary's Office Records, 68:3), and the ship did not sail until early June. Unable to continue on to Melbourne, the Leonowens/Glascott group decided to stay.

Anna and Tom settled in Swan River. Anna advertised to begin a little school, but apparently was unsuccessful at starting one. Tom got work as a storekeeper. By the beginning of 1854 he had joined the Swan River Mechanics' Institute, a kind of early library and discussion center. Tom was a very active member of the discussion class, which met most Monday evenings to debate fixed topics. The Institute's minutes record that the topic for the summer of 1854 was "the alledged inferiority of the Coloured races." Most of the discussants agreed that the "coloured races" were not inferior, but Tom was particularly eloquent. He stated emphatically that "there is no inferiority of intellect in the Coloured races. Solomon, the wisest of all men, was a coloured man—and from the East, and God himself spoke from the East—and all lands shew the superiority of the Coloured races" (Mechanics' Institute Minutes, 6/12/1854).

A week later Tom elaborated on this point:

> In regard of the inferiority of one race from another, it may appear where the Coloured Races are debarred from the advantages of education and refinement—to be inferior in intellectual acquirements to those who have had such advantages—The East Indian have not the means of education as in England—which accounts for the absence of the high requirements discernable in our own country. The Native Troops being officered by Europeans no proof of their inferiority in intellect—they may be physically so. These officers are very often inferior in mind to the Native troops they command—many of whom possess a fund of sound knowledge did one but know their language—they are excellent mathematicians, astronomers, and particularly well versed in the history of their own country. (Mechanics' Institute Minutes, 6/19/1854)

Tom was well respected at the Institute. He would be elected auditor in 1855, and that June of 1854 he was invited to present a public lecture. On September 11, 1854, he delivered his lecture, titled "The Study of History." It "was listened to with marked attention and at intervals during its delivery elicited rapturous applause."

The year 1854 was intense for the Leonowens family. In March grief came again, as their second child died. The death notice in the *Inquirer* on March 22 noted simply the death, on March 16, at age nineteen months, of "the beloved and only child of T. Leonowens." And once more, as she buried one child, Anna was pregnant with the next. On October 25, a daughter, Avis Annie, was born to "Harriette Annie" and "Thomas Leonowens" in Perth. This one would live.

While Tom and Annie were in Perth, Uncle William had taken a job ninety miles north. Mr. W. V. Glascott was the storekeeper at the Barrack Branch Commissariat in the convict depot of Port Gregory (*Western Australian Almanack,* 1855, 21). Port Gregory had begun as a convict depot in 1853 and was little more than a small clearing in the wilderness, a shabby collection of tents with a few wooden huts, one of which was the store. Sometime in 1855, William left Port Gregory and, in fact, left Western Australia. His dreams of emigration over, he went home. William was back on the list of residents in the *Bombay Calendar and General Directory* for 1855 (the 1856 edition), recorded as the head of the boys school at the Indo British Institution in Sonapoor, Bombay.

Tom seems to have taken over William's job in Port Gregory. Perhaps he was transferred there from his job in Perth; perhaps he went for higher pay. By 1856 he is listed as the clerk of the commissariat at Port Gregory. Also in 1856, Anna gave birth to her fourth child, Louis Gunnis, his father's residence listed as Port Gregory. His birth is recorded as October 22, but the family seems to have celebrated on October 25, the same day as Avis's birthday. Anna may well have been in Port Gregory with Tom when she was due, but I think it more likely that she stayed in civilized Perth for the birth. Conditions in Port Gregory were famously appalling, with brackish water, rocky soil, disgruntled convicts and settlers, angry locals, and a dangerous landing for ships.

In 1856, perhaps as late as when Louis was born, or even in early 1857, Tom and Anna decided to abandon Australia. The government would choose to close the unsuccessful depot at Port Gregory by the end of 1857 anyway, and Tom would have been out of a job. The depot was a dangerous place to raise a family, a crucial issue for the young parents, and the alternative of Anna staying in Perth while Tom worked so far north would have been unacceptable. Tom and Anna may well have been disillusioned with Western Australia even earlier and simply not had the fare to leave when William Glascott did. I have wondered whether they asked Patrick Donohoe for financial help in paying their passages and were turned down, and whether Tom had to take the job in Port Gregory to make the passage money. Certainly, the family of four sailed on the *Lady Amherst* on February 3, 1857, to Singapore. The Australia adventure was over. But unlike William, they did not return to Bombay. The family stayed in the Straits Settlements, going to live in Penang, where Tom was employed to run a hotel. And there the family stayed for the next two years, until Tom died and Anna decided to be reborn.

When Anna stepped off the *Hooghly* in Singapore that June day in 1859, she launched an identity that would be hers for the rest of her life. She probably added some details and refinements as she went along, but the fundamentals of who she was going to be were now in place. And there is no doubt that she enjoyed this new Anna, not just the role itself but the very fact that she had simply made it up. The many accounts from her later life of her extraordinary sense of the injustice of social inequality and her hatred of inequity make clear that when Anna rewrote the facts of her birth and upbringing she was perfectly conscious of what she was doing. And perfectly delighted to do it.

Many years later in Canada her granddaughter, Avis, who unquestionably assumed Anna's narrative to be the truth, recalled in a letter to Margaret Landon, April 9, 1943, that one of Anna's favorite quotations was "the most important thing in life is to choose your parents." What a delectably edgy moment that must have been for Anna, gazing benignly at her admiring granddaughter while making such an outrageous statement. How she must have savored her private knowledge that Avis had not a glimmering that Anna meant quite literally what she said, that her account of her parents—and therefore of Avis's own origins as well—was a complete invention. Anna had done exactly as she described in offering that quotation to her granddaughter. She had defied and vanquished the rigid social inequities of her time and place. She had chosen her parents. And she had chosen her class.

The results of Anna's choices must have been more than even she had dared to hope. Her children never doubted their heritage. The conviction that they were born in England, were British and upper class, significantly shaped both their futures. When Thomas Fyshe was courting her in America, Avis was quick to remind him that, though living in the United States, she was an "English" girl and was to be understood as such. Louis also saw himself as English, as very much the public school boy, and was accepted as such by the European community in Siam. He was one of the founders of the Chiengmai Gymkhana Club, a sporting club for Europeans only, begun in 1898. When his first wife died in 1893, Louis wrote Anna "in great grief" that he was going "to leave for home" and went to England (Bristowe, 87). Sitting in Canada in the house of the rich banker who had married her daughter, her son a wealthy businessman and herself a well-known author and lecturer as well as highly respected cultural and social leader, Anna could only feel that, for her and for her children and grandchildren, her grand lie had worked out superbly.

After the sad departure in November 1852, I believe that Anna never saw India or her nuclear family again. John T. Pratt, the sixth of the Pratt sons and Boris Karloff's older brother, contacted Anna's daughter Avis in 1899. Writing from the British Legation in Peking, he told Avis that his mother, Lizzie (Anna's niece), had spoken of "Mrs. Leonowens' unhappiness and trouble." He went on to say that Eliza Julia (his grandmother), hearing by chance from "a certain Captain Baldwin" that her sister Anna was in Siam, had written to her

> and received a very strange reply evidently under the influence of strong emotion and showing what great suffering Mrs. Leonowens had endured. She said that in consequence of these sufferings she had determined to cut off all communication with her relations with whom her sad past was bound up, that it was enough for them to know that she and her children were happy and rich, that she would answer no further communications from her relations and she even went so far as to say that if anyone came to Siam to find her she would commit suicide. (LC, VI C, 4:2)

John Pratt, then twenty-four, also told Avis that his mother was having "a flood of old recollections" and that Lizzie's "married life has been almost as unhappy as that of Mrs. Leonowens," and she wanted to renew the connection.

It would be easy to read something extreme or melodramatic into this view of Anna's break with her family in India. But such a reading is not justified by the evidence. The statements of Anna's attitude are third-hand at least, and at quite a temporal distance. John Pratt is recalling what his grandmother told his mother (who presumably told him) in summarizing a letter from Anna written thirty years previously, before he was born. Moreover, the recipient of the letter lacked the context for understanding Anna's situation. Neither Eliza Julia nor her daughter, Lizzie, was aware that what Anna was doing in Siam was passing as a British lady. Pratt's invocation of a recollection of what yet someone else said that Anna said, and that someone else not knowing the real facts, hardly constitutes a reliable source.

What seems certain, perhaps all a biographer can be certain of without succumbing to the temptation of sheer invention, is that Anna was absolute in insisting that all connections with her relatives were severed. But this makes plausible that they had originally broken the connection with her and Tom when the couple decided to emigrate. She must have been shocked to hear from a sister after so many years, not to mention horrified that her relatives now knew her whereabouts, and terrified that her sister might appear in Bangkok. Her new identity, and her children's, would be destroyed. We can guess that when her family went ahead with Ellen's wedding rather than postponing it out of respect for Selina, Anna's heart could have withdrawn from them. We can guess that Patrick refused the couple financial help in Australia.

But that is only guessing. What is certain is that Anna had changed inside as well as out in her identity since Tom died. What is also certain is that her new life and livelihood depended on having no contact with her Indian family.

As to John Pratt's line that his mother felt drawn to renewing the connection, after forty years, and "her married life has been almost as unhappy as that of Mrs. Leonowens," he was probably referring to the deaths of Anna's first two children and the fact that both women had long been sadly widowed. He was, after all, writing to Anna's daughter, his "first cousin once removed." He was writing not about dreadful family secrets but about what he termed "the romantic nature of this story." What we can conclude here is that Anna's reply to Eliza's letter to Siam, probably sent sometime in 1863, was probably Anna's final contact with her Indian family.

Anna went on to lead a life filled with brightness, vitality, and accomplishments. As her granddaughter wrote, "hers was a spirit broad awake—to action, to literature, languages, beauty in people and in scenes" (LC, VI C). The world was all before her when she disembarked in Singapore as the British gentlewoman in 1859. But Tom Owens, the passionate young Irishman she had met at seventeen, remained the only romantic love of Anna's life. And for all her later adventures, the early part of their short decade together was a golden era, in spite of all the grief it brought.

Anna's decision to create an entirely different identity was motivated by her very practical sense of the social and economic disadvantages of her race and class. She needed a way around those disadvantages for her own sake as much as for her children's. She made for herself an opportunity to develop her considerable intellectual talents. And develop them she did, creating, in her granddaughter's words, "a life sublimated above the ordinary."

But the choice to become a different person had another dimension as well, one that will be familiar to those who have suffered the grief of losing a beloved partner or spouse. For all its practicalities, Anna's choice was also very much an emotional decision, driven by her extreme grief for the man she had believed she could never bear to be apart from again. When she lost Tom she did lose everything, herself as well as Tom. Having buried him, she dealt with the enormity of her loss by also burying the girl she had been and the entire life she had known, for they were gone as much as her husband was.

Yet Anna did gain that rarest of life's possibilities, a fresh start. And even as she made a future by erasing the past, who she and they two together had been, Anna never forgot the time when she was a very young woman, full of the happy belief that her future lay in making a domestic life with her loving husband and children in Bombay. In 1878, writing from New York City to her daughter away on her honeymoon, Anna told Avis, "darling, remember that to be a wife is the sweetest boon God has given to woman." She wrote again in January 1881 of meeting an Englishman, Mr. Powell. She was still telling the lies, still playing the British lady, writing falsely that Mr. Powell was "quite familiar with a great many of mine and your father's friends," as they talked of "Bombay and Indian days before the Mutiny." But the conversation did recall true feelings and memories. And thinking of Bombay, Anna ended her account to Avis with the poignant comment, "I seemed to have stepped back at least 25 years into the glamour and sunshine of the brightest and most delusive part of my life."

The "major's widow," the brightness of her life much dimmed by the loss of Selina and of her second infant, and then of Tom, settled down in Singapore that summer of 1859 with her two remaining children. If passionate love was gone, practicality and self-discipline were not. With the help of the sympathetic foreign community, Anna was able to make a little money at the one acceptable profession for genteel ladies in need of funds. She took in students, being a kind of governess or nursery school tutor for the young children of British officers. This was a convenient task for the mother who had her own young children to look after, since in June 1859 Avis was four and Louis two.

Singapore in 1859 was an exciting city. A tiny island at the southern tip of the Malay Peninsula, it was only a fishing village when Sir Stanford Raffles leased it in 1819 and developed it into a trading center and port for the East India Company. In 1824, the Company officially received the entire island from the Sultan of Johore, and Singapore expanded rapidly. Driven by the desire to beat out the Dutch in Batavia (now Jakarta), the Company made Singapore a free port (no dock charges, customs duties, or sales taxes for goods landing there). It was the main port between India and China, and one of the centers of the China trade. By midcentury this tiny island had become an enormous economic success, making huge profits for British businesses. It was the busiest port in Southeast Asia.

Singapore was peopled almost entirely by immigrants, more than half of whom were Chinese. These were in two major groups, the rich businessmen from the Straits Settlements and the poor workers from China. There were some Malays who had moved over from the mainland and also some Indian workers brought in by the British. Everyone who lived in Singapore had come to make money. Its population was neither indigenous nor stable.

Singapore was the gateway to the East for almost all European and American visitors, so it had a fluid international population almost as engaged in leaving as in arriving. Most of the travelers who passed through Singapore in the nineteenth century loved it, and many wrote glowing accounts of the place. Elizabeth Scidmore, visiting near the end of the century, commented vividly that arriving at most places in Southeast Asia was a matter of "landing in small boats among the screaming heathen," but Singapore was blessedly different. There "one walks down the gangplank in a civilized fashion" (Scidmore, 1).

Descriptions of nineteenth-century Singapore sound a lot like the descriptions of the other extraordinarily bustling British port of Bombay. Walking the vibrant streets, Anna must often have recalled scenes from her past. The emphasis was on commerce, on the multitude of ships in the harbor, and the docks full of coolies loading and unloading goods. As P. J. Begbie put it so fulsomely in 1834, Singapore "inspires the spectator with an idea that he is gazing upon a settlement which is naturally rising in importance under the united influences of English capital and an advantageous locality" (Jayapal, 33). Readers were repeatedly told that one could buy anything, absolutely anything, in the multitude of shops. It was a landscape of apparent chaos that was in fact a "glorious profusion," a commercial heaven, the streets filled with a "strange motley crowd," with the "Babel of languages," with people of every color from every climate and wearing every kind of dress (Burbidge, 16–17). Isabella Bird, with an unpleasantly familiar British condescension, assured her readers, that "here is none of the indolence and apathy which one associates with Oriental life" (Bird, 118).

Behind the glittering goods of the shopper's paradise there was another city. The dirty truth of Singapore was that its commercial success, and the money that allowed it to stay a free port, was based to a great extent on the opium trade. This included the standard business practice of deliberately addicting its poor Chinese, so that they represented virtually a slave labor force of dock and farm workers. The British government of Singapore financed the cost of running the colony largely through selling hugely expensive opium "licenses" (rights to monopoly) to wealthy Chinese businessmen, through which they controlled their poor workers. "Raffles' liberal capitalist Singapore not only created the opium-smoking Chinese coolie; it literally lived on his back. He paid for free trade" (Trocki, 2).

Governance of the Straits Settlements had always been directly under the control of the Company's governor general of India in Calcutta. The small British bureaucracy that made up the government of Singapore was just a branch office. When Anna arrived in 1859, two years after the Indian Rebellion and one year after the Crown had taken over India from the Company,

Singapore was celebrating what the business and commercial leaders of the city saw as its independence at last. They had spent several decades agitating for their separation from British India. In 1858, by an Act of Parliament, Singapore was officially named a separate Crown Colony and placed directly under the authority of the Colonial Office.

We can now appreciate the irony of political "freedom" being defined as a matter of being ruled directly rather than indirectly from the imperial state, not, as we would understand it, actually being an independent state. But the mood in Singapore in 1859 was joyous, as residents saw themselves out from under India's shadow at last. The newspapers were full of the growing agitation in the American states, with the Singaporeans representing themselves as newly freed and therefore avid supporters of emancipation for their American cousins. There was no mention of the plight of their own coolies.

The next three years were a crucial time in Anna's history. She came into her own in Singapore, settling into her new identity as an intellectual British lady, much given to studying language and literature. Her heart was slowly healing, as she adjusted to what her days looked and felt like, and the kind of person she now was, without Tom. Anna had begun the process of fleshing out the person she would be for the rest of her life. She made friends who accepted her as a proper lady and, even carrying the weight of her sorrows and deceptions, she began to breathe again.

Anna settled in to live in Singapore at a time when cries of liberty and individual rights were in the air. She struggled to make a living from her small pupils. She got to know Francis David Cobb, a young American from Boston, whom Anna's granddaughter said lived in a bungalow in the compound next to Anna's (his daughter, Louisa, wrote to Margaret Landon in 1945 to point out that he did not have tuberculosis, as Landon had supposed, and also was not rich [LC, VI C]). Frank lent Anna a copy of Emerson's *Essays* and the two became lifelong friends. Frank Cobb was originally from Barnstable, a small town on the coast of Massachusetts that had bred Cobbs for several generations. Born in 1840, Frank was only nineteen or twenty when Anna met him, and full of the idealism, outrage, and enthusiasm of the young.

Through Frank, Anna became familiar with many of the well-known American authors and also many of the political issues facing the United States from 1860 to 1862. A strong abolitionist and supporter of Lincoln, Frank was deeply worried about the developing civil conflict between the Northern and Southern states. Yet he was also passionately committed to the principles of equality and individual worth, which for him were represented by the Northern side.

And, of course, like most Americans, he had no idea at that time of just how heavy the price of a war fought for those principles was going to be. Through Frank, Anna had an entrée to people in the American community in Singapore, who often talked of the political situation in Singapore and at home.

It was a lucky moment for Anna when she moved in as a neighbor to Frank. It was the beginning of decades of friendship with him and also of years of connections with Americans in Southeast Asia, which would culminate in Anna immigrating to the United States. Anna was drawn to the very idea of the United States, the notions of equality and the right to happiness. Her low birth and culturally rich childhood in the East India Company cantonments had bred in her a strong belief in the wonderful range of human beings of all classes and colors. Her recognition of her own talents had brought home to her the falseness of "pure" birth and social class as measures of worth, even as she pretended to that purity and status. Anna had responded to the rigidly hierarchical world of British India by creating an elaborate deception that provided her with the fake credentials necessary to develop her very real abilities. In the American social and political system she encountered a set of beliefs that, at least ideally, spoke to her own deepest belief in human equality. In hearing about America she imagined a culture where being well born and well bred was not the fixed currency of social life.

This general difference between Great Britain and the United States was particularly visible in the early 1860s in the public tensions and debates over slavery and states' rights. The Americans Anna met in Singapore were Northerners and abolitionists, people who spoke eloquently of the immorality of treating the darker race as lesser than the white. To the mixed-race, lower-class Indian Army brat, such conversations must have been balm to her heart. In Singapore the line of Anna's life changed. Her social connections with Frank Cobb and his friends were a practical choice, of course. With Americans she need not be constantly on guard in terms of her background and her speech. But they were also an emotional choice, providing a public validation for her private belief that she had every right to present herself as a lady.

In Singapore Anna began a permanent realignment of her cultural focus, from England to the United States. That shift in gaze was intertwined with her metamorphosis into an independent and free-thinking woman. Like so many women before her, she found that when she lost the man she loved best in life, she lost the woman she had seen reflected in his eyes as well. The old Anna died with Tom, and she became a different person, as so many women had to do before and have had to do since. But part of the glory of Anna's story is that she was strong enough to accept and even embrace that change, to take charge of it, as it were. She could not prevent losing who she had been, but she could have a say in who she became. Anna used not only the personal moment but also the historical and cultural moment in which she found herself to shape a new viewpoint about herself and the world. A key element in that reshaping, that metamorphosis, was Anna's deepening interest in Americans and American culture.

Anna did make a new identity. She became a lady, but a lady with a professional skill. Nonetheless, after a while it became obvious that the life she was attempting to make for herself and her children in Singapore was not going to work, financially anyway. She later told her grandchildren that this little school of hers did not do well. She could barely earn enough to keep herself and the children. After almost three years in Singapore Anna had become perfectly comfortable inhabiting her new identity. But her financial situation was close to desperate. She needed to find another way to make a living. And, with the help of an amazing bit of serendipity, she did.

In 1861, King Mongkut, ruler of Siam, sent a letter to his agent in Singapore, Mr. Tan Kim Ching, asking him to find a British lady to be the governess to the king's children. Mr. Tan applied to his European business acquaintance, Mr. Adamson, manager of the Singapore branch of the Borneo Company Ltd. The British community in Singapore was in fact quite small. Mary Turnbull has pointed out that in 1860 the number of Europeans numbered "466 in Singapore, 316 in Penang and only a handful of officials in Malakka" (Turnbull, *A Short History of Malaysia, Singapore and Brunei*, 106). Almost all these people were men. In Singapore the number of "European" women would have been more than twenty and not more than fifty at the outside. Almost all of them were wives.

Clearly, King Mongkut's agent was not going to find too many British ladies in Singapore who were obviously qualified to be governesses and whose personal circumstances would allow them to go off by themselves to live in Bangkok for an indefinite period of time. In fact, there was probably only one such lady in all of Singapore, a genteel and scholarly widow, without family ties, who kept a small nursery school, which was not a financial success, and who found herself at that very moment in need of funds and open to a new position.

The whole arrangement happened very fast. Anna immediately used her promised salary to arrange for Avis to go to school in England. She could not do anything about Avis's birth. Except lie, of course. But she could do something about her education. It was a wonderful opportunity. She sent her little girl to England, to become in reality the genteelly educated lady that Anna herself could only pretend to be. But she and Louis had to leave for Siam, sailing on the *Chao Prya* with Captain Orton before they could even put Avis on the boat. Frank, who had come to love the little girl as much as he admired her mother, took over. He arranged for Avis to travel on the *Ranee* to England in the company of a family who was going home, Mr. and Mrs. Heritage and their little daughter, Susan. They delivered her to the Misses King's school.

Before Avis had even left Singapore, she received a letter from her mother:

> We are at Bangkok love, a very pretty river runs through the town. Mamma and Louis are staying at the Prime Minister's palace, it is so beautiful darling, even the walls are covered in gold. Louis is going to get a boat and bring Avis here. We went to the King's palace which is even more beautiful. The King was so kind to Louis, he took Mamma's hand and led her to the Queen who put her on the ground as soon as the King came to her. The little princesses are pretty children, almost as pretty as Rosalee your friend. Louis sends you a necklace which he made on board. My darling must be good, love and obey everyone. God bless my own dear Avis—and take her safely to England. Give Mamma's love to Susan. Read every day dear, Mamma will tell you much more in her next letter about Bangkok. Mamma is very comfortable but not happy without her darling; God bless you—love—always, your Mamma

Anna was in Siam. The great adventure of her life had begun.

SEVEN

A Teacher and a King

MRS. LEONOWENS AND HER SON, Louis, age five and a half, arrived in Bangkok in March 1862. Anna was thirty years old. The daughter she left behind with Mr. Cobb was seven and a half, considered old enough in those times to be sent from her family to board at school. But Anna kept Louis with her, perhaps because she could not afford to, or bear to, lose both children, and certainly because Louis was too young for boarding school anyway. He was not yet six, usually the youngest age at which British families would consider sending their children away, the youngest age at which a school would take them.

The little steamer *Chow Phya*, named after the river running through Bangkok, could not go up the river to the city. It stopped near the mouth of the Chow Phya (often misnamed by foreigners as the Menam, or Meinam, actually the Thai word for river), "at the bar," a large shoal about ten miles from the city. This shoal was a most effective barrier for keeping unwanted strangers out of Bangkok. Large ships could go no closer, and those arriving had to wait for small boats to come out to pick them up. The travelers said good-bye to Captain Orton. His descendants assured Margaret Landon that he had never made romantic advances to Mrs. Leonowens, though citing no information that would provide the grounds for their certainty. Her descendants were convinced that he had pursued Anna, her granddaughter claiming explicitly that after Anna got to America in 1868 she received a letter from Captain Orton proposing marriage for what was not the first but would be the last time.

A few years after Anna arrived, the river was dredged to clear out the impediment of the sand bar. But the Siamese still appreciated the defensive charm of having some sort of blockade to protect Bangkok. For many years it was the custom to keep a heavy chain across the river, which would keep out unwanted foreigners but could also be moved to let in large trading ships. But in 1862, a

FIGURE 3. Anna Leonowens in midlife.
Margaret Landon Papers (SC-38),
Special Collections, Wheaton College.

little boat was sent out to convey Anna and Louis across the shoal and up the river to the dock. They were settled temporarily as guests of the prime minister while housing was arranged for them. On April 3, "Mrs. Leonowens, an English lady, commences services" as governess to the royal children of King Mongkut, Rama IV, of Siam (Bradley, *Bangkok Calendar*, 1863).

The king's wishes in his search for a schoolmistress had been explicit. He wanted someone to teach English to his children but not to try to convert them to Christianity. He had excellent reasons for that stipulation. In his first attempt to bring in teachers, he had hired three of the wives of American missionaries in Bangkok, at $1 per two hours (Feltus, 207). They came to the palace over the course of three years, supposedly to give lessons in English language. But they had shamelessly used the time to proselytize, teaching the children to recite Christian prayers and read Christian pamphlets.

After Mr. Adamson and his wife recommended Mrs. Leonowens for schoolmistress, there was the traditional bargaining. Anna began by asking for $150 a month (in Singapore dollars, a great deal of money) and residence among the missionary community and then accepted less. The king wrote Adamson that "now we have learnt that the said lady agree to receive only salary of $100 per month and accept to live in this palace or nearest place thereof [for the practical reason, "to save us the trouble of conveying such the lady to and fro almost every day"], I am very glad to have her be our School Mistress if the said information be true" (LC, VI C, 4:6, 14).

There was some delay in finding a house. King Mongkut had two important reasons for wishing his new schoolmistress to live in or near the palace. First, there was the completely practical point that Bangkok was a city of canals, called *klongs*. There were no roads. Virtually the whole city was built on water. As Mrs. Charles Hillier pointed out about this wonderful city in 1856, "floating houses line either side of the river for five miles, and they line, also, numerous creeks that branch off in either direction." A house was built on a bamboo raft "secured to the shore by ropes and chains," or it was "fixed to beams anchored in the bed of the river" (Hillier, "At Home in Siam," 482). Living away from the palace would entail not only the inconvenience of distance but also the extra complication of providing the new teacher with a boat and a boatman who could be on call.

The second, more substantive reason reflected King Mongkut's accurate sense that he had already been taken advantage of once in this matter of an English teacher and was determined that it not happen again. Anna's request that she be housed near the missions, really about her desire to be living among some Americans in this unfamiliar country, was to the king a red flag.

In his February 26, 1862, letter to his Singapore agent, he responded directly to "hearing that she wish to live at Missionaries establishment far from this palace." He feared that "her appearance is in pleasure with the Missionaries" and that she "in doing her education may endeavour to convert our Children to Christianity more than education for knowledge of English language and literature like American Missionaries and their wives have done here before." He wryly concluded that "we need not have teacher of Christianity as they are abundant here" (LC, VI C, 4:6, 14).

The debate about where Anna would live took place within the context of King Mongkut's determination not to hire another missionary type, out to convert the heathen. He actually wanted someone to teach his children to understand and be able to converse in English. His refusal to have the new teacher live at a distance from the palace was in no way an indication, as some commentators have imagined, of the king wanting Anna for his "harem" or trying to get some sort of control over her comings and goings or wishing to save himself the expense of providing a boatman and boat.

As the king pointed out in the same paragraph, he had reason to be concerned about the lady's possible attitude. First, his trust had been deliberately and repeatedly violated by the previous teachers, people he had known for years. He was also well aware of the general contempt with which Westerners viewed Buddhism, the Siamese, and Siam. He explicitly referred to "our countrymen whom English called inhabitant of a Benighted land." He was committed to finding someone to teach the English language and English literature to his children and wives whom he could trust to do so without her own agenda and without either condescension or contempt.

In his letters to his Singapore agent negotiating for the schoolmistress, King Mongkut insisted that she live in or near the palace grounds. He also generously offered to provide a brick house in the vicinity of the palace at low or no rent. He offered brick because wood, in this climate of many white ants, did not last. He was actually saying that he would provide one of the very rare structures built not on stilts but on land. The king had no particular house in mind, and it took some time to find one near enough to the palace not to require transportation. After being shown at least one possible lodging that she considered unacceptable and insisting to the king that she must have something decent, Anna did receive a small house on the same side of the river as the palace and in easy walking distance from it.

E. B. Lewis, an Englishman who visited Bangkok in 1862 and published an account of his visit in 1867, included his version of Anna's struggle to get lodgings:

On the first arrival of the governess for the royal children, the accommodation fitted to an English lady had been but very shabbily provided. After repeated applications through the first minister for the redress of these grievances without effect, she took the opportunity of remonstrating (on the occasion of an interview) with his majesty in person, declaring her determination not to remain in the royal service unless his majesty could more fittingly discharge the duty of a host to a lady. The king, whose subjects of every degree tremble and prostrate themselves before him, was so much astounded at the independence of spirit displayed towards his august person by a simple individual and a lady, that he sent for his minister in all haste, and ordered that whatever she demanded should be given her immediately, but that on no consideration could her services be dispensed with, or could she be allowed to depart. (LC, VI C, 4)

Lewis offered this anecdote as an example of how the king, "with all his wealth and magnificent public display, was said to possess the Oriental characteristic of a love of parsimony in his private affairs."

Now, all this is nonsense. Note the mythmaking, the manly tone of outraged gallantry, as the sequence of events is cast in the chivalric frame of how to treat a lady, rather than in the business frame of how to fulfill an employer's agreement. We hear in such loaded phrases as "accommodation fitted to an English lady," the "duty of a host to a lady," and "astounded at the independence of spirit" the language of the European narrating the old familiar story of British principled individualism versus Eastern corruption and weakness (including the very odd claim that being parsimonious is somehow "Oriental"). We see exemplified the power of the True British Lady, carrying the sword of justice, to bring to heel the foreign despot. Deborah Kerr and Yul Brynner would do a lot with this scenario a century later.

But if we look through the jingoistic language, we can discern the series of events. When Anna and Louis arrived, they stayed at the prime minister's while lodgings were being sought, since there was no appropriate house immediately available near the Grand Palace. No one acted in a hurry, Anna herself being the person most concerned, and the prime minister having more pressing business than how quickly a foreign governess got her own place to stay. She pressed him when she could, but he was not very attentive since she was, after all, very comfortably lodged in his own luxurious home, but at some point she was offered something not very good. After a week or so, she complained to the king, who told the prime minister to make it a priority, and a house—probably evacuated by someone else—was found.

Anna could well have told this story to Lewis herself in 1862, when the events had occurred fairly recently and when she still might have been feeling irritated at having to argue for her own place. Who knows how much in the telling she played up her role as an English lady. But we do know that by April 18, Frank Cobb had already received a letter from her in Bangkok announcing that she was in her new house. He wrote back to her from Singapore to say that "it affords me pleasure that you are to be agreeably housed and not confined to the palace" (LC, VI C, 4:2).

The country Anna had come to teach in was utterly unlike anything she had experienced. For the first time in her life, she was in a world that was not a British colony, not driven by the Colonial Office or the directors of the British East India Company, not a place culturally and politically defined by its inferiority to and dependence on England. Quite the opposite. Siam was an independent nation, outside British control. In fact, the translation of *Thailand* is "Muong Thai," or "Land of the Free." Siam was the first free country Anna had ever lived in. Moreover, it was an absolute monarchy, and its monarch's heartfelt goal was to improve life for his people while at the same time keeping his country out of foreign, particularly British, control.

Western imperialist attitudes to the small kingdom of Siam in Southeast Asia were a different matter from imperialist attitudes to other parts of the East, particularly to the Middle East and the Far East. The United States, for example, was simply not interested in Siam the way it was in, say, China or Japan. The United States had appointed its first consul in Bangkok by 1856, but the position was unpaid. It was filled by one of the missionaries on-site, Stephen Mattoon, who had been in Bangkok with his family since 1847. The consulate was his own house on stilts. No money was approved by Congress for a consular salary until 1864. The major U.S. presence in Bangkok throughout most of the century was religious, in the form of three Protestant missions: the Baptists, the Presbyterians, and the AMA (American Missionary Association), starting in 1850. This last was represented by Dan Beach Bradley, the most visible figure in the foreign community in Bangkok. Dr. Bradley had been in Siam since 1834, first sent by the ABCFM (American Board of Commissioners for Foreign Missions), which had withdrawn its mission funding in 1847. At that point Dr. Bradley was forced to go home, where he waited until he got another mission in 1850.

Britain's major imperialist attention and efforts were directed to trying to maintain India, which the government had taken over from the East India Company in 1858. That goal had been the reason it was gradually taking over Burma, Siam's neighbor on its western border. After the Bowring Treaty in 1855, Britain also established a consulate in Bangkok, in 1856, sending out

Charles Hillier to be the first British consul. He arrived with his wife in June 1856 and lasted only four months, dying in Bangkok in October.

Though both England and the United States might well have been willing to scoop up Siam if given an opening, they showed no special eagerness to do so. They did not have any pressing political or economic reasons to decide that the effort could justify the cost. And the lack of those pressing reasons was a result both of Siam's strategic diplomacy, carefully choreographed by King Mongkut, and of the economic success of the various forms of Western involvement in Siam.

The major reason that the British did not feel pressed to use their superior force to take Siam was that in 1855 the British had successfully negotiated a treaty that gave them most of what they wanted anyway. Sir John Bowring, the British governor of Hong Kong, negotiated an agreement that resulted in opening up Siam to "the full force of international trade" (Wyatt, *Thailand*, 200). The Bowring Treaty allowed Britain to trade freely in Siam with minimal taxes or duty, allowed British subjects to reside in and own land in Siam, and provided British consular jurisdiction over British nationals. Effectively, the British could now live in and do business in Siam, with their host country not being able to have much to say about it (though Siam's revenues did double as a result of the increase in trade).

The terms of the Bowring Treaty were in many ways denigrating to the sovereignty of Siam. The loss of state control was extensive. The king and the Siamese legal system had to relinquish civil and criminal jurisdiction not only over British nationals but over those, including Siamese, employed by British nationals. What the British owned was considered British territory, and the Siamese government was liable for all damages to British property. Finally, Britain's most-favored-nation status meant that whenever Siam signed any treaty with another nation, Britain would automatically receive at least the same concessions. The Thais had been pressured to give away much of their economic potential to the British primarily because of the ominous threat, recognized throughout the regions of Southeast Asia, of the British Navy. Sir John Bowring was personally vivid evidence of that threat, ruling as he did the territory China had lost by daring to defy British trade demands.

After signing the Bowring Treaty with Britain, the Thais signed similar agreements with several other countries, including the United States. By the time Anna arrived in Siam seven years later, Bangkok was in commercial terms an international city, with more and more foreign businessmen coming in. Leonowens's appointment was just one of many examples of King Mongkut's established policy of ensuring that his country would be as well prepared as possible in the dangerous business of staying independent. His goal throughout his reign was to evade successfully "the direct colonial control of the Western powers" and thus provide for the "survival of an independent Siam" (Wyatt, *Thailand,* 166).

While Britain was taking over Burma on Siam's western border and also taking the Malay states on its southern border, France was moving to make colonies out of the states on Siam's border to the east. There were imperial aggressors on three sides. Geographically and politically, Siam was that small and continually threatened open space between the British and the French. The threat went on for decades. Britain did not take Upper Burma until 1885, when the French also completed their conquest of northern Vietnam. The French took over what had been Siamese Laos in the 1890s. It was no small feat, arguably even a great political and diplomatic feat, in spite of its heavy costs, for Siam to remain independent amidst the general takeover of the states of Southeast Asia by the countries of Europe during the nineteenth century.

Credit for sustaining the sovereignty of Siam during a time of generally uncontrollable European aggression and in a region littered with collapsed states is generally given to King Mongkut, and to his son and heir, King Chulalongkorn. They were successful in the extraordinarily difficult task of directing Siam to a strong national independence. Thailand is the only country in Southeast Asia that has not been colonized or occupied. King Mongkut saved Siam's political independence in part because the British attack was a matter not of literal force but of economic invasion. King Mongkut was explicit and insightful about his country's difficult international position. He clearly recognized that the British and French viewed the Siamese as "wild and savage," even "as animals," and that British policy consisted of "intimidation of us until we are afraid to go about our own business" (Moffat, 119, 121).

A substantial factor in the success of Siam's defense was the royal harem, named in Thai "Nang Harm." This was within the walled Inner City, or *fainai* (Hong, "Of Consorts and Harlots," 341), of the Grand Palace, where the king's female relatives, his wives and concubines and their slaves, and his children lived. Nang Harm was filled with girls and women given to the king by their noble and/or powerful families all over Siam and Laos. Tamara Loos has pointed out the complex ways in which the Inner City served as a site for generating and sustaining political power, both functionally, in terms of the king's being able to establish and sustain powerful relationships through women, and conceptually, in using male control over women to sustain a definition of "elite masculinity" (Loos, "Sex in the Inner City," 897). The royal harem helped to keep Siam independent because it helped to keep Siam united and the king of Siam perceived as most powerful because, in part, of his masculine virility. Unlike India when faced with the British threat, Siam did not present itself as an uneasy grouping of disparate regions ruled by competing and quarrelsome princes, none of whom qualified as the head of state.

The harem, with its group of royal mothers coming from families all over Siam, had a key political function as a unifying force, existing in relation to one central paternal figure with the power to make state decisions for all the territories of Siam. Through the royal harem, almost everyone else with any power in the country was a relative of the king. If we consider just King Mongkut and his eighty-two children, his relatives from those children constituted a staggering family group. The combination of monarch and harem helped to limit the internal disputes that could make civil decision making a struggle and thus could weaken Siam's resistance to foreign takeover.

When Anna met King Mongkut, he was close to fifty-eight years old and had ruled the Kingdom of Siam for twelve years. The king was the grandson of the founder of the Chakri dynasty in Siam, Rama I. Mongkut's father, Rama II, was a great Siamese poet, some say Siam's greatest poet. As was required by Siamese custom, Mongkut entered the Buddhist priesthood to serve for a few weeks in 1824. He was twenty years old, already with a wife and the father of two children. But his father suddenly died, and his older half-brother, though not the official heir and not of as royal blood as Mongkut, took over the throne, as Rama III. In an era when princes, and even kings, could be poisoned, Mongkut made the wise choice to stay in the priesthood until, if ever, he might ascend the throne. He would remain a monk for almost twenty-seven years.

By this accident of history, King Mongkut's background was far different from the typical background of those destined to be kings in any country. The Buddhist priesthood proved to be an extraordinarily rich training for an absolute monarch. "It gave him an acute sense of reality and a knowledge of the people he could not possibly have got amid the artificialities of palace life" (Griswold, "King Mongkut in Perspective," 13). Mongkut first learned the discipline required. Monks rose by four or five. Owning nothing, they took their begging bowls and received as alms from the people whatever they would eat for the day. They ate nothing solid except fruit after noon. They lived under strict vows of celibacy and were committed to studying Buddhist scriptures. It was a challenging existence, and the young monk developed ascetic habits that stayed with him throughout his life. Even as a king, his typical meal was a little rice with salted fish.

During his years as a priest, Mongkut developed into a highly accomplished and serious scholar. He learned Pali, the written language of classical Buddhism, and also French and Latin from a Catholic priest and English from an American Protestant minister. He traveled the country to read and gather up religious scrolls, often rescuing them from terrible storage conditions in various Buddhist temples, called *wats*. From his studies Mongkut evolved a "new" Buddhism, which he saw as not new but old. He created a reform movement in religion, the Dhammayutta sect, which returned to the old principles and practices of the true Buddhism, which had been corrupted and filled with errors over time. In seeing the conditions of the Siamese during his journeys, he developed a strong sense of duty to his people, along with the belief that there were many ways in which Siam needed modernization and reform. He founded a new order of Buddhism, with a new temple in Bangkok, attended by eager students and funded by his half-brother, the king.

In 1850, when his brother died and Mongkut ascended the throne, he was almost forty-six years old. He brought to the throne decades of experience as one of the "poor" of Siam, a reputation as a devout Buddhist and extraordinary scholar, a solid knowledge of European as well as Eastern languages, and a commitment to educating his people and helping his country modernize. He was a thin man, and small by European standards. Bowring described him as "of middle height, thin, with a somewhat austere countenance" (Griswold, *King Mongkut of Siam,* 30). In photographs, he appears without the self-consciousness of the typically handsome, but with an impressively serious mien (see figure 4). Even his greatest admirers admit some flaws. Griswold acknowledged that "there is no doubt that he was quick-tempered" (*King Mongkut of Siam,* 45). There are multiple historic references to his bad temper; he was quick to explode but also fairly quick to recover.

Mongkut's complex strategies to protect Siam from the rapacious Europeans and Americans included having his heirs become familiar with foreign ways, to the point of having the members of the royal harem trained by an Englishwoman. The king and his younger brother, the sub-king, understood that speaking and reading English would be necessary criteria for successful international relations. They knew it would be crucial for Siam's future that Thais be able to read not only documents such as the Bowring Treaty but also the newspapers in London, New York, and Singapore.

Among Anna's royal pupils, the most important, and the one most charged to develop a fluency in English, was the king's son Crown Prince Chulalongkorn, who was eight and a half years old—three years older than

FIGURE 4. His Majesty, the King of Siam (King Mongkut).
Margaret Landon Papers (SC-38), Special Collections,
Wheaton College.

Louis—when Anna and her son arrived in Bangkok. Over the years, Anna taught many other princes and princesses as well, along with any of their mothers and other women in the king's harem who wished to take advantage of this opportunity to study the English language, English literature, and English ways. For five years and four months, Anna had daily access to the inaccessible female world of Nang Harm, though she lived outside its walls. She and Louis walked into Nang Harm almost every morning and, just as incredibly, walked out of its gates again at night.

The professional arrangement between Anna and the king was an enormous bit of luck for them both. It was one of those accidental, unpredictable, and yet peculiarly appropriate partnerships that can make history such a delight. Anna, whose claims about her national and ethnic origins, social class, and educational background were, after all, false, got a well-paying and high-status teaching job. But the job attained under false pretenses, with false credentials, in some sense made those pretenses come true. Anna's position as schoolmistress to the royal children and ladies of Siam provided her for the rest of her life with total credibility about her being an English "lady." It catapulted her into the class she had fraudulently claimed to be in all along.

Along with credibility, Anna also got a whole world of women friends, many of whom were mothers, and a world of children who embraced her child, one of whom was the future king of Siam. Louis's childhood friendship with Prince Chulalongkorn would shape his entire life and be the basis for his future success. And finally, Anna found herself in a position unique in the history of Siam, for the Siamese as well as for foreigners, of being an outsider granted daily access for five and a third years to the intensely private inside world of the royal harem of Siam.

On his side of this bargain, King Mongkut got for his wives and children a deeply intelligent, scholarly, and enthusiastic teacher, an experienced teacher who was as committed as he was to the power and importance of education. In June 1864, when Avis was only nine years old, her mother wrote, "I am most anxious that my darling should love study—for itself alone because knowledge is as necessary to the mind as love is to the heart and air light food and exercise are for the body" (LC, VI C, 4:2). If King Mongkut believed that the route to beating the British and the other Western powers was to learn their language and culture so as to meet them, in knowledge at least, as their equals or betters, he simply could not have picked another teacher who shared his belief as strongly as did Anna Leonowens. Had she not experienced the power of education to transform herself from her poor beginnings as little Harriette Edwards in the barracks at Ahmednuggar into the respected schoolmistress at the royal court of Siam?

In hiring Anna, King Mongkut also got a teacher who, almost miraculously in a "Western" woman, came without the usual jingoistic baggage that saw the Siamese as an inferior race and Buddhism as an inferior religion. Anna would later write that "there are influences in the religions of the East to render their followers wiser, nobler, purer" (*An English Governess*, 184). In truth, the miracle of the teacher's openness to Siamese culture was not really a miracle at all. The real beauty of the arrangement was that the Westerner the king found who was capable of respecting his Eastern people and religion, who did not see them as savage heathens in need of conversion, was able to do so precisely because the Westerner was really just another Easterner as well. She had not only been born in the East but spent her childhood among Buddhists, Muslims, and Hindus and was well aware that the English Christians, though they had more public power, were not an inherently superior race. Anna was not an English lady. She was a fake. And it was precisely because she was a fake that she could meet her employer's criteria so well.

Anna's job did not remain solely being the governess to the king's children. During the decade when international business affairs were involving Siam as never before, she claimed that the king turned to this English teacher to take on the second duty of providing him with secretarial help, at least in the matter of writing his letters in English, often rephrasing them with correct spelling and grammar. His official letter to George Virgin, the American vice consul, on July 3, 1865, to offer his condolences on the assassination of Lincoln as a "very improper occurrence of calamity which will be heard with great surprise around the globe" is in Anna's handwriting.

To the scoffing of twentieth-century American and British "experts" on Thailand, Anna described this part of her job as occasionally including as well the task of providing a sounding board for the king's ponderings about how to deal with the Western powers who were competing for trading rights and power in Siam. He consulted her not on policy matters but rather on Western customs and attitudes, on possible Western responses to positions he was planning to take. Having some sense of those responses could help him in gauging Western political motives and in choosing his own stratagems.

What we can be sure of about Anna's job is that this thirty-year-old woman from India found herself in the amazing and utterly unique position of daily moving between two normally inaccessible spheres: the female world of some of the most powerless people in Siam, in the royal harem, and the world of the most powerful person in Siam, who in the 1860s still ruled by divine right. And in certain limited ways she became the confidante, and the advisor, to each.

There is no way of knowing in any depth how King Mongkut and Anna got along. He was an absolute monarch, a very devout Buddhist whose religion viewed women in complex ways as more earthly than men. Buddhist monks would neither look at nor touch a woman, lest they be tainted by the encounter. Also, King Mongkut believed that Anna was English, belonging to a nation that he correctly viewed as a threat to Siam, given England's habit of taking over states in South and Southeast Asia. For her part, Anna was a woman of strong intelligence, studious and self-reliant. She was also a person of strongly held beliefs, one of which was in the sacredness and equality of all people. In her thirties when she worked in Siam, Anna was well past the age of girlish dependence. She knew her own mind.

But Anna and King Mongkut had much in common. As Susan Kepner reminded us in her 1995 unpublished essay, "if the King of Siam was a complex individual who defies facile analysis, Leonowens too was enormously complex" (27). They were both serious people. Unusually strong in both of them was the commitment to education, the certainty that knowledge was a great value and that the self-discipline brought by the endeavor to learn was among the highest human virtues. They were both moral people, dedicated to walking the paths of virtue, though each had a different idea of what virtue entailed. He may have thought it did not include lying to one's employer (and everyone else) about one's birthplace, nationality, family background, and education. And she may have thought it did not include requiring people to kneel and crawl in one's presence, enslaving women, and ordering people with whom one was displeased to receive the lash. But each had a firm belief in the Divine, in the sacredness of life, and in the idea that a virtuous life required a ceaseless effort to improve oneself and to serve the public good. They were both intense in their passions and found it difficult to tolerate those who chose paths of laziness or ignorance or personal greed.

This brings up the question of the possibility of either of them having a passion for the other. Who can forget Yul Brynner dancing with Deborah Kerr, or the gazes that passed between Jodi Foster and Chow Yung Fat? John MacNaughton, a Scottish professor who knew and admired Anna when she was an old woman in Montreal, wrote a privately published tribute to her, in which he addressed this question: "He would have gladly raised her even to royal dignities, if she had been willing to accept a fraction of his conjugal condescensions. Of course, she would have none of him, either in whole or in part. She would have much preferred a nice little clean grave. Once he gave her a magnificent ring. She took it in perfectly good part, and entire singleness of eye. *Honi soit qui mal y pense.* But when he saw that her innocence had not caught the squint of its parable, he took care to have his ring back" (LC, VI C, 4:2, MacNaughton, 13).

MacNaughton's story plugs in to a set of attitudes similar to those shown by Lewis, and is just as nonsensical. He calls up for his Canadian audience the leering Oriental potentate, full of "conjugal condescensions," offering a sexual bribe but being nonplussed by the "innocence" of the English lady, who simply does not understand his crude message. MacNaughton's version is particularly full of what I would label "imperial condescensions." Most twentieth-century American versions are more generous and more romantic, assuming at least some interest on the part of both the lady and the king.

But there was no conjugal condescension or romantic interest. Hollywood notwithstanding, it is time we all just accept that. There is simply no evidence to claim any kind of attraction on the side of either Anna or Mongkut. Asserting that the king wanted to make Anna a part of his harem, either because he was lecherous or because he was parsimonious or a combination of the two, is nothing more than a completely invented projection, and a highly insulting projection, on the part of those Western commentators who have suggested it.

Moreover, there is a lot of reasonable historical evidence to contradict any such suggestions. On the king's part, he was approximately sixty years old, a man of dignity and high position, and a person long used to dealing with the foreign community in Bangkok, both men and women. He was hardly a man given to carnal indulgence, having chosen to spend twenty-seven years of celibacy as a Buddhist monk. As a king, he was engaged in the very delicate business of working to keep his country out of the hands of the British. That business did include having frequent sexual relations with young women. The harem system provided him with an ample number of young women with whom it was his duty to have sexual relations and hopefully impregnate. I doubt he had to force himself. But this private pleasure was also a public obligation both to produce heirs and to continue extending connections between the royal family and other families of the region. And the suggestion that King Mongkut wanted Anna for his harem just to save the cost of her salary is as fantastic as it is offensive.

Anna for her part was in her thirties, well past what was considered an age of sexual charms in the mid-nineteenth century. She was also quite tall, with a pointed nose, and had never been considered conventionally pretty. But apart from such questions about her supposed attractiveness, there is the question of her own situation and wishes. The central truth about Anna's heart was that she was a widow, and not just any widow but a woman who had lost the husband with whom she had been deeply in love, and to whose memory she remained true for the rest of her life. When Anna went to Siam, her days of romantic life were behind her. She was a permanent widow, a mother, and a serious professional.

Of course there was no romantic interest between Anna and King Mongkut, on either of their parts. He was a monarch utterly engaged in protecting and improving his kingdom, and she was a teacher mourning her beloved husband and struggling to make a professional life for herself and a future for her children. To cast their relationship in the frame of conventional romance is to do an injustice to them both. And it is also to do an injustice to what really is interesting about Anna's life. We tend too often to think, as George Eliot said, that the greatest stories are those of romantic love. But there are other stories, stories of the shaping of a character or a career or a country, that are at least as passionate and as deserving of being told. One such story is that of Anna Leonowens in Siam.

EIGHT

A Job in a Palace

By THE EARLY SUMMER OF 1862, Anna and Louis were comfortably settled near the Grand Palace. They missed Avis terribly. She had sent a simple note to them after they left Singapore, "Mamma good-bye now goodbye for Louis, your own child, Avis Leonowens." Anna wrote a cheerful letter back:

> Birds sing sweetly and brightly the sun beams as Mamma reads her darling's dear little note, be good and brave my Child and never cry when kind friends are near for that will make them and Mamma too sad, but look up to the fair blue sky every evening for Mamma looks there then; and think how much comes from there—sunshine and rain cool winds, and breezes, dew drops, and rainbows, while only one thing brings these bright visitors to us—that is love, God's great love small in dew drop but how large in the sunshine so be good in the smallest and brave in the largest act of your sweet young life. (LC, VI C, 4:2, 10)

Anna closed this letter full of love and of the consolations of Sunday school metaphors on a more mundane note. She told Avis that "Louis sends his love and this flower to you dear, we often speak of Avis and miss her now."

Avis sailed on the *Ranee* from Singapore on April 16, 1862, with Mr. and Mrs. Heritage and their daughter, Susan. Mr. Cobb reported in a letter to Anna written two days later that the seven-year-old "was gay, talkative and merry as a lark—seemed in high enjoyment of the novelty and could not remain motionless one second." He told Anna that she could expect to hear from Avis around October 16, in other words, in about six months. Mr. Cobb also sent to Anna from Singapore a "small parcel entrusted to my hands by Mrs. Heritage" (LC, VI C, 4:2, 29) before they left. It was a portrait of Avis, done by Mr. Heritage.

That October 1, at about the time Avis was arriving in England and shortly before her eighth birthday, Anna wrote to "My own sweet bird":

I look at your dear face morning and evening as my only comfort. I hope you all are safe and happy in England. I am longing with a breaking heart to hear again from you. Again I pray to Him who loves little children to care for my own sweet my precious Child. Avis dearest be always good my love be always brave to bear and brave to forgive. I hope to be able to send you dear Mrs. Heritage and Susan each something pretty for Christmas, were only waiting to hear you are safe in England. Louis is quite well and sends you his fondest love also to dear Mrs. Heritage and Susan and her papa. (LC, VI C, 4:2, 10)

Because Avis arrived in England in October, she remained at the Heritages until after Christmas, going off to her school at the Misses King after the holidays, in January 1863.

Anna wrote to her daughter in December, full of pride and maternal advice for this child who was about to fulfill her mixed-race Indian mother's dream that she attend a proper school in England:

You are now I expect preparing for School and that when this gets there— you will be already at home with dear Miss King and your school mates— and striving to be ever kind and gentle to all you know. Avis my fondly loved child never be idle or willful. Learn with all your heart Mamma knows you will try if you can, to be such as she fondly hopes to see you grow—Love dear Miss King and obey implicitly every command of hers or any other Lady who kindly teaches you—I expect to hear well of you darling always. And in every way strive to improve, now is the time for study and improvement.

We hear in this Anna's hopes for Avis, but also the familiar themes of Anna's own deep respect for teachers and learning, and her fundamental conviction that education was the route to personal fulfillment and success in life.

The letter moves on to more daily concerns. Anna does not fail to assure Avis that "Louis is writing to you, he thinks so fondly of you darling and has saved 1 tical to buy you a doll which I hope to send in a box I am getting ready for my darling." Anna adds a sad but truthful note, that "Mamma is as happy and comfortable as she possibly can be without her sweet bird's voice to gladden her lonely home, but I won't come to England until my pet grows quite a clever little woman" (LC, VI C, 4:2, 11). They all knew the separation would be for several years.

In January, Avis wrote to "my dearest Mama," probably not yet having received Anna's December letter. She writes to announce the good news: "I am going to school tomorrow with Mrs. Heritage and Miss Collingwood and I am packing up all my dolls today to take to school with me. Mrs. Heritage is going to buy me a new doll and Mr. H says that if I am a good girl he will buy me a large one next Xmas when I come home." Avis understood as well as the adults that she was not going to be joining her mother and brother, that from now on the Heritage household was "home." She would have long summer vacations from the Misses King's school, but the plan was that she spend them in Ireland, staying with her father's brother-in-law and cousins, the Wilkinsons, in Enniscorthy.

Anna deeply loved her children, and her distance from her daughter was a continuing hardship. She strongly believed that the parting was in Avis's best interests, that she was using her salary as the royal schoolmistress to provide her daughter with a wonderful educational and cultural opportunity. Avis would really have what Anna could only claim to have, an education in England. But the pain of absence was one that neither Anna nor Avis ever forgot. They were apart for almost six years, and once reunited both spoke often in later years of the sweetness of being together. They were never separated again for any length of time, until Avis died and Anna experienced the final terrible pain of a grown child dead before her parent.

On her honeymoon after her marriage in 1878 in New York, Avis wrote eloquently to her mother about visiting her old school in London and the memories it brought back: "Those seven years were spent away from you my darling and so are counted in my mind as seven years of my life lost. I contrasted them with the ten years that I have been with you as your daughter and friend, years never to be forgotten, so happy and blessed they have been to me, and I felt that only then did I begin to live and feel and love and I realized more than ever what a noble, loving, true and faithful Mother you have been to me, dear, dearest Mamma" (LC, VI C, 4:2, 29b).

Avis's numbers were off. The separation had lasted less than six years. But it is the kind of letter a mother dreams of receiving. Returning to that childhood scene, with her wonderful new husband at her side, Avis took an accounting of her growing up, including the long years of separation. The conclusion of that accounting was to pay joyful tribute to Anna's love and faithfulness. After Avis and her husband, Tom, returned from their honeymoon, an important part of her happiness was that her mother moved with her to live permanently with the couple in their new home in Halifax. One extended separation had been quite enough, for both daughter and mother.

After Anna and Louis left Siam in July 1867 for a much-needed leave of absence, Anna went immediately from Singapore to pick up Avis. Unsure of her plans, Anna ended up in the United States, where she published two memoirs of her time in Siam. The first was cast in the form of a descriptive travelogue and the second in the form of a "romance." They offered many clearly fictionalized incidents, but all were presented as true. Many readers have been critical of what they have seen as the false picture of Siam presented in Anna's writings. They have been particularly critical of the dramatic horror stories about life in the royal harem and about King Mongkut's moments of apparently capricious cruelty that she offered in her second book, *Romance of the Harem*, in 1873.

There is no plausible justification for reading Anna's two books about Siam literally and then castigating her for getting the facts wrong. She was not writing history. It is obvious that her books are imaginative visions of Siam and that many of the incidents she depicts are exaggerations, amplifications of rumors, and retellings of stories about the wicked past that circulated in Bangkok while she was there. But that does not mean her writings can simply be dismissed as all lies, either. For a biographer, there is nothing simple about telling Anna's life. Her books are emotionally intense, draw on real events and people, and are highly imaginative. They are also, if approached with caution, rich sources of biographical and cultural information.

One example is the place in her first book, *The English Governess at the Siamese Court,* published in 1870, when Anna described coming to terms with having sent her little daughter away to England and adjusting to her new life in Siam. Even with the grief of separation from Avis, we can believe that Anna and Louis did come fairly quickly to enjoy their Bangkok days in the "cool pavilion" of the *wat* that was Anna's schoolroom. In spite of her maternal grief, Anna's attitude, typical of her belief in being strong, looking forward, and always struggling to make life a "living poem," was that "I had flung off the dead weight of my stubborn repinings, and my heart was light again" (90). She loved teaching, and throughout the following five and a third years in Bangkok she found her job and her pupils, the king's children and women, to be a continuous delight.

Days at the palace had a clear pattern. The king and his household rose at five. Their first act was to take their places—the king, his children, his sisters and other relatives, his concubines, and their slaves—along a strip of matting that started from the "Gate of Merit" and was laid "through all the avenues to another" gate (*English Governess,* 95). The Gate of Merit was opened, the Amazon guards lined up on either side, and one hundred ninety-nine priests walked through, receiving their daily offerings of food from the members of the royal household. Then came an hour of quiet prayer in Wat Sasmiras Manda-thung, followed by a nap for the king, and breakfast about sunrise, at which Anna and Louis were often present. After breakfast everyone went about their morning tasks. The king retired to do his reading and correspondence. Anna, the children, and those women who wished to join in went off to do their lessons in the schoolroom. There was a little break for tiffin, or snack, between eleven and twelve.

At two o'clock it was time for bathing and fresh clothes, followed by the major meal of the day. Anna and Louis sometimes went home for lunch at this rest time in the heat of the day. But they were always welcome to stay for the palace meal along with the whole household attending the king. Here Mongkut "chatted with his favorites among the wives and concubines, and caressed his children, taking them in his arms, embracing them, plying them with puzzling or funny questions, and making droll faces at the babies" (*English Governess*, 98–99). After this main meal and family time the king went to the Hall of Audience or attended to official matters with his ministers while Anna and her students returned to the schoolroom for afternoon lessons. These lasted until early evening, when everyone in the palace met again for a light supper. The king retired to his private apartments around nine.

One of the striking things about this schedule is how often during the day King Mongkut spent time with his women and children. He saw them first thing in the morning, and ate all three of his daily meals with them, with plenty of time to play with the children. Anna's dramatic phrase was that "the love of children was the constant and hearty virtue of this forlorn despot" (*English Governess*, 99). But it is hardly persuasive to call a person with more than sixty doting children (more than eighty of them by the time of his death in 1868) in any way "forlorn." Moreover, the love of children was "the constant and hearty virtue" of all of Siam. Siamese culture revered, and reveres, children to an extent unknown to Europeans and Americans. The Siamese understood Anna's devotion to her son and her longings for her daughter, including the self-sacrifice entailed in sending Avis away.

Anna and Louis were free to go home after lessons were over, before the evening meal. But as the months went by, more and more often they chose to linger at the palace after school. Louis frequently ran off to play with some of the children, in the open pavilions and gardens or in their quarters. Anna stayed alone in the schoolroom for a while, preparing the lessons for the next day. Sometimes the king consulted her about phrasings in his correspondence. Sometimes Anna and her son were invited to visit with one or more of the harem women or stayed to supper. Gradually, not only Anna's professional life but a great deal of Anna's and Louis's social life took place in the Grand Palace.

It was quite common for the king at state dinners or when entertaining foreign guests to call for some of his children to be brought and introduced to the guests. Occasionally he would even escort a guest on a visit to the inner palace. A young Frenchman, the Marquis de Beauvoir, who visited in January 1867, described being led "through great halls, sparkling with brilliancy, amongst a troop of laughing children," and found to his astonishment that he was being taken into "the harem!" The women in the room, perhaps 160 of them, "taken by surprise by this unexpected visit, instantly threw themselves down on the covered mats which covered the floor, supporting themselves on their elbows and knees" (Smithies, 206). Mongkut then gathered for the marquis's appreciation about thirty of his sons. (The marquis was one of those condescending Westerners who described the king as looking like a "monkey.") For the king, as for all Siamese, one's children were a source of enormous pride, and Mongkut was no different from any other Siamese parent in being eager to present his children to his guests.

King Mongkut grew increasingly fond of Louis as well. When J. M. Hood arrived in Bangkok in the fall of 1865 as the newly appointed American consul, Louis was the only "Westerner" among the hosts at the banquet welcoming him. Hood observed of Louis, who was then about to be nine, that "this bright boy his Majesty seemed to regard as an adopted son" (LC, VI C, 4:5, 10). In 1862, Louis at five and a half was a happy child, as much in need of his mother's schoolroom lessons as the Siamese children with whom he went to school. Everyone learned their ABCs together. Bristowe (32–33) described Louis rather romantically as "like a shaft of sunlight, with quicksilver in his veins, radiating uncurbed enthusiasm for the life around him." In a world that loved and welcomed all children, this easygoing and friendly little boy soon charmed virtually everyone. Louis was "intensely happy amidst the gorgeous temples, the fairytale pageantry, and the King's harem of wives" (Bristowe, 32). He was "completely at ease with the King" and loved the palace, with its inner city filled with children and the innumerable adults who lived to make them happy.

The other group of people with whom Anna and Louis had social connections was the European community in Bangkok. Their world was divided between the palace and the other "Western" foreigners. But the foreigners were not themselves a large or unified group. Probably the most important point to realize in trying to reconstruct Anna's life in Bangkok is that there were very few Westerners living there during her time. In 1851, just before the Bowring Treaty, when King Mongkut came to the throne, a typical estimate was that out of about 250,000 inhabitants in Krung Tep, the City of Angels (as Bangkok was called), only about twenty were Europeans. By 1868, when the king died, the population of Bangkok had exploded and the number of Europeans was probably between one hundred (eighty-four having entered the king's service over the years) and one hundred fifty (Smith, 13–27).

There were many foreigners in Bangkok from the surrounding states: Cambodians, Burmese, Chinese, Indians, and Malays. The few Western foreigners could be described as four groups. In some ways we could think of them as factions, given to spats among themselves. First there were the few merchants and military people, the ships' captains and soldiers, adventurous men who had come to Siam to make some kind of living. Many of these worked for the king or were agents for trading companies. They tended to like Siam and its culture, certainly including the practice of polygamy (the more precise modern term is *polygyny*—one man, more than one mate). Second, there were the temporary people, quite a lot of them, passing through Bangkok, a very few visitors but mostly sailors. The third group, from 1856 on, was consular people, British, American, French, and others. In the late 1850s and 1860s, this was not quite a group, since often the consulates were staffed from people already in Bangkok—a missionary or a merchant.

The final group, and probably the most visible presence, was the missionaries, who were mostly Americans. There were one or two French Catholics but almost all were Protestants from three American missions. Their social leader was Dan Beach Bradley, who was in Bangkok from 1835 to 1873, with a three-year break from 1847 through 1850. Their very raison d'être in Siam was about not liking or approving of the culture. The laissez-faire, easygoing, or enthusiastic attitudes of the other groups—the merchants and military, those passing through, and the consular staffs—were all attitudes the missionaries disapproved of. On the contrary, they were intensely committed to the project of bringing to this godforsaken Siam a "better" way.

Dan Beach Bradley was a medical missionary and an impressive man. He was born in Marcellus, New York, in 1804, and in his teens became a store clerk. But he was transformed by a revival and received a medical degree in New York City. The ABCFM (American Board of Commissioners for Foreign Missions) sent him and his new wife to Siam in 1835 and supported them for twelve years. In 1847, the ABCFM withdrew its mission from Siam because of lack of converts. In 1850, Dr. Bradley managed to get another sponsor, the AMA (American Missionary Association), and went back to Bangkok for twenty-three more years, dying in Bangkok in 1873.

Dr. Bradley's list of practical achievements is extraordinary. In terms of literacy, he brought the first printing press to Siam, and introduced book binding and commercial printing. He bought the press in Singapore, and it came with Siamese characters, made by an Englishman and never used. Over the years, Dr. Bradley brought a great many Siamese texts into print, in English and Siamese. These included a Siamese dictionary, a Siamese-English dictionary, *Laws of Siam, History of the Kings of Siam,* royal proclamations, an annual almanac in Siamese, an annual *Bangkok Calendar* in English, and many, many biblical tracts. In terms of the practice of medicine, he introduced vaccination and inoculation to Siam and founded the first public dispensary and private hospital.

But for all his practical achievements, which are formidable, Dr. Bradley understood himself to be first and foremost a missionary. His primary purpose in serving in Siam was spiritual rather than practical—to save the souls of the heathen, who were otherwise all damned. And in that he could only count himself, and the rest of the Protestant missionaries, as failures. In terms of what he called "the greatness and nobleness of our work" (Feltus, 190), conversion did not go well. It really did not go at all. Even after decades of trying, they could get virtually no one to convert.

As Bristowe observed, "Dr. Bradley never did master or take into account the true meaning and merits of Buddhism as a way of life. For the most part he concentrated on criticisms of their deeply rooted religion, sparing not even the king from personal attack in a singularly underbred manner." While I would describe Dr. Bradley's views as more a matter of narrowness of ideas than of being "underbred," I understand Bristowe's (19) estimate of Dr. Bradley's occasionally rude ingratitude to the king, a ruler committed to the principle of religious tolerance and "by whose generosity the teaching of Christianity was permitted."

The Siamese, including the king, were polite to Dr. Bradley and the other missionaries. But they did not see a reason to convert. As the king told Dr. Bradley, "what you teach people to do is admirable, but what you teach them to believe is foolish" (Griswold, *King Mongkut of Siam,* 21). The Siamese objections made good sense. They could not embrace or respect a theology according to which God, supposedly "the father of all men," did "not reveal his will to eastern as well as western nations," and yet damned unbelievers (Griswold, *King Mongkut of Siam,* 20).

The king's insight was reinforced by the constant quarrelling between the Catholic, Baptist, and Presbyterian missions, a quarrelling exacerbated by their different national loyalties. By the 1870s, the American missionaries could count just one convert, an orphan child whom they had adopted and sent to America for an education (Bristowe, 18). As the king pointedly commented in his February 26 job appointment letter to Anna, "the followers of Buddha are mostly aware of the powerfulness of truth and virtue as well as the followers of Christ" (LC, VI C, 4) and did not need a new religion.

The doctrinal rigidity, the cultural blindness combined with a boundless willingness to criticize everyone else, and the heavy-handed proselytizing of the Protestant missionaries was a little tiring even for the other Christians in Bangkok. As Dr. Bradley acknowledged in his journal, almost no one "of our foreign community" attended Sunday services (Feltus, 208). For the more than thirty-five years Dr. Bradley spent in Bangkok, the mission's church services were attended by the missionaries themselves and their servants. Other people did occasionally come, for special occasions or, I suspect, out of politeness.

The other foreigners in Bangkok quite frequently found themselves, along with the Siamese, unintentionally offending the moral sensibilities of the missionaries, who worried a lot about lewdness. In a typical journal entry, Dr. Bradley noted that, in the strictness of their principles, he and Mrs. Bradley would not attend a dinner party given by the British consul, Mr. Schomburgk, one night in 1861, because "there was a theatrical performance" planned for the evening (Feltus, 324). They did attend another party at Schomburgk's in January 1864, "not thinking for a moment that there was to be a theatrical performance and dancing." But they were "greatly disappointed" to discover that the evening, though without theatricals, did include dancing "bordering close on the confines of lewdness, especially their waltzing" (Feltus, 288). Nor would they attend the ball at the American consulate celebrating July 4, 1864, because American missionaries, though almost all invited, "could not of course take part in such kind of celebration" (Feltus, 288).

Anna's and Louis's initial contacts were with the missionaries, arranged through the American community Anna had gotten to know in Singapore. Among them she met Rev. and Mrs. Johnson, with whom she became friendly. Also, Anna met early with Mrs. Mattoon, Mrs. Bradley, and Mrs. House, wanting to consult with them because they were the three missionary wives who had preceded her as tutors in the Grand Palace. They gave her their views of life in the inner palace, including their horror of the sin of polygamy.

It is worth emphasizing that, unlike the permanently horrified missionary community, Anna never in her writings condemned the Siamese practice of polygamy in religious or sexual terms. What she repeatedly declared her disapproval of was not sex but slavery, the injustice of a man imprisoning the women of the royal harem for life.

The Americans were welcoming to Anna and Louis, and she was grateful. After all, in spite of their religious inflexibility, the Americans had certainly been in Bangkok the longest of the Westerners, were fluent in Siamese, and knew the details and practices of the culture better than any other foreign group in Bangkok, even if they did not approve of them. To a newcomer, their information and practical help were invaluable, and they appear to have welcomed her. Dr. Bradley told of meeting Anna at a dinner party in January 1863 at the Telfords, Rev. and Mrs. Robert Telford also being with the AMA mission. Also at the dinner were missionaries Dr. and Mrs. Campbell. Dr. Bradley recorded that Anna, as the schoolmistress, had to accompany the king and his children and ladies on a trip to his summer palace north in Petchaburi, in July 1863. And it was to Dr. and Mrs. Bradley that Anna turned for suggestions about what she should do when she came back from Petchaburi in late July and discovered that her house had been broken into and robbed.

But in spite of continuing friendly relations with the missionary group throughout their years in Siam, and connections to other foreigners, Anna and Louis did not quite fit in to any particular one of the four loose groups of Westerners in Bangkok. The few merchants and military were busy professionals, mostly out to make their fortunes, often engaged in dubious business dealings, often traveling, and often with harems of their own. They were not particularly interested in entertaining socially the schoolmistress and her son. Those traveling through, the visitors and sailors, were just that, traveling through. They hardly composed a social group that Anna could rely on with any regularity, though she did try to meet what visitors she could. There were virtually no foreign women with whom Anna could become friends. She was a friendly social acquaintance of Rosa Hunter, who did live in Bangkok and was the Eurasian Catholic wife of Robert Hunter, himself the son of a Scottish Presbyterian named Robert Hunter and his Siamese wife. Hunter senior was the first European trader in Bangkok and was very successful for twenty years. But he was ultimately thrown out, primarily for importing opium, which the king had wisely banned in Siam. Hunter the son worked for King Mongkut as his first harbor master, in charge of organizing shipping.

The third group was composed of the consular people. Even they did not provide much of a social option for Anna and Louis. The French consuls were at odds with everyone, other foreigners and the Siamese. The American consulate consisted mostly of ambitious businessmen. First there was Aaron Westervelt, an entrepreneur, the son of a shipbuilder, who arrived just before Anna. He served from February 2, 1862, to October 1, 1863, the first consul to receive a consular salary. When he left, he appointed George Virgin as acting vice consul; Virgin served from October 1, 1863, to September 13, 1865. Virgin was a rum seller with a very low reputation. He was replaced when a new consul was finally appointed. This was James Hood, who was consul until January 21, 1868.

Hood had a reputation for being something of a scoundrel and a crook. He used his appointment as consul to create a little side business, selling American citizenship papers to Chinese for a fee, thus providing them with extraterritorial rights in Siam according to America's treaty with the king (LC, VI C, 4:4, 3). Recalling "The Olden Days of Bangkok" many years later in an unpublished interview with George McFarland, Rev. S. J. Smith revealed that "these Asiatics" would "hoist American flag on their boats and sell liquor on the river to floating house residents" (McFarland Collection, N). Hood was a man with a choleric temper about whom so many complaints were made to the Department of State that he was not reappointed. Clearly, Anna did not find the makings of a group of friends among the men at the American consulate.

Then there was the British consular staff, again not a sterling group, though perhaps not quite as unscrupulous as the Americans. When Anna and Louis arrived in Siam in March 1862, Sir Robert Schomburgk was British consul, remaining so until the end of 1864, when he retired to Berlin, where he died in March 1865. Sir Robert was a far cry from a public school Englishman. Indeed, he was not English at all. He was German, a protégé of Prince Albert, Queen Victoria's husband. Educated in Germany, he was said to speak English with a thick German accent, and to be a heavy drinker (LC, VI C, 4:5, 18). Sir Robert came to Siam after having served many years as British consul in Santo Domingo. He did not speak much Siamese and spent almost all of his time in Siam in places far from Bangkok. He was a committed naturalist, and he made long excursions around the country and neighboring countries as an amateur geologist and surveyor. Any notion that Anna was shunned by the British consul, and that this was because he recognized her as not truly a British lady, in part because her accent gave her away, is not only an invention but one that notably does not fit the facts.

Sir Robert was replaced by Thomas George Knox in January 1865. He would be the British consul for the next fourteen years, until 1879. Thomas Knox was an actual public school Englishman, one who had been in the Indian Army, fighting in China. As Rev. Smith recalled the gossip at the time, "it is said he resigned, or was compelled for some misdemeanour or other" (McFarland Collection, M). He came to Bangkok and was hired as a "drill master," to train the troops of the sub-king, King Mongkut's brother, who was fluent in English and committed to Western ways. Knox soon learned the language, married a Siamese woman, Prang, whom he met at the sub-king's court, and had three children with her, Fanny, Caroline, and Spencer. Caroline grew up to marry Louis Leonowens. While Anna was in Bangkok, she occasionally went to Sir Thomas with complaints about how the king treated his wives, pointless because Sir Thomas himself had at least two wives. But Sir Thomas and Anna were quite friendly. Still, he and his Siamese family hardly constituted a social world.

Moreover, the king, along with many other people in Bangkok, both foreign and Siamese, did not particularly like Thomas Knox. In a culture that believed strongly in being polite and calm, he was considered ill-mannered. He often spoke aggressively and interjected himself into the middle of problems. Sir Thomas was finally recalled by the British in 1879 for improperly using the power of his consular office to intervene in internal Siamese affairs. He had threatened the Siamese government with calling in the British gunboat in an effort to prevent his Siamese son-in-law, fairly convicted of embezzlement and murder, from being executed. But the Foreign Office did not care to have the British Navy in the business of rescuing its consuls' non-British sons-in-law from the legal consequences of their crimes.

Surveying the English-speaking population of Bangkok in the early 1860s, we soon see, as did Anna, that they were actually a very small population, widely diverse in their interests and beliefs, and fairly fractious. They were almost all men, a very few single but most, like Siamese men, with small harems (first and second wives and a few "minor" wives and/or debt slaves). Virtually all Western foreigners in Siam, with the exception of the missionaries and priests, found the custom of polygamy quite endearing and rushed to embrace it themselves. If in their private lives they thought a great deal about sex, in their professional lives they thought a great deal about money. Many of them were ruthless businessmen committed to taking whatever advantage they could of the Bowring Treaty and the other treaties Siam had made since 1856 in order to gain fortunes for themselves. Most of them were not particularly thoughtful and were uninterested in topics such as raising and educating children.

The missionaries attached to the three American missions formed the largest English-speaking social group in Siam. By sheer process of elimination, they were pretty much the only group of foreigners in Bangkok socially available to Anna and her son. On the most basic level, they had wives, and they invited people to dinner. However rigid their beliefs, the missionaries were concerned with and could discuss topics beyond getting more wives and more money. In particular, Anna could talk to the wives about children. Social occasions with them provided a rare safe venue for a widow on her own who was not in the market for a second husband.

While Dr. Bradley was in many ways the missionary most experienced at living in Siam, and the one to whom Anna turned for advice, the people with whom she became most friendly were Dr. Stephen and Mrs. Mattoon of the Presbyterian mission. The acquaintance between them had been established when Mrs. Mattoon and the other two missionary wives briefed Anna on their experiences teaching in the inner palace. But it developed into a friendship when Anna became ill in the spring of 1863. She had been in Siam a year. It is not clear what was wrong, but it was serious enough that Anna and Louis took the *Chao Prya* to Singapore for a few weeks.

From Singapore, Anna wrote to Avis in April 1863, "I am trusting that my birdie is well and happy at School—and loving and obedient to her instructresses." Avis probably had some initial difficulties fitting in. Her mother advises her to "never complain of nor retaliate upon your schoolfellows or playmates however offended you may feel; it is much better and braver to forgive." Anna's concern for her daughter's loneliness and her attempt to reach across the distance separating them shines through when she tells Avis that a friend from when they lived in Singapore, "your kind old friend Mr. Burrows," has friends in London and has written to them. "Mr. Grennell with his dear wife are very good people and much respected here" and will come to visit Avis and take her away from school for a day's outing.

Louis wrote to Avis too about their Singapore visit, offering his usual forthright cheer: "We had to go to Singapore because dear Mama was very ill, and I enjoyed myself very much and had no lessons to learn. Dear Mama is better and we have come back to Siam where they all love us well. Mr. Cobb gave you some presents and told me to ask you if you still loved him—and old Mr. Burrows too—I had very many pleasant days at Singapore dearest Avis, I wish to come to see you" (LC, VI C, 4). It was wonderful to see their friends in Singapore, to remember that people still thought and cared about them.

It was also wonderful to return to Siam and be welcomed in a way that let both Anna and Louis understand that their new friends in Siam cared about them as well. When they got back to Bangkok, Anna was still not feeling strong, so Mrs. Mattoon simply brought the two to stay at her house for a few weeks until Anna felt fully recovered. The times at the Mattoons' pleasant house, with its long verandah, marshy gardens, and nearby *klongs,* was a pleasure for all. Louis particularly enjoyed running around with the Mattoon children. Mary was nine and Emma was six. Anna and Mrs. Mattoon built a friendship on that verandah that lasted for decades.

Mrs. Mattoon and Anna visited often, sometimes at the Mattoons and sometimes at the palace. Mrs. Mattoon was also helpful in getting Anna school supplies. She sent a letter back to her mission friend in the United States: "I write now to gratify our friend Mrs. Leonowens, the English lady teacher in the King's palace. She wishes me to send an order for some books for her use in teaching and also for Wilson's sewing machine. We brought one with us on our return to Siam which has run beautifully. Esther, the native girl I had with me in America works it very expertly and Mrs. Leonowens wishes one like it. She hopes to get it at the reduced price given to ministers and missionaries." Along with the sewing machine, Anna had Mrs. Mattoon ask for some of the typical school texts of the time, McGuffey's *First Reader,* Parker's *Juvenile Philosophy,* Charles Davie's *Primary Arithmetic,* and Pasley's *Universal History.*

Anna did have warm connections with a few members of the Western community in Bangkok. But she also kept herself and Louis at a little distance from the group most available to her socially, the religious Americans. She never shared, and did not admire, the kind of fundamentalist religious fervor and the accompanying disdain for Asian cultures that characterized the missionary community. She could not respect the very concept of their mission to Siam, that non-Christians, whatever their beliefs, were barbarians and were wrong, and that only Christians were right. Proselytizing for Christianity in a Buddhist country seemed to her narrow and blind. Worst of all, it seemed to her to cover ignorance in the cloak of faith.

Although Anna became true friends with two or three of the American women, they were not at the center of her social world. There were just not enough people in the Western community with whom she could become close friends. Her closest ties were with some of the women of the inner palace. Louis thought of the palace and, by extension, their little house nearby as home. He was very happy there, settling contentedly into Siamese life as perhaps only a child can do. It became his real home. Anna did not find the same kind of contentment. Yet most of Anna's social and emotional life during the next five years was lived not with the foreign community but entwined with the women and children of the Grand Palace of Siam.

NINE

"The Noble and Devoted Women Whom I Learned to Know, to Esteem, and to Love"

ANNA'S SCHOOLROOM IN THE PALACE COMPLEX was the marble-floored grand hall of one of the many temples—Wat Khoon Chom Manda Thai, Temple of the Mothers of the Free. This beautiful *wat* (temple) was located behind the inner wall of the Grand Palace, within the royal harem. The king's children who were old enough were expected to attend Anna's classes. But anyone in the harem was welcome to come to the schoolroom, just to observe or to participate. Anna and the king shared a strong belief in the enormous value of learning. The king encouraged his various wives and concubines to go to the lessons, and Anna welcomed them. Many women did come. Initially, the mothers brought their children and stayed with them to give them the support and encouragement the presence of a mother can provide. But it was also true that many women without children began to come to the schoolroom, and many mothers stayed long after their children were comfortable without them there. The lessons, the teacher, and her son were fascinating novelties in an existence that for many women grew very stale.

Nang Harm was the name the Siamese used to refer both to the place, the inner palace, and to the people who lived in it. There is no direct translation, but *Nang Harm* has been variously translated as "Veiled Women" (a bad translation—there were no veils) or as the "Inside" or as "women of the In-side." Dan Beach Bradley offered his own translation: "all the wives of the king are designated Nang-ham,—literally a lady forbidden, that is forbidden to go out of the palace" (Bradley, *Bangkok Calendar,* 1863).

The absence of a direct or literal translation highlights the fact that we do not have a cultural concept that matches the Siamese institution called Nang Harm. *Harem* is an impossible word in English. Virtually all Western images

FIGURE 5. The king's son, heir apparent to the throne
(Prince Chulalongkorn). Margaret Landon Papers (SC-38),
Special Collections, Wheaton College.

of harems are variants on Hollywood fantasies about the harems of the
Middle East. Nang Harm—and possibly any other harem, including those
in the Middle East—does not fit this image. What, then, was it like, the royal
harem of King Mongkut of Siam?

Nang Harm in the 1860s was a walled city. Wide avenues with graceful
houses, parks, flower gardens, and small streets crowded with apartments and
shops were all enclosed by an inner wall inside the Grand Palace, with the
whole palace complex enclosed by an outer wall four and a half miles long.
Malcolm Smith, a doctor who arrived in Bangkok well after Anna had gone,

described it as "a town complete in itself, a congested network of houses and narrow streets, with gardens, lawns, artificial lakes and shops" (Smith, 56).

In the *Bangkok Calendar* for 1871, Dan Beach Bradley also described the royal harem as "in fact a compact little city of brick buildings, all of them covered with earthen tiles. Our readers may well conceive that it must needs require a large space to furnish room for 100 or more distinct palaces, and numerous streets of ample width, and a bazaar and market of respectable size, and many other brick buildings too numerous to mention." Mary Cort, an American missionary, also stressed in her 1882 memoirs of her time in Siam that the harem was "this little city," and "not without its tradespeople and shops" (Cort, 50).

Anna estimated the population of Nang Harm to be about nine thousand people, all (with the exception of the priests, who visited every morning) women and children, and almost all captive there. Nang Harm functioned in many ways as its own city, with inhabitants in a range of classes, having a range of functions. The highest class consisted of members of the royal family, the queens, consort mothers, and princesses. These women would never leave Nang Harm until, in Anna's phrase, they would "have by age and position attained to a certain degree of freedom" (*Romance of the Harem*, 13).

Bradley's explanation was that "in all former reigns this class of persons have been rigorously confined in the royal palace; but in this reign, they are allowed much more freedom. . . . [T]hey may never go away from home, beyond the palace walls, without a royal permit, and this must not be sought very frequently, and then only on extraordinary occasions" (*Bangkok Calendar,* 1863). This most likely would be to accompany the king and the children on some outing. For other purposes, Malcolm Smith confirmed, permission "to visit outside was always difficult to get." Permissions would often be delayed until the date of the outing had passed, so the women learned not to ask. When an outing was granted, chaperones were required. And on the lady's "return a full account of the trip had to be given, the time of her leaving and returning, where she had been, and whom she had met. A report of it was then made out and sent to the king" (Smith, 63).

Mary Cort was in Siam in the 1870s and Malcolm Smith arrived in 1902, during the reign of Mongkut's son, King Chulalongkorn. He had loosened the restrictions on the ladies of the royal palace, mostly liking to travel himself and often having some of his wives and children accompany him. Cort observed that "there are no 'zenanas' strictly speaking, in Siam, and even the ladies in the royal harems are often allowed to go outside the walls and witness state ceremonies." But even in the presumably more modern era of King Chulalongkorn, Cort emphasized, the royal ladies "occupy retired positions—

often behind curtains or screens—and are not allowed to mingle with other spectators" (Cort, 50).

When there were guests for dinner at the palace, the members of the inner palace, the women and children, ate by themselves and did not attend. This was a constant rule for the women of the harem. This injunction was not lifted until 1908, when Queen Saowapa, King Mongkut's daughter and a half-sister and wife to King Chulalongkorn, attended the state dinner for the Grand Duke and Duchess of Mecklenburg (Smith, 80). The rule confused some of King Mongkut's Western visitors, who wrongly concluded that the women always ate by themselves.

The crucial point about the women of Nang Harm is that they were the exception to the typical condition of women in harems in Siam, found in virtually every elite household. Polygamy was not practiced among the rural and urban poor, and Siamese women were not kept locked up at all. On the contrary, they usually "had considerable liberty of action" (Smith, 80). But the women of the "Inside" were forbidden to leave. They were effectively imprisoned in the Grand Palace. On the other hand, even though the royal ladies were not allowed to be present at court dinners for visitors, this should not be understood to mean that they were required to hide themselves from the many people of the outside who came to visit the palace.

King Mongkut had a vast number of sisters and aunts, for whom he inherited responsibility when the previous king died. The women under King Mongkut's care included the dependents of his father and even his grandfather, as well as his elder half-brother. And the dependents included not only all kinds of relatives but also leftover concubines and all the ladies' slaves. The royal family of a few hundred people also included King Mongkut's wives, his children (eventually eighty-two of them), and various other relatives. As was considered proper, King Mongkut took for consorts several of the princesses, who gave him children.

The possibility of a royal princess being allowed to marry and leave the palace was nonexistent. The sons of the kings had to leave Nang Harm at puberty, but the daughters might well remain there forever. The most important function of the royal princesses was to be considered as possible consorts for the next king, since it was important that at least some of the king's children have royal blood on their maternal as well as paternal side. Another very small possibility was that they might become a wife of one or another of the next king's (and thus their own) half-brothers. In fact, the inner palace was full of unmarried daughters of all ages, of various kings, who would never leave.

Their most likely hope for something to do in life, apart from the long shot of being selected as a possible consort by one of their half-brothers when he became the next king, was to be appointed to one of the various offices inside the palace. Some of these appointments were strictly ceremonial, but some were not. Princess Somawadi, King Mongkut's fifth child, became keeper of the palace keys (a revered job, sort of head housekeeper), while Princess Napapon, King Mongkut's sixty-eighth child, became deputy of the security forces inside the palace (LC, VI C, 4:6, 27). Several of King Mongkut's daughters were chosen as consorts to their half-brother after Chulalongkorn became king.

Apart from the women and children of the royal family, Nang Harm contained other women, consorts not of royal blood and also a vast number of women who performed the functions needed to maintain the community of Nang Harm (Loos, "Sex in the Inner City," 884). Many of the residents, including children, were slaves. Some of the women were or were hoping to become concubines (a title, complete with a decoration, gained by sharing the king's bed at least once), or had been concubines for a night or a week or longer. Some underwent the rigorous training needed to become dancers or performers in the royal theater. Women of royal blood who were selected to share the king's bed were consorts. A few of the women were or had been the king's "favorites." Even fewer were lucky enough to have conceived during their time with him, thereby becoming consort mothers or concubine mothers. A fair estimate is that there were several hundreds of potential concubines, several scores of concubines, three dozen mothers, and perhaps a score of consorts.

The rest of the thousands of women were all the varied kinds of people it takes to sustain a world. There were endless domestic slaves, cooks and tasters, seamstresses, nannies, teachers, soldiers (whom Anna named in English "the Amazons"), who kept order and guarded the inner gates, and even doctors and judges. "This women's city is as self-supporting as any other in the world: it has its own laws, its judges, police, guards, prisons, and executioners, its markets, merchants, brokers, teachers, and mechanics of every kind and degree," she wrote (*Romance of the Harem*, 13). In short, Nang Harm was an entire society of women and children.

This "town of women, controlled by women," was an elaborate and absolutely unique world, inaccessible to Westerners and, I stress, to almost all Siamese as well: "Men on special work of construction or repair were admitted, and the doctors when they came to visit the sick. The King's sons could live there until they reached the age of puberty; after that they were sent to stay with relations, or with the governors in the provinces. But the only man who lived within its walls was the King" (Smith, 56). Although Anna was not literally the first Western woman to have access to the royal harem, she was the first really to do so.

Eleven years earlier, when King Mongkut had first tried to provide the women and children of his harem with formal instruction in English by hiring Mrs. Mattoon, Mrs. Jones, and Mrs. Bradley, the ladies came only at designated lesson time a few mornings a week. Too driven by their proselytizing agenda and their narrow-minded views of the Siamese as godless heathens, with few exceptions the ladies did not teach their charges much English or make many personal connections with their students. The king's next effort, bringing in an outsider, was much more successful than he could have imagined. The schoolmistress made deep friendships with several of the women in Nang Harm. Anna corresponded with them long after she had moved to North America. They were united by being mothers or longing to be mothers together. The women shared Anna's sorrow at her separation from her daughter. And they apparently all loved little Louis, that easygoing boy who loved Bangkok and the palace and just about everybody in it.

What did Anna think of Nang Harm? The best evidence we have of her attitude to her experiences is her published writings, particularly the two "memoirs" of her time in Siam that she published after moving to the United States, *The English Governess at the Siamese Court* in 1870 and *The Romance of the Harem* in 1873. Both must be used gingerly as biographical sources.

Anna certainly saw her role as romantic and daring. The court of Siam, like any other court, was filled with political intrigue and could be dangerous to one not knowing its ways. As Griswold commented, Anna "was a brave woman." Yet he also rather smugly denigrated her courage by adding that she was "in fact a good deal braver than necessary if she could have seen how groundless her fears were" (Griswold, *King Mongkut of Siam,* 44). I do wonder on what Griswold based his easy certainty that Anna's fears were "groundless." After all, what we know of absolute monarchies from English history is not particularly reassuring. And there are certainly several references in nineteenth-century Siamese history to people vanishing from court or to people whose deaths seemed suspiciously like poisoning. The king could, and did, have people killed. Certainly Anna began her time in Bangkok acutely aware of her own ignorance and vulnerable position, and worried about what her life would be like as the employee of an absolute monarch in a strange country.

Anna was particularly troubled by the situation of the women of Nang Harm. To her the world of the inner palace was one in which numbers of women and children were being crushed, most of them spiritually and some of them physically. She saw the inner palace with a kind of personal immediacy, paying attention to how the girls and women there really felt. Looking through the eyes of its powerless inhabitants, Anna thought Nang Harm to be a world of suffering and despair.

Many of the women in the inner palace had either been born in Nang Harm or been brought there as very young girls, victims of their families' political aspirations or the king's random and roving eye. It was the common practice for locally powerful or noble families all over Siam to solidify or improve their relations with the king by being "pleased to make an offering of their handsomest daughter, or grandchild, or niece, to the prince for the honorable station of royal concubine." Because of these customs, "the royal concubines of the kings of Siam have ever been very numerous, numbering many hundreds, and even a thousand and upward to each" (Bradley, *Bangkok Calendar*, 1863). Once the girls were born into or placed in the royal harem, there was no exit for them. They were there for the rest of their lives.

In 1861, King Mongkut did issue a "Royal Proclamation Pledging Royal Permit to Ladies of the Inner Palace to Resign" (Kukrit Pramoj and Seni Pramoj, *A King of Siam Speaks*, 211; Loos, "Sex in the Inner City," 897). Many Western commentators have chosen to read this as a proof that the women of the inner palace were, in fact, free to leave Nang Harm. Against that reading stands more than Anna's claims that the women of the inner palace were required to live there regardless of their own consent. There are also Dr. Bradley's reports that the women of Nang Harm were kept "Inside" and also the point that it was King Mongkut's son, Chulalongkorn, whose decrees abolished slavery in Siam. Moreover, the women of the inner palace were held there by the laws of polygamy. A possible way to reconcile these apparent contradictions has been offered by Loos, who points out that "one version of this proclamation is explicit about how government officials would go about requesting the withdrawal of their daughters from the Inner City" ("Sex in the Inner City," 897). In other words, women could be "free" to leave not by their own will but by the will of their families. This was, effectively, an arrangement between men.

There is certainly legal evidence that women in the inner palace could not themselves choose to leave. Polygamy was governed by an elaborate series of laws, based on Palatine law. Loos ("Sex in the Inner City") and Hong ("Of Consorts and Harlots," "Palace Women at the Margins of

Social Change") have discussed the ways in which adultery was a form of treason, as was corresponding with men outside the palace. Running away was severely punished. Moreover, women could even be kidnapped and given to the king by men "whose status as relatives was highly suspect" but who were more powerful than the women's relatives (Loos, "Sex in the Inner City," 893). King Mongkut ruled in favor of a powerful official and against the parents in just such a case involving three women in 1857. There was absolutely no question of the women having any say. The accumulated evidence clearly indicates that, in actual practice, the women themselves did not have the right of decision, in terms of sexual choice and in terms of their being in Nang Harm.

From the point of view of most men, Western as well as Siamese, polygamy in Siam should be understood as "a recognized instrument of statecraft" (Griswold, *King Mongkut of Siam*, 43). It was a system that served the families and the state well, and it was devised for the greater good. But clearly it was not devised for the individual good of the women who were its pawns. The tragedy of their fates, from their own points of view, was not simply that they were virtually imprisoned for life and, since permission to visit outside was officially possible but rare in practice, most of them were not to see their homes and families again. The great majority of them had nothing much to do with the king. The several dozen who were lucky enough briefly to catch the king's favor and the thirty-five women who actually conceived and bore royal children to King Mongkut and therefore were "consorts" were actually the exception in the inner palace. The rest of the thousands of women, from princesses to slaves, were doomed to virginity and childlessness, in a society where status for women came through motherhood.

In this grotesquely artificial universe, Anna's presence was certainly exciting, even extraordinary. Though a good Christian, at least by the testimony of her writings, Anna was neither rigid nor doctrinaire in her beliefs. Dr. Bradley is said to have wished that "she had appeared more frequently at church on Sunday" (William Bradley, *Siam Then*, 103) and her granddaughter Anna later remarked that she seldom attended church. One advantage her background gave her was that Anna never thought it her Christian duty to try to convert her Buddhist students. She was one of those rare Christians in the East in the nineteenth century who knew better than to judge the Buddhists, Muslims, and Hindus she was acquainted with as somehow inferior in their beliefs and practices.

Writing of being invited by her friend Lady Talap to a particular Buddhist ceremony, Anna commented, "Many have missed seeing what is true and wise in the doctrine of Buddha because they preferred to observe it from the standpoint and in the attitude of an antagonist, rather than an enquirer" (*Governess*, 186). I cannot help but think that Anna was in part directing this comment at the American missionary community in Bangkok, with their endless remarks about the Siamese as godless heathens.

Anna taught her students English language and culture as she knew them, she got to know the students, and she came to feel more and more involved in many of their lives. She felt particularly close to some of the women she came to know. From her perspective, she had been placed in the position of trying to help these lost women. Leonowens presented her second book, *The Romance of the Harem*, as a series of stories of some of the more memorable incidents she had observed or been told about during her years of acquaintance and sometimes friendship with the women of Nang Harm.

It is clear that Anna deeply disapproved of Nang Harm. To begin with, she simply could not take what so many nineteenth-century Siamese and male visitors and twentieth-century male historians have considered as the larger or objective view. She did not see the royal harem as an empowering social institution that brought unity to Siam and strengthened its resistance to British imperialism. The idea probably did not occur to her. But her distaste was not produced by sexual prudishness. One of the common claims of later American "experts" on Thailand, who have dismissed out of hand the only known eyewitness account of life inside Siam's royal harem, was that Anna was rigid or "Western" in her beliefs. The argument has been that Anna did not have the larger political vision to understand or evaluate properly the life she witnessed in Siam (as the "experts" presumably do) because she was blinded by her religious and/or Western narrow-mindedness, possibly through being unduly influenced by her association with the American missionary community in Bangkok.

The problem with this kind of dismissal is that it does not fit the evidence. Anna did not complain on sexual or religious grounds about the existence of the royal harem. She explicitly defended Buddhism on the grounds that Christians are "prone to ignore or condemn that which we do not understand" (*English Governess*, 184). Anna did not object to the harem as promiscuous or even as an illicit offense against the principles of Christianity. Whatever her private opinions of Siamese sexuality may have been, she did not express them in her writings. What was wrong with Nang Harm, from her point of view, was not polygamy per se. What she did write about, and continually offered as her key objection to the harem arrangement, was that, from the perspective of the women living in Nang Harm, their lives and their sexuality were not a matter of their own choice.

For Anna, the political value of an integrating, even democratizing, social institution that could continually feed the royal blood lines with new connections from other families in a network of relations large enough to be a significant force in uniting a country did not have the kind of priority it had for King Mongkut, many other Thais, and many twentieth-century political historians. Perhaps this is not a sign of cultural ignorance and political blindness. Perhaps instead it is a sign that her priorities were radically different from those of her detractors.

Are these different priorities a matter of applying "Western" values, whether rigid or liberal, to an "Eastern" culture? The difficulty with that question lies in the assumption that Anna and/or Anna's values were "Western." We know that Anna's own identity cannot simply be labeled Western. But what of her values, in particular her abhorrence of slavery and commitment to the right to freedom of person and body? There are problems with placing her critique of Nang Harm as a reframing of polygamy "within Western imperial discourses of civilization" (Loos, "Sex in the Inner City," 898). Anna could well have learned her values during her childhood in India, not from the British but from the Indian rebellions against British occupation and from Anglo-Indian rejections of dominant British hierarchies of race and class.

After all, is it not a Western value, I might say a Western prejudice, to argue that believing in people's rights to freedom and equality of justice is primarily or exclusively a Western value? The nineteenth century saw slavery both in the West and in the East. It is surely more historically accurate to see a rejection of slavery as an Eastern as well as a Western value, just as a belief in slavery is a Western as well as an Eastern value. And what of the social institutions that put women's sexuality at the service of men? Surely this has been as much a Western as an Eastern practice, though taking a range of particular forms. Is it not possible to critique the royal harem from an Eastern position? And if so, must that position only be Siamese? The problem with that view is that, of course, it tends to foreclose *any* possibility of critique. The Siamese most likely to object to the sexual control of women in Siam and their confinement in the Inner City were the women themselves. But, as many commentators have noted and as I emphasize here, "there are no 'voices' of women from the Inner Palace of King Mongkut available to historians today" (Loos, "Sex in the Inner City," 884). Indeed, the closest we can come to hearing those voices is, first, in the writings of Anna Leonowens, who frequently represents her stories as mere written records of oral narratives told to her by the women in the palace, and second, in the few letters the women in the palace sent to Anna after she left Siam.

Moreover, there are complexities to the historical insight that the sociopolitical institution of having one or more women—be they consorts, major wives, minor wives, or slaves—compelled to be at the service of one man was a positive and powerful force in Siam's keeping its territorial freedom. If Thailand has inherited many of the benefits of that institution, it has inherited some drawbacks as well. Hong has argued that in the nineteenth century "the moral inclinations of individual women is not the key to understanding their entry into prostitution" but, rather, "prostitution was tied to the institution of debt slavery" ("Of Consorts and Harlots," 344). As she goes on to point out, "women who were sold by their husbands or parents, or who sold themselves as slaves were expected by their creditors to engage in prostitution in order to pay off their debts." In other words, women's sexuality was quite literally currency, exchanged among men. This has, of course, been true in some form in most cultures, Western and Eastern. My point here is that it has been true in a particular way in Thailand. It is plausible to argue that the nineteenth-century customs of debt slavery, including offering female relatives to others, have their twenty-first-century incarnation in the widespread prostitution in Thailand. Thai prostitution is big business and is crucial to Thailand's economy, complete with child prostitution, poor families selling their daughters, and slave markets where you can buy young girls and young boys.

Anna took the personal view. She took the actual women's view. She objected to King Mongkut's harem not because she supported British imperialism, not because she was a repressed Victorian prude who was under the sway of the rigid American Protestant missionaries in Bangkok and rejected sexuality, but because she came to know and care about some of the women in the harem. As a matter of principle, she was opposed to slavery. For her, Nang Harm was a form of sexual slavery. And she was perfectly clear about it. As she explicitly explained in *The English Governess*, "how I have pitied those ill-fated sisters of mine, imprisoned without a crime!" (103).

Any defense of the social institution of the Siamese royal harem also involves, however unwittingly, a defense of the social institution of slavery. In Nang Harm, the two were intertwined. Without slavery the harem could not have existed. That this relationship is undeniable is easily seen by the positive chorus of various Western apologists asserting the benign quality of slavery in Siam. An early expression of what would become a familiar Western attitude was Sir John Bowring's assertion in his 1857 account that "I saw few examples of harshness in the treatment of slaves, they are generally cheerful, amusing themselves with songs and jokes while engaged in their various toils" (Griswold, *King Mongkut of Siam*, 35). Bowring went on to cite the observations of a presumed authority, a "European gentleman living in Bangkok," who assured Bowring that "in small families, the slaves are treated like the children of the masters."

Quoting Bowring with some acceptance, and possibly even approval, Griswold articulated what is probably the standard Western attitude in written accounts that do more than simply note the widespread existence of slavery in Siam. Griswold's claim, offered in his admiring book on King Mongkut, was that "slavery in Siam was not the terrible institution it was in some other lands" (35). The particular "other land" of terrible slavery that Bowring's account and Griswold's supportive summary invoked is, of course, the United States. Bowring's account of slavery in Siam is similar to contemporaneous accounts in America describing darkies singing happily on plantations, looked after by their benevolently paternal masters. I have often thought that Anna tolerated Dr. Bradley's religious narrow-mindedness, blind dislike of Siamese culture, and personal rigidity—all qualities of which she strongly disapproved—because he was one Western man who did not just smile tolerantly at the idea of slavery entwined with polygamy.

Western readers now know enough about the grotesque inhumanity of slavery in nineteenth-century America and in the British colonies in the eighteenth and nineteenth centuries to be skeptical about lenient judgments of slavery, and thus of the harem as one form of slavery, in nineteenth-century Siam. Yet those lenient judgments have been common in studies of King Mongkut's achievements, particularly in terms of crediting him with the heroic feat of taking the first major steps in modernizing Siam while guiding it to be the only state in Southeast Asia to maintain its independence from Western control.

Anna's professional relations with her employer were in many ways harmonious. This harmony occurred because the two shared an unusually strong love of learning and belief in the value of knowledge. But Anna's attitude to the king was also marred, continuously and irretrievably marred, by her relations with her students, specifically the women, in Nang Harm.

What many readers have found particularly offensive and deceitful about Leonowens's writing about life in the Grand Palace has been her negative portrait of King Mongkut's rule over the harem. She attributed atrocities that are fictional or from the far past to an actual historic figure, one with real claims to being considered enlightened and progressive. As well as citing the distorting destructiveness of Leonowens's portrait for Mongkut's international reputation, readers have objected to the sheer ingratitude her writing shows. The first 1873 review of *The Romance of the Harem* in the *Athenaeum* ended by questioning "the propriety of the writer's conduct in spending years in the service of the Siamese King, taking his pay, accepting his kindness, and afterwards publishing" such accounts. And in 1961, Griswold quoted the Siamese ambassador to London, who reproached Leonowens for "slandering her employer" (*King Mongkut of Siam*, 49).

There are many problems with the general claim that Leonowens's accounts of incidents in the royal harem are "slander." In the first place, there is a lack of supporting evidence on either side. Leonowens's two books about what she saw inside the royal harem are without question heavily fictionalized. But they cannot be dismissed as all lies. Moreover, they are the only accounts we have of the women of the royal harem. There is nothing else. Certainly, the royal court records of trials within Nang Harm during King Mongkut's reign would provide a superb source for discovering something of what went on in the harem. But they are not available.

In the absence of substantial direct evidence, writers who are engaged in what they see as restoring King Mongkut's unjustly slandered reputation point out that Leonowens's harsh critiques are implausible, given what they do know about nineteenth-century Thailand and the particular character of the king. Rejecting Anna's writings, with their intense attacks on slavery in the royal harem, and defending King Mongkut as an enlightened head of state rather than an occasional despot toward the women whose bodies he controlled have depended on enumerating the special qualities of Mongkut's character and of his life.

No one can deny the extensiveness of slavery in Siam during Mongkut's reign, or the extensiveness of his royal harem. But Mongkut is hardly personally responsible for the institution of slavery in Siam. He was a victim of his historical context, a product of his culture. And it is true that he was more modern than his predecessors. As Griswold and others have pointed out, through some of his edicts King Mongkut specifically addressed the miserable conditions of slaves and worked to improve them.

And yet, after all the qualifications, after all the information that there were seven categories of slavery in Siam and that people could in theory, by King Mongkut's royal edict at least, buy their own freedom, we are left with the fact that in nineteenth-century Siam a few of the people had absolute control over most other people, usually for their entire lives, and usually over their children as well. Anna's fictional instances of Mongkut's cruelty were slanderous in attributing to him specific instances of cruelty that I do not believe happened as she said. Did King Mongkut really build a scaffold outside Leonowens's window for Tuptim and her accused lover and there have the tortured and mutilated bodies burned alive? Of course not. On the other hand, it was hardly mere religious narrow-mindedness for Anna to claim that there was a fundamental evil here. Even if we believe that the institution in Siam was benevolent compared to its counterpart in the United States, slavery is, by its very nature, violent, abusive, and cruel.

While Anna's first book, *The English Governess,* is sometimes harsh in its portrait of King Mongkut, her second, *The Romance of the Harem,* often borders on the fantastic. The more extreme specifics of Leonowens's tales in that book are melodramatic and surely false. But we need first to acknowledge that the two books are quite different in their form and content, one in the genre of travel narrative and the other in the genre of "romance." Nonetheless, the claim of *The Romance* is that it is offering the "truth," which is not the same as factual reportage. From Anna's perspective, compared to previous kings and many of his contemporaries, King Mongkut may well have been an enlightened master. But he was a master. He was a nineteenth-century man with absolute power who was instructed by both his religion and his culture to view women in terms of their functions rather than their selves.

Dan Bradley in the 1860 *Bangkok Calendar* described a real event that is clearly the basis of Anna's story of "Boon," one of the more extreme tales in *Romance.* His report, cryptic and tantalizing, was that on June 29, 1859, "a young Siamese Nobleman was executed for the crime of seeking to win one of the 1st King's concubines for a wife. The wife of the man was also executed for having abetted him in his designs" (50). Nothing was publicly known of what happened to the concubine. It is perfectly plausible that Anna's account of events is historically accurate. It is certain, after all, that the king's concubines were his absolute property. Moreover, it was generally and quite publicly known that for the women in the Grand Palace, as Chow Chom Manda Kian, King Mongkut's twenty-fourth consort, assured her granddaughter, "whippings were not too unusual in those days" (Knight, 27). Many Siamese men, including the king, had their slaves whipped, and that definitely included women. In other words, some of Anna's tales of cruelty were grounded in actual events, though they did not stay on the ground.

Did Mongkut, on occasion, order his slaves, including his consorts, concubines, and minor wives, imprisoned, chained, beaten, or whipped? Many of the less extreme specifics of Anna's tales involving the king were probably true. One such incident is Anna's and Louis's painful eyewitness account of the public whipping of a consort mother who had repeatedly committed the serious crime of gambling. Anna described "the king furious, striding up and down," and the harem ladies and children required to attend, crouching and hiding their faces. Did the guilty woman's eight-year-old daughter, Princess Wanne (Wanirattanakanya), fling herself "across the bare and quivering back of her mother" and cry out to receive the lash instead? Anna wrote that it took "the united strength of several women to loose the clasp of those loving arms from the neck of an unworthy mother. The tender hands and feet were bound, and the tender heart was broken. The lash descended then, unforbidden by any cry" (*English Governess*, 115).

This is a telling scene in understanding the complexity of Anna's perspective on King Mongkut. Imagining watching the scene, I can accept that it was a sight full of horror. But we can also read the scene from a different perspective. We remember that flogging was a familiar form of punishment in the nineteenth century, in the West as well as the East. The British Army and Navy used it as a centerpiece of discipline until 1881, so commonly that the Indian sepoys' nickname for Crown soldiers was "the bloody backs" (Waterfield, xiii). Men in England had the legal right to beat their wives. And the scene Anna describes is, after all, a punishment. Nor does the crime seem minor. Anna's own account is that the consort mother, "Lady Khoon Chom Kioa" (111), has become addicted to gambling and has received warnings. She has virtually abandoned her daughter and already "squandered all the patrimony of the little princess," who is now poor. What has finally prompted this extreme punishment is that this mother has gambled away her small daughter's last slave, a woman devotedly attached to the little girl, who loved her in return. We may share Anna's perspective and feel that no person, certainly no woman, should be whipped. But we can see the king's perspective as well. It is Anna, after all, who allows us to do so.

Finally, perhaps it is enough to say that based on situations and events that we already know to be true rather than on situations and events that I fully believe were true, we could claim that King Mongkut did treat with injustice the women of the "Inside." Was not the mere fact of their being imprisoned for life in the inner palace, no matter what the particulars, for many of them a form of spiritual torture that broke hearts and deadened joy? Isn't it true that these women's own hearts, and their own sexual desires, or lack of desires, were irrelevant to their sexual usage? Isn't it also true that some of the women were physically hurt as "punishment" and possibly even killed? And should not King Mongkut be held at least partly accountable?

It seems to me that these questions reflect Anna's point of view. In doing so, they give us a way to explain and understand her attitude and motives in writing so harshly of King Mongkut. Anna's representations are not best described as exaggerations, as if there is an objective truth that she has somehow distorted. She has certainly played fast and loose with many facts. But what she offers is not objectivity nor exaggeration nor distortion. Those are all terms of dismissal. Anna's view does not deserve to be dismissed. Her vision does have its claims to truth. She offers a particular angle of sight, of how events looked seen through her eyes, of how she believed they looked through the eyes of many of the women of the "Inside" as well, reminding us that opinions about Nang Harm are, after all, a matter of perspective. And hers is both unique as an available written account and invaluable.

From the historically masculine perspective that slavery in mid-nineteenth-century Siam was a useful and not particularly cruel institution it is not far to Griswold's conviction that the women in the royal harem, with a few exceptions, liked it there and were "contented with their lot" (*King Mongkut of Siam,* 45). Against such convictions, formed from a distance and formed by men, stands the testimony of the only outsider who saw firsthand, saw in depth, and saw from the point of view of being a woman herself.

Anna's eyewitness report was quite different from those offered by Western men. Her opinion was that in the harem the women

> have the appearance of being slightly blighted. Nobody is too much in earnest, or too much alive, or too happy. The general atmosphere is that of depression. They are bound to have no thought for the world they have quitted, however pleasant it may have been; to ignore all ties and affections; to have no care but for one individual alone, and that the master. But if you become acquainted with some of these very women . . . you might gather glimpses of recollections of the outer world, of earlier life and strong affections, of hearts scarred and disfigured and broken, of suppressed sighs and unuttered sobs. (*English Governess,* 107)

These are intense lines, emotional rather than rational, involved rather than detached, full of the passionate conviction that marked Anna's life. Unarguably, there were women in the Grand Palace who were happy. But, also unarguably, there were a great many women of the "Inside" who were not.

Anna's eloquent and sometimes sentimental writing style is tied to the fantastic and "romantic" quality of the particular events it narrates. Why did Anna so often give us the fabulous yet use actual historical people and label the whole combination real? The question, I think, leads back to another. To whom in Siam did Leonowens really owe her gratitude? In other words, for what in her experiences as the governess in Nang Harm did Leonowens most deeply feel grateful? The explicit claim of her writing is that Leonowens is most grateful for the friendship and the example of the Siamese women with whom she became acquainted inside the palace.

Among the women in the palace with whom Anna became friends were two old pupils of Mrs. Mattoon, Ladies Talap and Klin. In September 1863, after Anna had returned from Singapore and finished her recovery at the Mattoons', Mrs. Mattoon wrote of going to the palace for a visit and "taking my girls, Mary and Emma [ages nine and six] with me." Ladies Talap and Klin provided some tiffin and "the little girls were much amused at seeing the gold chains and jewels worn by the King's children." Clearly, Mary and Emma had not been inside the palace before to visit with the royal children, a privilege Anna had arranged. Each of the girls "received a Siamese gold ring from Lady Talap and were taken to see some white monkeys." The visit was a great success.

Lady Klin was already Anna's closest friend in Bangkok. Lady Talap also became a good and constant friend. Anna also got along particularly well with Lady Thouapp (or Thao App), the respected judge of Nang Harm. Another friend was Lady Thieng (or Thiang), King Mongkut's head wife. These were the special four. But Anna had friendly relations with several of the women in Nang Harm and was very fond of many of their children.

In spite of the opinion of many of its detractors, Anna's second book, *The Romance of the Harem*, is a tribute to Siam. But it pays tribute to the women of Siam as opposed to the men. Moreover, that the women were opposed to the men is not an emotional but a structural truth. This opposition was inherent in the very institution of the harem; and it was created not by the women but by the men. Anna's writings paid tribute to the women of Nang Harm by displaying the power of their characters as they responded to their state of oppression, for the oppression of its women was the overlooked truth of Nang Harm.

Anna's stories about Nang Harm, for all their excess, uncovered that consistently hidden, politically inconvenient truth. The stories also offered another truth, that the women in Nang Harm were not mere victims, any more than they were less fully human than men or their lives and personal suffering were less important than the greater good of a unified Thailand. *The Romance of the Harem* was particularly notable in presenting Siamese women to American audiences as great heroines. It did not do so through an objective or sociological account of the facts.

Anna's fictionalized tales constituted a grand gesture, in which the evils and the heroics were both painted larger than life. The stories pitted all-powerful masters, carelessly unaware of the full humanity of their human possessions, against outwardly powerless yet indomitable women of many kinds: Tuptim, the innocent sixteen-year-old Buddhist bricklayer who defied torture and death; Ore, the Muslim slave and daughter of a slave who bore years of misery for the right to be free; May Peah, the stalwart Laotian whose loyalty to her friend outwitted the forces of the whole Siamese penal and legal system; and Boon, whose selfless love was stronger than the weakness of women and the fickleness of men. The major tales in *The Romance of the Harem* were preposterous. But all of the stories spoke for the women of the harem as no other writings about the royal harem of Siam have spoken. Their excess was their gift. Anna did not allow her readers to conclude that the women of the royal harem were "contented." She never wrote blithely of a system that violated so many women's bodies, so many women's lives.

The irreducible factual basis of Anna's stories about Nang Harm was one woman looking at other women's lives, seeing how many of those lives were blighted, and being horrified. She insisted on responsibility by actually naming the times, the place, and the man in charge of this blight. Yet the emphasis of Anna's writings fell not on the situation but on how these women dealt with it. As Anna's dedication in *The Romance of the Harem* said, her book was written for "the noble and devoted women whom I learned to know, to esteem, and to love in the city of Nang Harm."

TEN

Settled in Bangkok

ANNA HAD AN ENTHUSIASTIC AND INTENSE PERSONALITY, always fascinated with the world about her. She was a sociable being who liked to be among other people, and she made many friends during her years in Bangkok. Most of her friends were Siamese women. These relationships evolved both because she spent almost all of her time among the women and children of the royal harem and because there were very few foreign women in Siam anyway. As with the friendships of most of us, Anna's friendships were forged among the group of people daily surrounding her.

The basis of Anna's friendships was not that of teacher and students, though that was primarily a pleasant experience on both sides. The sturdier foundation that linked Anna to the women of Nang Harm was the bond of motherhood, in terms of sharing both the joy of having a child there and the sorrow of not having one there. It was not the scholarly woman but the absent little girl and the laughing little boy who guided their mother into the hearts of the royal women. In a culture that deeply loved children, every woman in the palace who had lost or never had a child understood and could empathize with Anna's grief at her loss of her daughter, just as all could join in her delight at the cheery mischievousness of her son. They understood all too well, at Nang Harm, what self-sacrifice for the better good of the family was, and what it felt like to be far apart for so many years from those you love.

When Avis said good-bye to her mother and little brother in Singapore as they sailed to Bangkok in March 1862, she was not quite seven and a half years old. Avis did not see her mother and brother again until she was thirteen. A good part of Anna's grief during those long years of missing Avis in Bangkok was how inevitably distant their relationship became, how faint a connection remained. In the Misses King's school, for the fee of fifty pounds a year plus incidentals, Avis was instructed in "English, French and music," along with "other accomplishments (as Drawing and Dancing)" (LC, VI C, 4:2). Over the almost six years of separation, the little girl whom Frank Cobb had described as "merry as a lark" on the decks of the *Ranu* before it sailed, "gay and talkative," who "could not remain motionless one second," evolved into a young English lady.

Anna wrote to "my dear sweet bird" on her birthday, October 25, 1862, "my glad thoughts go out this pleasantest of pleasant days to picture the dear face that it gave to comfort my heart." She told Avis, "No mother was ever more blessedly happy and no love came in deeper richer glow to my bosom than the love that eight years ago welcomed you into it darling." She went on, "Very dear are the memories that come to me of the day which brought first light of your little face. God's mercy was surely hidden in the little Baby and now it bursts forth into such beautiful promise as I am thinking of my little girl" (LC, VI C, 4:2). Signing herself, "with fond love I am your Anxious mother," Anna then added a typically mundane postscript: "Dear Pet I forgot to tell you that Louis cried on the first thought that came to him of you this morning but bye and bye he got very merry and drank your health."

Anna's deep love for her daughter continued as strong as ever. But the tenor of the letters between them inevitably changed as the years went by. It was clear that the "family" available to Avis in England was the Heritages, who had brought her from Singapore. It would be Mrs. Heritage who sat for hours at Avis's bedside in March 1865 when she had the measles. On Avis's ninth birthday, October 25, 1863, Miss King wrote to Anna to let her know that the Heritages had not been allowed to visit the little school in Fulham, the day falling on a Sunday, and neither the Heritages nor the Misses King could approve of Sunday visiting. But Avis had been allowed to treat her schoolfellows to wine and cake.

By the summer of 1863, a little more than a year after her mother and brother had left Singapore without her, Avis was writing rather formal letters. She had spent the summer holidays with the Heritages since her own relatives decided they could not arrange to see her. Thomas Wilkinson, her father's brother-in-law in Enniscorthy, Ireland, had declined to take her until the following summer, for "as we have not direct railways communication from Dublin I could not send a young lady of your years, though being such a great traveler, a hundred miles in Ireland with several changes of trains and coaches."

On August 1, 1863, Avis wrote describing that summer in London:

My dear Mamma, I have come back to school, and I have had very happy holidays. I went to Madame Tussaud's and saw the wax work figures, and they are so natural I was going to bow to one of them. I have also been to the Crystal Palace and there I saw the Plantains and other plants which reminded me of Singapore. Yesterday I went to the Bishop of London's School treat and drank tea with his small daughters at Fulham Palace. Miss Caroline Sandall is their Governess. We had a very pleasant afternoon. Give my love to dear Louis and accept it for yourself. I remain,

Your Affectionate Child, Avis.

Anna must have taken real comfort from this polite and well-written letter. Madame Tussaud's, the Crystal Palace, tea with the daughters of the bishop of London; these were surely the kinds of childhood leisure activities that the woman who had spent her own childhood running freely among the tents, barracks, and bazaars of army outposts in southern India had hoped to provide when she sent her beloved child away.

Just as important as the intellectual and social education Avis was receiving was that she was well liked and well treated at her school. On February 2, 1864, she wrote after the Christmas vacation, "I have enjoyed my holidays very much," but emphasized, "I am at school again now, and am very happy here." She was particularly delighted that "now there are two young ladies younger than I am," one only six years old. Avis went on to tell her mother, "Miss Clark is now my teacher. She is very kind; and I love her very much." The teachers at the school seemed to return that love. On March 24, 1864, Miss King wrote to Anna the kind of report from school that every parent would love to receive. Miss King assured Anna, "You will readily believe that it is a labour of love gratifying and satisfying in itself to teach and to care for your precious child." She went on to amplify the compliment by noting, "I have seldom seen the unaffected simplicity of the child so beautifully blended with the thoughtfulness of the woman, as we see them in your dear child" (LC, VI C, 4:2).

On June 20, 1864, well over two years since they had been parted, Anna wrote one of her many loving letters to her absent daughter, now in her tenth year. At the actual moment Anna was writing, Avis had already left school for her summer vacation. She was having the promised visit to the Wilkinson relatives. The Wilkinson family was headed by Uncle Thomas, who had married her father's older sister, Mary. There were at least five girls: Selina, Martha, Mary, Lizzie Avice, and another (Nell?). Avis also had at least one male Wilkinson cousin, Thomas Leon, named after her father. And there was Aunty Avice, another of her father's sisters and her own namesake. For the first time in her life, Avis was actually meeting and even staying with real relatives. Anna had told her daughter in a letter that February that the trip was being arranged through Uncle Thomas's correspondence with Anna, and Avis was "to visit your dear Papa's native place and try to like it." Avis loved it all. "Oh; it was *beautiful; beautiful!*" were her words about that journey (LC, VI C, 4:2).

In Anna's June letter we again get a glimpse of Avis's life as a school boarder without family nearby. "My own darling Avis, I have received your pretty little precious note and am quite happy in all that you say of yourself— especially in hearing that you found it pleasant remaining at school and continuing your studies during the Easter vacation." We do not know the particular reason why Avis did not go to the Heritages that Easter holiday. She would stay with them again the following Christmas, for the holidays.

The Heritages were definitely not at peace as a couple. In late 1865, Mr. Heritage abandoned his wife and child and was never heard from again. The Heritages and their daughter, Susan, continued to have Avis visit from school up through the fall of 1865. Then their visits stopped, primarily because Mrs. Heritage began to make criticisms to Avis about the school, and Anna decided that it would be better for Avis if she stopped her visits. Of course, the late fall of 1865 was a time of terrible tension and pain for Mrs. Heritage and her daughter. Their grief and shame at being so totally abandoned by husband and father was great, and they were now without an income. It was probably easier not to have Avis as their guest, and Avis enjoyed holidays at school anyway. The longstanding friendship between the two mothers and the two daughters continued throughout Avis's years at school.

It was in this June letter that Anna exhorted Avis to "love study—for itself alone, because knowledge is as necessary to the mind as love is to the heart." Anna was here repeating to Avis one of her own deepest beliefs. She went on to promise her daughter that if she did well in French and English "I mean to indulge you dearest [in the sense of paying for the extra lessons at the Misses King's school] in the true and valuable pleasure of acquiring the German language." It may not be a form of indulgence many girls not quite ten years old would have appreciated or would now appreciate.

Nor did Anna stop there. This woman who herself had a love of languages went on in the letter, dreaming her dreams of her increasingly scholarly daughter: "When we meet again I hope your mind will be sufficiently cultivated to make you like Arabic, Persian, Hindoostani and Siamese—and then we shall have the delight of reading together some of my favorite books— particularly the Kasamah and other fanciful but really beautiful books which I have been selecting." And we suddenly catch a view of the lonesome mother, comforting herself by picturing which of her favorite books Avis might most like when at last Anna is with her daughter again.

After this flight of wishful thinking and the pretty picture conjured up of mother and daughter happily reading together someday, Anna caught herself, recollecting that Avis was still but nine years old. "I fear I am writing hard words, and too closely for you my pet," she confessed, then went on to relate a funny anecdote of Louis also sitting there writing his letter to Avis, and struggling mightily with spelling and with writing as well. And lest I give the impression that Anna's letters to her daughter were too serious or academic, I turn to the ending, with its by now familiar reassertion of the great value of love. After helping Louis spell, "finally I have to hold his hand to write your Affectionate Brother—which I am quite sure his heart writes without any holding at all. Be very gentle and Kind to all love, remember that there is nothing so priceless as love and Kindness, it makes the heart rich in its possession" (LC, VI C, 4:2).

Interwoven through Anna's time in Bangkok was her correspondence with, and longing for, her absent daughter. We can remember that Anna had endured the death of her first daughter, Selina, and surmise that this first loss led to valuing her one living daughter even more. But I am not sure that is true. It is enough to say that Anna loved and deeply missed Avis throughout the long years of their separation. Avis was enough of a topic of conversation among the ladies Anna knew particularly well in the Grand Palace that they too sent letters to Avis, and little presents as well. As early as Avis's ninth birthday, her mother is advising her to "ask Miss King to help you to write notes to the Ladies Koon Talap and Koon Thowapp," for a "box of silks presented to you on your birthday" (LC, VI C, 4:2). The practice of the Siamese ladies and children occasionally corresponding with Anna's little daughter continued throughout Anna's years at the Grand Palace. It made sense to all as a lovely combination of practicing English and also doing a kindness for Anna and for Avis.

Although threaded throughout Anna's years in Bangkok was the pain of missing her daughter, she and Louis led a busy life. During 1862 Anna and Louis spent their first months getting settled in Bangkok, getting to know the people there, both the foreign community and the people of the Grand Palace, and generally establishing their lives. Professionally, Anna spent the six or seven months of 1862 getting her classes functioning, selecting and developing teaching materials, and learning the ability and knowledge levels of her many pupils. The first classes were around twenty children. But the numbers gradually increased as more children, and several of the women of Nang

FIGURE 6. House of Mr. and Mrs. Mattoon, Siam, 1864. Margaret Landon
Papers (SC-38), Special Collections, Wheaton College.

Harm, regularly attended. Anna had been in Bangkok about a year when she
developed some sort of lingering illness. She and Louis spent part of that
spring of 1863 in Singapore, and then the early summer at the Mattoons' back
in Bangkok, while Anna recuperated and the women and their children became good friends. The Mattoon house was particularly delightful because
it was a roomy bungalow, and on dry land (see figure 6).

Louis and Anna's regular life in Bangkok was marked by occasional incidents that disrupted their daily concerns. Perhaps the saddest was the death
of one of Anna's pupils from cholera in May 1863. Fa-ying (Somdetch Chou-
fa Chandrmondon), of fully royal descent as she was the daughter of the late
queen and full sister of Prince Chulalongkorn, was only eight years old. Not
only was Fa-ying the same age as Avis, she was by all accounts an exceptional child—extremely bright, sweet, and pretty. She was said to be King
Mongkut's favorite child. Everyone in the palace adored her, including her
teacher. Anna was grief-stricken at Fa-ying's death. She also told Dr. Bradley,

who recorded it in his journal, that she saw the king shortly after the sad event and "he was entirely overcome by it and wept like a child" (Bradley, "Abstract of the Journal," 233).

Two months after Fa-ying's death, in mid-July 1863, Anna and Louis did have a pleasant vacation trip for a week at Ayuthia (the "Old City," Siam's previous capital), with the king and several of his wives and retinue. But the trip was marred when Anna returned to Bangkok and "found to her great grief that her house had been broken into during her absence and plundered of all its valuable contents which she estimates at $800" (Bradley, "Abstract of the Journal," 234). Since Anna did not have much money, it is fair to assume that most of the stolen "valuable contents," the value of which had to be estimated "at $800," were the gifts Anna and Louis had received from the ladies of the Grand Palace, items such as silks, rings, and little gold figures.

Of the various events that disrupted the tenor of Anna's days as a schoolteacher, perhaps the most frequent were the arrivals in Bangkok of Westerners, some come to stay and some just passing through. There had been, of course, Mr. E. B. Lewis in the summer of 1862, who had written with such chivalrous outrage of the delay in finding Anna a house and referred to the women of Nang Harm as "caged doves." One visit, which Anna missed because she was in Singapore, she heard all about when she returned. It was the exciting and quite accidental arrival of an American woman, Mrs. A. Vernon Rose Eastlake. The U.S. clipper ship *Hotspur* was shipwrecked in late February off the coast of China. Mrs. Eastlake, her small son, and some of the crew spent twenty-one days drifting at sea. They were picked up at last and brought to Bangkok, where they spent two weeks recuperating from the ordeal. Mrs. Eastlake and her boy were sweetly tended by the American missionary community and also kindly treated by King Mongkut, who gave them an audience, spent some time with them and his children, and took them to visit his white elephant. The children spoke to the rescued pair in English, telling them of their teacher (LC, VI C, 4).

Anna and Louis were at home in Bangkok for the arrival in April 1864 of the new French consul, Captain Aubaret of the French Navy. They were there for the arrival in January 1865 of the new British consul, Thomas George Knox, and for the arrival in September 1865 of the new American consul, James Hood. They were there when Amelia Bailey, the famous singer, came to perform for the king and his court sometime between 1863 and 1865. And in June 1865, they were there to host Mary Atkins from California, Mrs. Bradley's old college roommate from Oberlin. As Dr. Bradley put it in his inimitable way, Mrs. Leonowens "took us to a royal theatrical performance to show Miss Atkins the heathenism of Siam. She there had such a view of it as quite horrified her." He goes on to acknowledge that "Mrs. Leonowens gave Miss Atkins an introduction to His Majesty," who "had the generalship of all parts of the performance, being on his feet nearly all the time moving from place to place and directing by word of mouth and by pointing his cane" (Bradley, "Abstract of the Journal," 240).

The New Road, the first major road in Bangkok, ordered by King Mongkut and going along the east side of the Chao Prya to the Grand Palace, was finished in March 1864. Foreigners particularly loved it because it gave them a place in Bangkok to ride. Louis rode there on his pony, Pompey, just about every day, and Anna usually rode as well. Louis wrote to Avis on February 2, 1865, to announce with his usual good cheer, "I am very happy. All the people loves me and Mama and my pony can race Mr. Knox's big horse (Bristowe, 133)." He was eight and his sister was ten. Louis wrote again on March 2, 1865, gleefully telling Avis that "Pompey is good and fat but Mama's poney is wicked and kiks." He also told his sister, "I am learning sanskrit and siamese [the written language] and when I know them well I will go to England." Louis ends, still cheerfully, with a detail that reminds us that his mother was sometimes unhappy. He tells Avis that he has met "a pretty lady" who is French, and he has learned a few words himself. "When Mama crys and is naughty and wont do as I tell her I call her une Mauvaise Sugete" (LC, VI C, 4:2, 29).

One of the many small mysteries of Anna's life comes from a remark of Louis's in that February 1865 letter to Avis. He tells her, "I am well but Mama has been sad because her Uncle is dead but Mama says he did not think of us." Who was that uncle? And why would there be any possibility that he left Anna and Louis anything in his will? In terms of Anna's family, he would not have been a relative of Thomas Edwards, her father, or of Patrick Donohoe, her stepfather. I do not believe Mary Anne's children, and probably even Mary Anne and her husbands, had any contact with the families the two farm boys had permanently left behind. The Glascotts of England were always out of the picture.

Anna had a maternal uncle, her mother's brother, William Glascott. He had been baptized William Frederick but, in a move I find socially telling and personally touching, he changed his name in 1848 or 1849 to William Vaudrey Glascott. It was his father's, the English officer's, name, although originally spelled Vawdrey. William and his exceptionally bright niece shared a commitment to learning that Mary Anne and the rest of Anna's siblings did not have. Anna's beloved uncle had encouraged her in her studies, been a witness at her wedding, been close to Tom and Anna during those happy times in

Bombay, and gone to Singapore with them at the end of 1852 after the horror of Selina's death and then on to Western Australia. But he had returned home and gotten a good job as a master (teacher) in a boys' school for Eurasians, the Indo British Institution.

The uncle whom Louis mentioned could not have been William, though he had become much better off than during his days as a clerk with Tom and Johnny Donohoe. He had been promoted to headmaster of the Indo British Institution and was well enough established to make the "List of Persons Qualified to Serve as Jurors," in the *Bombay Gazette,* a list reserved for those propertied men who occupied houses of at least 300 rupees in value. Sadly, William had died of acute dysentery while Tom was still alive and before Louis had even been born. He died on February 5, 1856, only in his late thirties, almost a decade before Louis wrote his letter.

Although we may never know to whom Louis referred, perhaps the best possibility is that the uncle who died in late 1864 or 1865 was not literally an uncle, that the term was just a euphemism for some kind of relative. I believe Anna was referring to her stepfather, Patrick Donohoe, who died at the end of October 1864 and left everything to his wife. In any case, by 1865 Anna felt virtually no links to her past. She had been particularly fond of her uncle William, but he was long gone. She loved her sister Eliza, but the two had made different choices and gone different ways. Eliza had apparently not shared Anna's interest in learning, perhaps not having similar abilities. Eliza had followed their mother in choosing the marriage path typical of mixed-race girls in India. And even Eliza was gone. She died shortly before Patrick, in June 1864 in Bombay, age thirty-four, of peritonitis.

Anna was a different person from the daughter and sister and wife she had been in her youth in India. Her family ties were to some extent with her husband's family in Ireland and with her dear friends in Singapore and Siam. But even that was changing. Her closest friend in Singapore, Frank Cobb, left there for good in the fall of 1865, when at last the American Civil War was over and he could head for home. But he made sure to arrange to stop off in London, specifically to visit the Misses King's school at Fulham House and bring his love to Avis. Then on December 4, 1865, Anna wrote to Avis that "one of my best friends here is about to leave for America." Rev. Mattoon was leaving the mission to go home to America to join his wife, who had been Anna's closest friend among the foreign community. She had gotten ill in Siam and left for home with her two daughters in July 1864. More and more completely, Anna's remaining ties were with the ladies of the Grand Palace.

Lady Thiang (Chao Chom Manda Thiang), though not a queen because not of royal blood, was perhaps King Mongkut's most important consort. Said to be the official holder of "the keys to the Inside," she was the child of a noble family in Siam, whose members had served the Chakri dynasty since the reign of Rama I. Lady Thiang was among the very first group of women selected to be one of Rama IV's "Ladies of the Inside" when he took the throne. It was a fruitful choice, for Lady Thiang bore Mongkut ten children. Her first was Princess Somawadi (or Somawati), the king's seventh child but fifth as king, since as a young man, before he became a monk, he had had two sons. Both died early, one in 1862 and one in 1867. The princess, who lived until 1930, grew up to be one of the most respected and powerful members of the royal family. During the reign of King Chulalongkorn, the princess, like her mother before her, was in charge of "the keys to the Inside."

Somawadi was the last of the five children born to the king during 1852, the first full year of his reign. The first, born on January 21, almost exactly nine months after the king took the throne, was Princess Ying You Wahlacks (Phra-ong Chao Yingyaowalak), whom Anna also taught. Yingyaowalak held the official title of eldest daughter to the king. Anna encouraged her students to write letters in English to Avis. Since all mail to the inner palace was sent to the king, in May 1864 Somawadi wrote to Avis, "Your little note came to Papa His Majesty who handed it to me and it pleased me and my dear Mama very much." She admitted that "your Mama our kind Governess [urged] me to improve my handwriting before I wrote to you," and ended by saying, "We wish much to see you and England to, which we read of in our History of England." Princess Yingyaowalak's letter is more telling. She also politely announced her wish to see England. But she began more personally, saying, "I have much pleasure in writing to you and though you do not know me, yet I feel as if I knew you quite well" because "your dear Mamma is always speaking of you" (LC, VI C, 4:6).

Throughout the letters sent to Avis by members of Nang Harm we hear that Anna spoke often of her beloved daughter and also that the students had real affection for their teacher. One of Anna's adult pupils was Lady Koon Thouapp, not one of the king's consorts but the woman who held the highly respected position of judge in Nang Harm. Lady Koon Thouapp's letter to Avis on her eighth birthday, October 25, 1862, began by saying, "Your Mama is my teacher and I love her quite well." The judge went on to tell Avis, "You must let me have the pleasure of showing my love by presenting this silk frock on this your birthday and you must wear it for the sake of Lady Koon Thouapp." We hear the warmth in this letter, even through the formal English.

Anna got along well with Lady Thiang, whom she consulted in regard to many of the little arrangements of daily life as a schoolmistress. The two were frequently together, discussing mundane but important details such as Siamese customs that would help Anna in her classroom conduct, in celebrating holidays, and in securing schools supplies. They grew used to conferring with each other and trusting each other within the limits allowed by Lady Thiang's loyalty to the king. Close in age as well, they became friendly. Each saw in the other both a desire to have Anna's work be successful and a real affection for the women and children who came to Anna's schoolroom.

The topics Anna addressed with Lady Thiang sometimes became more serious than questions of numbers of pencils and amount of paper needed or when school needed to be canceled because of a ceremony. When a pupil was absent from the schoolroom or seemed to be troubled and not doing well at the lessons, it was Lady Thiang whom Anna consulted. Occasionally the absences were because the pupil was in disgrace. Lady Thiang and Anna from their different perspectives were both concerned that the king be at peace with the women under his control. His anger, when strong enough, when the woman's violation was considered offensive enough, could lead to the lash or even confinement in chains. Lady Thiang was utterly devoted to the king. Anna was an outsider. Yet it was Lady Thiang, according to Anna's published account, who evolved the harmless ploy of trying to distract Mongkut from his anger at one of his consorts by sending for Anna, who would rush in and ask him a question of scholarship or translation.

Anna's warmest relationship in the palace was with Lady Son Klin, or Sonn Klean (Chaochom Manda Sonklin), whose name, that of a beautiful flower, translated as "Hidden Perfume." Sonklin was another of the king's consorts, mother number twelve. Her grandfather had come to Siam from Burma. I believe her mother was also in Nang Harm and Sonklin had been born in and grown up in the confines of the inner palace. From her family's point of view as well as from the point of view of the Chakri dynasty, Sonklin was a success. She was taken to bed by the king, and the result was a fine son, Prince Krita-bhiniharn. Anna and Lady Sonklin built their friendship on talking about their two boys, Louis and Krita. Prince Krita was almost seven when Anna and her son arrived.

Prince Krita, later named Prince Nares Worariti, was of particularly high status during Anna's time as royal schoolteacher, though subordinate to Prince Chulalongkorn. According to the order of births to Mongkut while he was king, Prince Chulalongkorn was the seventh born (ninth of all) and first living son, therefore the heir apparent to the throne, although officially a king did not name his selection of successor until on his deathbed. Krita was the fifteenth born (seventeenth of all) and the second living son. In 1892 Prince Nares "was Minister of Local Government and Police, and a member of the Privy Council. He became the father of a very powerful family, who are listed in the *Directory for Bangkok and Siam, 1939–40* . . . as the Second Family descended from King Mongkut" (LC, VI C, 4:7).

It would be hard to overestimate the social and political importance of Prince Nares in Siam during the reign of King Chulalongkorn. Henry Norman, in *People and Politics of the Far East,* described him as "for some years Minister in London, and now practically governor of Bangkok." We hear Norman's British smugness in his claim that Prince Nares "in his instincts and point of view . . . resembles the type of the mind of the English gentleman more closely than does any other Siamese." Perhaps Norman meant that "except for the king he was the first Siamese to secure a European tutor for his sons, one of whom is about to take his degree at Trinity College, Cambridge, while the other is high up at Harrow" (449).

But Norman also observed that Nares was "one of the few princes who really understands and sympathizes with the common people." Prince Nares was one of the highly distinguished group of King Chulalongkorn's half-brothers whom David Wyatt called "an extraordinary generation of talent" (*Studies in Thai History,* 281) in Siam. This was the very generation that comprised Anna's students. A group of young men, mostly the king's brothers (perhaps especially Damrong, Devawongse, and Nares) and some lesser nobility, "brought into being"—almost literally from scratch—the "entire structure of modern Thailand" (*Studies in Thai History,* 282–83).

These young reforming Siamese were guided by the genius of their leader and king, Chulalongkorn, whom Wyatt appropriately called "one of the truly outstanding men of the world in his day." King Chulalongkorn's great achievement was that, in the face of enormous opposition but with the help of those forward-looking men, he transformed a "traditional Southeast Asian kingdom" into "a modern nation" (*Studies in Thai History,* 282). As Wyatt so eloquently put it in evaluating that achievement, "I can think of no one else in the world, in his day, who, at his age, did single-handedly so much in so creative and visionary a fashion" (284).

But this great future was still to come, and Prince Nares was still little Prince Krita when Anna was in Bangkok. Krita had been born right after Princess Chou-fa, in May 1855. He was almost a year and a half older than Louis, who was five and a half when Anna's little school began. The two boys, along with many other of the royal children, including Krita's older half-brother

Chulalongkorn, who was already eight and a half, played together happily. Prince Chulalongkorn always had a warm spot for his schoolmistress, and his childhood friendship with Louis became for the two of them a slight but permanent bond. All the children attended Anna's school lessons, as did Sonklin, along with several other inner palace women. But Louis also found himself seeing a lot of Krita outside school hours because Krita's mother regularly gave Anna private lessons in Siamese in her apartments.

In the Grand Palace the status of the child did not necessarily reflect the status of the mother, except possibly in the matter of annual allowance. Sonklin's allowance was a good one, befitting the mother of the second son. We know that Sonklin had been bedded by the king in the fall of 1854 and had given birth to Krita in May 1855. But ever since that brief period of having the king's attention in the mid-1850s—though we cannot actually know how many weeks or months the attention lasted—Sonklin had been out of favor. Some of his other wives continued to hold Mongkut's interest and produced several children for him over several years. Not Sonklin. By the 1860s, when Anna met her, the king had long been uninterested. Krita was clearly the only child Sonklin would ever have. At the court Krita was much petted and adored, but his mother was generally ignored.

Sonklin and Anna developed a strong friendship. Sonklin was a few years younger, and her heart opened up to this foreign woman who was not part of the inner palace. Among the earliest notes extant from her to Anna were those (undated) when she heard of Anna's illness in the spring of 1863. She wrote on a Sunday morning, "My dear friend, I hear you are sick. I am very sorrow with you indeed and I thinking of you always my dear and because you both kindred and give my love to dear Louis. I am prayed to my God to make you well soon."

Anna did not get better soon, and Sonklin wrote an even more worried letter on Tuesday. "My dearest friend, I hearing that you are very ill and I am very much sorrow and can't happy for you and Louis and I send my very kindness to you and dear Louis." Sonklin went on to plead that if Anna cared about them she would take the medicine she and her mother had sent. "Perhaps will you like me and my mother a *little* more you please drink medicine mine and dear Mother for three day." Sonklin grew even more insistent, arguing that "you can't like me and my very dear Mother truly you do not drink." By Thursday she wrote again to press that "truly I dream of medicine will you please to drink some" (LC, VI C, 4:6).

Sonklin wrote other notes as well, on the little occasions of life when she and her friend were separated. When Anna went to Ayuthia in the summer of 1863, Sonklin was not of the party. She wrote, "I am always thinking of you and dear little Louis and I am quite sorry when I cannot see your kind dear face and now I hear you come from Ayuthia today I am very glad to see you both today." Another time Sonklin was included in a royal trip and wrote to Anna, "I am quite sorry for I go . . . from you for 9 or ten days I thinking my heart like 9 or ten months." She ends asking, "my very dearest Friend don't forget me very goodbye for a little longer my dear Friend." And there is the sweet note after a quarrel, responding to a message from Anna, who seems to have reached out to apologize first. "Many many millions thanks for your very kind note and I am very most sorry because I am very badly and made you angry for a little thing and I made my face very ugly." Then Sonklin offered a warm testimonial to her deep affection for Anna. "I love you and your child more than anyone and more than my elder sister indeed I love you like my Mother too my dear Teacher."

Anna and Sonklin's friendship, like Anna's love for her absent daughter, was one of the constants of Anna's time in Siam. Sonklin became quite fluent in English. She wrote to Avis sometime in 1865, 1866, or even 1867, thanking "my dear little Friend" for a gift, her English now graceful. "I shall always look upon [the gift] as from my dearest Avis reminding me of my dearest Teacher's daughter." Sonklin then wrote of her own child, whose studies had become quite serious. "My dear Son Prince Kritabhinihar tries his best to learn Siamese Pegu [spoken in Lower Burma] Cambo Sanscrit and English lessons every day five hard languages and he bravely goes on with it all." Wishing that "when my son is grown up to be a very great man I will perhaps go to England to visit you," Sonklin ended by saying, "I am your Mama's best friend here I hope" (LC, VI C, 4:6, 28).

By 1863, Sonklin was signing her notes "Klin Harriett Beecher Stowe" or some variation of this name (Son Klin Harriett, Harriett Beecher Stowe, Son Klin H. B. S.). The practice of taking on a Western name of an admired person, as a sign of respect, was not unknown at the court. One of the sons of the second king at the time of Mongkut famously called himself George Washington. In 1863, Sonklin would not have had the fluency in English to read *Uncle Tom's Cabin* for herself. But her source of knowledge about Stowe and her writing must have been her schoolteacher and friend.

Anna was a great admirer of Stowe's work. I think she had read at least selections from *Uncle Tom's Cabin* well over a decade before, when the *Straits Times* in Singapore was running excerpts in December 1852 and on into the spring of 1853. Singapore was *the* cosmopolitan center in Southeast Asia during the second half of the nineteenth century, and the *Straits Times* was *the* weekly English-language newspaper in the region, eagerly awaited and just as eagerly read by everyone, including the foreigners in Bangkok. Anna probably read some and possibly all of Stowe's novel when she lived in Singapore from 1859 to 1862 and discussed it with Frank Cobb. Anna may well have told the story of Stowe's novel to Sonklin or even read to her excerpts from the book. I think it most likely that she told the story in the schoolroom, using it not as fiction but as a plausible historical resource in attempting to explain to her students the workings of American slavery and in relation to the causes of the American Civil War.

The Civil War was a major focus of interest for the foreign communities of Southeast Asia. It is hard to overestimate the extent to which these communities in the early 1860s attended to what was going on in the United States. American slavery formed a constant part of the public conversation in Bangkok and Singapore during the 1860s and was a continuing topic under discussion in the *Straits Times,* as it covered in its headlines most of the major issues and events of the American Civil War. The newspaper did reprint a series of articles from the *Evening Mail* edition of the *London Times,* which were vehemently anti-North. One of my favorites is the easy dismissal of Lincoln and his Emancipation Proclamation: "impotent maliguity *[sic]* is apt to be a very contemptible spectacle" (Nov. 22, 1862). But generally the newspaper took the "moderate" view that Americans should let go of the institution of slavery, given that the war had already "permanently undermined its foundations" (Jan. 18, 1862).

Dr. Bradley and the rest of the American missionaries in Bangkok were certainly riveted. They were already, for religious reasons and in terms of their ongoing criticism of Siamese culture, antislavery. They had spent decades overlooking the fact that slavery was a legal institution in their own, supposedly superior, Christian nation. It helped that most of them, like most of the Americans in Singapore, were from the Northeast. It also helped that many of the businessmen in Singapore profited from the embargo on cotton from the American South, seeing it as easier just to bring cotton from India. Everybody read about the war, everybody talked about it, and almost everybody, including Anna, was on the side of Lincoln and the North. King Mongkut himself greatly admired Lincoln, and believed that the North was right because a country should not rebel against its ruler.

In *Romance* Anna offered a telling and believable anecdote about her friend. After a dinner in her apartments, Sonklin announced to Anna that she was "wishful to be good like Harriet Beecher Stowe." In a reenactment of

Lincoln's 1862 Emancipation Proclamation, she declared the freedom of her 132 slaves and made them all salaried servants. At this narrative moment, forestalling any narrow reading of this story as simply a lesson taught to an Easterner by a Westerner, Anna "quoted" Sonklin, who invoked Buddhism as the true source of her belief in equality. "Her sweet voice trembled with love and music whenever she spoke of the lovely American lady who had taught her, 'even as Buddha had once taught kings,' to respect the rights of her fellow-creatures" (*Romance of the Harem*, 249).

Another of Anna's little stories, one that her detractors have pushed aside as fantasy (arguing that there couldn't be "dungeons" in Bangkok, because the ground was too marshy for there to be cells beneath the floor) but that I believe happened, also involved Sonklin. In *The English Governess* Anna wrote of how Sonklin was imprisoned for a few days beneath the main floor (which, as in all formal buildings in Bangkok, is raised many feet above actual ground level) of one of the palace buildings. She was chained by the ankle on a plank bed, in a cell with a high grated window and a damp floor. As Anna eloquently put it, in her sympathy and outrage when she went to visit the prisoner, "In such a cell, on such a couch, lay the concubine of a supreme king and the mother of a royal prince of Siam" (*English Governess*, 107). Sonklin's crime was the insult of petitioning the king to appoint her elder brother to a position that, unknown to her, he had already given to someone else.

Did Mongkut really have one of his consort mothers chained up in a dank cell with only a small window for light, because she had unintentionally said something that displeased him? Did he have Sonklin beaten on the mouth with a soft slipper, a punishment skillfully designed not to hurt her physically but to mortify her publicly for saying the wrong thing? I believe the answer is yes. Not one of the Western "experts" who over the years have condemned Anna's written attitude to her employer have ever attended to what happened to Sonklin in this incident, any more than they have attended to the incident in which Wanne's mother was whipped. Yet Sonklin's punishment calls to mind another woman's description of the king. Having met him in late 1850, Mrs. Charles Hillier wrote in the English magazine *Household Words* that, for all his excellent qualities of leadership of his country, King Mongkut had "a temper willful and capricious not to say cruel" ("A Pair of Siamese Kings").

Anna was appalled at the king's harsh and disrespectful treatment of her beloved friend, and filled with sorrow for the consort mother's shame and loss of face. She also shared the fear and horror of Sonklin's powerlessness in that dank cell, not knowing when or if she would be released, even though the consort was not physically hurt, was not whipped. Anna never forgot those feelings. Nor did she forget the tyranny created by a system that made one man a virtual god and made his chosen sexual partners, however many titles and ticals and slaves of their own they were given, lifelong slaves.

ELEVEN

The Paths to Good-bye

ANNA HAD BEEN ILL IN THE FALL OF 1865 and, though she recovered, in the summer of 1866 and on through 1867 she still felt worn out. She began to think seriously about taking some time away from Bangkok. Anna's plan was to start with a visit to Singapore. But her real goal was to take passage from Singapore with Louis for what would be their first visit to England, to see Avis again at last. Avis would be twelve years old in October 1866. She was arriving at the age when girls were finished with school. Louis was completely at home in Siam and seemed to belong there, generally reporting, "I am very happy. All the people loves me and Mama" (Bristowe, 33). But both he and Anna wanted to meet their Enniscorthy relatives, and she was eager for him to have some advanced schooling in Ireland.

Anna felt that her workload in Siam had become heavier and heavier. She had all her teaching, and the number of her students had steadily increased. She had close ties with many of the women and children in the palace, and they often asked her for favors. Her relations with her employer, the king, had also become more complex as well as more vexed. Anna had come a long way from being simply a governess, as her range of professional tasks had increased. She was involved in many small but significant ways in the business of state, in terms of writing letters in English and also in terms of His Majesty's relations with the foreign community.

One indication of the kinds of tasks Anna performed as an employee of the king of Siam can be seen by a letter Mongkut wrote to her from his summer palace in Petchaburi on April 6, 1866. It was a reply to a letter from her about some state business. He asked her to convey the king's thanks to the British consul George Knox, who had visited her and "assured [her] that he will be standing in favorable assistance to me and my government even but privily for the [hostile step of the] French Imperial deputee and monipilies of spirit sale[s]" (LC, VI C, 4:6, 14). The French were hoping to set up a monopoly of the importation of liquor to Siam by making it one of the terms of a new treaty they were working out.

As well as being a convenient secretarial go-between in diplomatic matters that could be kept private, Anna also received the king's confidence in terms of some of his practical plans. The April 6 letter contains a long paragraph evaluating the representative of an English company who was proposing terms for building a telegraph line. More tellingly, the letter closes with a "very private post script." In it the king takes up the worrisome question of Anna's advice that he publicly and officially name Prince Chulalongkorn as his heir (not the custom in Siam). The king was responding to Anna's apparent previous assertion that she gave this advice because there were some in Siam who did not like the king and therefore at his death would not support Chulalongkorn as king. Mongkut argued vehemently that he did not see how anyone would have told her such a thing because from her arrival everyone in Siam, including the foreigners, had believed that she was "really my partisan even may be my spy!" Therefore, he logically concluded, "who would say such before your audience!"

Apart from the specific arguments of this letter, the telling point of it all is how much it reveals about Anna's true role in the Grand Palace. The British consul passes on private political messages to the king through her, promising support against the French. Mongkut casually discusses the issue of whether a particular businessman has the best terms for installing a telegraph service in Siam. And he ends with a postscript that clearly reveals an ongoing argument between Anna and King Mongkut as to how best to proceed to secure his eldest son's ascension to the throne of Siam after Mongkut's death. It is obvious from his own rebuttal that Anna has previously argued to this absolute monarch that many of his people might not like him, and that Mongkut has considered her argument. It is also obvious that Anna was perfectly capable of arguing with him and of saying unpleasant truths to him.

Without having to exaggerate the extent of her influence or the political importance of her role, I can say that Anna was to a small but significant extent privy to matters of state and that the king did occasionally consult her on issues important to Siam. She often disagreed strongly with the king, in terms of his treatment of the women of Nang Harm and also in terms of some of his political decisions. But the important point here is that she was actually in a position to do so. Her job in the Grand Palace had clearly evolved over the years into a lot more than being schoolmistress to the royal children. And even in her role as a teacher, Anna had significant influence.

As Wyatt points out in discussing King Chulalongkorn's extraordinarily forward-looking vision, "his early reforming zeal suggests that he took seriously the injunctions and exhortations of Anna Leonowens and J. H. Chandler, his English tutors," as well as his father's deep moral convictions (*Studies in Thai History*, 226).

The 1860s were a challenging time for Siam and for King Mongkut. On July 6, 1864, George Virgin, the unsavory rum seller and acting American consul in Siam from October 1863 to September 1865, presented the king with a golden sword. It was a gift from Abraham Lincoln, in thanks for the gifts King Mongkut had sent to him. The king had even offered to send elephants, so the Americans could start a herd, but the president had declined. The United States was being pleasant to Siam. The British, while still paying close attention to this small nation, were not as threatening as they had been in the 1840s and 1850s. The Bowring Treaty was working out well, allowing them to take virtually whatever they wanted from Siam. The greatest threat in the 1860s was France (and England's determination that, if necessary, it would take over Siam as a colony before letting France have it). Siam had signed a treaty with France in 1856 that gave it rights similar to England's. But that did not seem to be enough.

Siam's worries about France had to do both with strategy and with personality. France was taking over territory in the region, determined not to cede the lands of what is now Southeast Asia to the British. The French occupied southern Vietnam in 1863 and were pressing for control of Laos. Norodom, on becoming king of Cambodia in 1860 after his father died, was faced with France, which coveted "the apparent wealth of his state and viewed the Mekong River as a possible golden highway to the hidden wealth of the interior of Southeast Asia and China" (Wyatt, *Studies in Thai History*, 185). The French considered it merely a minor problem that Cambodia had historically been submissive to Siam.

Norodom was pressured to sign a treaty with the French in 1863. But true to his country's traditions, he also almost simultaneously signed "a secret treaty recognizing the suzerainty of the Siamese—who held the coronation regalia of his father" (Wyatt, *Studies in Thai History*, 185). Unfortunately, when Norodom tried to go to his own coronation in Bangkok, the French moved into his capital. King Mongkut recognized that France was taking over Siam's sphere of influence in the region. That takeover continued in 1865, when the French man-of-war *Mistraille* arrived in Bangkok on April 9 to make very sure that Siam annulled its treaty with Cambodia and signed a new treaty with France, ceding major influence over Cambodia to the French.

Part of the difficulties the Siamese had with France can be directly attributed to the attitudes and actions of the French consul, M. Aubaret, who repeatedly overstepped his consular assignments and had a bad temper to boot. In May 1865, Dr. Bradley published the specifics of the French and Siamese Treaty for all to see in the *Bangkok Recorder,* before the treaty had officially been ratified. He included some critical comments about how the French consul had proceeded. He also included, "quite to the astonishment of all parties" (Bradley, *Bangkok Calendar,* 1865, 128), the terms of a secret "treaty" arrangement between M. Aubaret and a Siamese spirit farmer (licensed liquor seller) for M. Aubaret to be the sole supplier of liquor imported into Bangkok. M. Aubaret was incensed. He immediately demanded that King Mongkut shut down the American newspaper. The king, who had no intention of being such a fool as to suppress the paper, did offer the courtesy of sending a message to the paper's editor via the American consul, requesting that hereafter the paper publish no official document without direct license from the government. The paper agreed, but M. Aubaret was not appeased.

The next moment of conflict came when the *Bangkok Recorder* of September 16, 1865, offered an account of another instance of M. Aubaret's behavior. Early in a long series of incidents, M. Aubaret petitioned King Mongkut to remove a Siamese who was the official leader of the Cambodian Catholics in Bangkok, because he had quarreled with the head Catholic missionary, and replace him with a Frenchman. Ignored, he wrote again, now demanding that the Siamese be fired and replaced as he suggested or he would see it as an insult by King Mongkut to both Christianity and the French government. He had the note delivered at 2 A.M. to the palace, and the king awakened for this "emergency." When the king again made an effort to respond courteously to the French consul's outrageous demand and sent a Siamese judge to confer with the consul, M. Aubaret threw the king's emissary out bodily, by grabbing his topknot. As Rev. Bradley concluded, M. Aubaret "is not the man to get along with the Siamese, and we doubt if he could get along smoothly anywhere."

The final egregious moment came in December 1866, when M. Aubaret arranged to accost the king "accidentally," without having been granted an official appointment, as the king and his retinue were coming out of a temple after a ceremony. Claiming he was just out for a stroll, M. Aubaret began to "speak disparagingly of his Excellency the Prime Minister," then moved to the threat that the minister "must be humbled, or the most serious consequences would result" (*Bangkok Recorder,* Feb. 2, 1867). King Mongkut was understandably insulted by the French consul both forcing this audience with him and dictating to him in public, complete with threats, as to who his appointed officials should be. After this interview, M. Aubaret began to spread around Bangkok the accusation that the Siamese government (presumably the prime minister) had deliberately leaked the specifics of the treaty on Cambodia between France and Siam and to claim that all these events should be taken as an insult to France.

Everyone wondered whether the French emperor could possibly know how his representative was behaving. And everyone believed, as Mr. Hood, the American consul, reported in his letter to Washington back in June 1866, that "Mr. Knox [the British consul] is correct and the French will continue to make encroachments upon this territory until they finally get possession of the Kingdom of Siam" (LC, VI C, 4:3, 2). Dr. Bradley, in his account of this last offensive encounter, commented that the "demand he made in that interview" is "tantamount to requiring [the king] to cut off the right arm of the government . . . and how preposterous the thought that such matters shall not be published in this city without license from the French Consul." When M. Aubaret read this account in the February 2, 1867, issue of the *Recorder,* clearly describing for everyone his overstepping of his diplomatic privileges, he promptly denied that such an interview had ever taken place and sued Dr. Bradley for libel.

The suit was a huge issue in the spring of 1867 in Bangkok. Everyone was on the side of Dr. Bradley, of course. But the problem was that King Mongkut himself did nothing to contradict M. Aubaret's lying denial and forbade any member of his retinue who had actually been present at the horrid interview to admit that it had taken place and testify about M. Aubaret's demands at Dr. Bradley's trial. Effectively, Dr. Bradley was deprived of any witnesses to the truth of his report. Dr. Bradley was furious at the king for being a "liar for the purpose of pacifying the French Consul at the expense of my good name" ("Abstract of the Journal," Jan. 20, 1867).

Yet the king was right as a statesman to avoid a public legal confrontation with the French consul, however much it left Dr. Bradley out to dry. France posed too big a threat to Siam. Mongkut was engaged in a diplomatic war with the French consul, and what was at stake was the continuing independence of Siam. The Siamese were no match for a French man-of-war. But their king was a match for the arrogant M. Aubaret and all his trumped-up contrivances and charges. For the king to allow a Siamese to give public testimony in a Siamese court against the French consul, and thus for a Siamese court to find against the consul, would give M. Aubaret ammunition to claim to his emperor that Siam—and its king—had actively insulted His Majesty's representative. For the sake of his country, King Mongkut had to deny the incident and Siamese subjects had to stay out of the battle between Dr. Bradley and M. Aubaret.

But Anna had no such state obligation. Louis, who by then was dearly loved by the king, was one of those in Mongkut's retinue when M. Aubaret accosted him, and Louis had witnessed the whole encounter. As Dr. Bradley recorded in his journal, grateful, I believe, that he had an ally in the palace, Anna had been consulting with him about the trial. She knew that he had published the truth. He wrote on January 20, 1867, of her telling him that "she had seen the King the day before and said to him that her son, who heard all that the French Consul said to his Majesty on the occasion of the outbreak, would probably be subpoenaed as a witness for Dr. Bradley and that he would then speak the truth." Anna presumed that since Louis was not a Siamese subject he could speak. The king later notified her that because she was a palace employee it was important that she stay out of it, and that he would fine her if Louis testified.

Anna heeded his warning. Instead of allowing her son to appear in court, she sent a private letter to the Reverend Doctors House and Dean, who were the judges of the American Consular Court, and offered her testimony: "That the unprecedented demand made by the French Imperial Consul did create consternation in the minds of all orders of the Siamese, and that I heard the natives, to the very guards stationed under my chamber window, both agitate and discuss the matter of the Prime Minister's removal with nervous apprehension of what might come next—and that both myself and my son were very much alarmed" (*Bangkok Calendar,* 1867, 120). She wisely chose to leave Louis out of it, but said enough to make clear that M. Aubaret actually had on a public street in Bangkok demanded of the king of Siam that he fire his own prime minister, and that many Siamese knew of it.

Still, Anna herself had not been a direct witness to the incident. In fact, her letter was conveniently not admitted into the American consular records until after the verdict, on the grounds that Anna had presented it to the gentlemen as "for your own *private* information." Dr. Bradley lost his case and the official verdict was $100 in damages (M. Aubaret had sued for $1,500). The French consul rather condescendingly waived the fine, as "the defendant is a poor man with a numerous family."

When Mr. Hood, the head judge and American consul, and no friend of the American missionary community, notified Dr. Bradley of the judgment on February 5, 1867, he also suggested that the good doctor mention M. Aubaret's generosity in his newspaper. Dr. Bradley was outraged. He responded sharply that "it would be wrong in me to acknowledge in any way that I accept of the Judgment as being what is due to me by the laws and usages of my country" and paid the fine. We can all imagine Dr. Bradley's sense of justification in December 1868, when "the long rumoured misdeeds of the J. M. Hood U.S. Consul" (*Bangkok Calendar,* 1868, 126) came out, and he had to auction off his belongings and leave Bangkok. The doctor did print a sort of nonapology to M. Aubaret in the *Recorder,* noting that on a point or two he had been "a little misinformed." But all of Bangkok knew that it was M. Aubaret who lied and Dr. Bradley who told the truth.

After the public furor faded away, the verdict was quietly revoked. And there is one final touching detail in this story. In spite of his real diplomatic need to placate the French consul in order to protect his country and his annoyance at Dr. Bradley for being so heedless of the upsetting effect of his published accounts on the Siamese people, King Mongkut finally could not in conscience just abandon Dr. Bradley and the truth. "Before the trial had actually finished his Majesty the King coming to realize that the case might go against Dr. Bradley, directed one of his employees to serve as witness to the facts but he arrived too late" (Bradley, "Abstract of the Journal," 256).

Anna was angry at the king over his apparent tolerance of the intolerable M. Aubaret and over his refusal to become involved, or to allow any Siamese to be involved, in the libel suit. Once again, she was on the side of personal justice, even when it conflicted with the public good. To her, King Mongkut's forbearance and statesmanship seemed like just another example of how under his rule strategy trumped justice in Siam, of how affairs of state took precedence over the truth and the rights of individuals. The woman Dr. Bradley described in the *Calendar* as having "a mind ever remarkably well balanced" (1868, 123) was feeling discouraged and exhausted. Anna badly needed a break from the complexity and the emotional intensity of this job in the Grand Palace.

The year 1866 was full of changes in many ways. Bangkok was developing rapidly into a thriving city, complete with even such modern conveniences as gaslights and a foreign dentist. Many of the children in the Grand Palace were becoming old enough to end their days in the schoolroom. The princes, at puberty, moved out of Nang Harm and out of the Grand Palace. Avis was definitely growing up as well. She wrote to Anna in January that she had learned to play, and presumably to dance, "a very pretty waltz." She went to see a pantomime at the theater and spent the Easter holidays at the home of a "schoolfellow in Kent" (LC, VI C, 4:2, 29). Frank Cobb had written from Boston in February to announce that he was married. This may well have been a surprise to Anna, but I think she must have been happy for her old friend, now only in his mid-twenties, and she was eager to see him and meet his bride (to whom she would dedicate her first book).

Avis spent her summer holidays in Enniscorthy, from which she wrote, "I am always called Miss Owens by the old people, but my Cousins take great pains to tell them my name is Leonowens." She also tantalizingly assured Louis that "all my Cousins Aunt and Uncle wish to see you and darling Mamma so very much" (LC, VI C, 4:2, 29). By October, Anna was decidedly hoping that she could go to Britain in the coming year. She wrote to Avis on October 21, just before the children's birthdays, that "Dear Louis is very well and looking forward with bright anticipation to the 25th when I am going to have a juvenile party as D. V. [God willing] it will be his last birthday in Siam." After all the stresses of the libel suit against Dr. Bradley that winter of 1866–67, Anna became committed to finding a way to make the trip.

On June 24, 1867, Dr. Bradley recorded in his journal with matter-of-fact directness that "Mrs. Leonowens has determined to return to England and has this day had all her goods sold at auction." Anna was really leaving Bangkok. She had worked in the Grand Palace since March 1862 and not been out of Siam at all for the past four and a third years, since the spring of 1863, when she was ill and spent a very brief time in Singapore. She had been ill again, off and on since 1865, possibly with bouts of malaria. Whatever the cause, her feelings of being physically worn down and given to attacks of illness throughout 1866 and her need to take Avis out of and put Louis into their respective schools were the two major reasons for her decision to leave Bangkok.

Even at the moment she actually left Bangkok, Anna was not sure of her ultimate plans. She had thought only as far as going to Singapore and then England. She certainly did not quit her job at the palace. She worked out with King Mongkut a six-month leave of absence, enough time for her to go to England for Avis and come back, after which she would return to Bangkok and take up her teaching position again. The presumption was that her children would more or less switch places. She would leave Louis at a school in Ireland, for training for the university or a career, and pick up Avis at her school and bring her to Bangkok. Anna had written to Thomas Wilkinson in the spring of 1867 for his help in finding a school where she could leave Louis in Ireland, close to his cousins. On April 17, Avis had written her that "Cousin Tom" had notified Avis that they had found the right place for Louis. Anna had also written to the Misses King, to prepare them for her withdrawing Avis from their school.

Anna and Louis left Bangkok for Singapore on the steamer *Chao Prya* on July 5, 1867, arriving in Singapore on July 10. Anna immediately booked passage on a P. and O. (Pacific and Oriental) mail steamer leaving Singapore for England on July 21. Prince Chulalongkorn had sent her a note before she left the palace, with a photograph of himself, a present of thirty dollars, and his wish that they have "a pleasant and quick journey to Europe, and that you may meet with every enjoyment on your arrival." When she sent a thank-you note with a promise to buy him a present in London, he courteously replied to Singapore, "I shall esteem anything from you that will be useful as a special token of love and friendship; and if the beautiful and ornamental are combined with the useful it will be prized very highly." But he softened this rather stuffy suggestion by remembering Anna's love of learning and saying, "Perhaps you will get some good book to instruct and ornament the mind and make me useful" (LC, VI C, 4:2, 29).

Anna got a far different letter from Sonklin, who was worried about Anna's continuing health problems and grieved by her absence. Typically, Sonklin wrote without formality to the woman who had been her close friend and emotional support for so many years. "I am writing to you by my heart, which is very sad for you to be sick so long. I cannot see your face." Her plea was simple. "Oh, do get well very soon and come back to us." Sonklin and Anna never saw each other again.

When Anna and Louis arrived in England in the early fall of 1867, Louis was close to eleven years old and his mother was close to thirty-six. Anna was on English soil for the very first time. They went immediately to pick up Avis, who was waiting at the Misses King, then right on to the Wilkinsons. Avis was ecstatic to see her mother and little brother again, and they were just as thrilled to see her. The happy reunion was made even happier because of the very warm welcome Anna and Louis received from the Wilkinsons. Mr. Wilkinson Sr. was delighted to welcome the widowed wife of his wife's brother, as were Cousin Tom and the rest of the cousins as well. It was a particularly joyous moment for Anna, the girl from Poona who had walked away from her nuclear family, to be welcomed into the family of her beloved Tom.

The Wilkinsons appear to have been a warm and open family, eager to welcome the pair from Siam as their own. Their easy affection reflected not only their happy memories of Tom Leonowens as a boy but also their growing love for his daughter, Avis, who was a sweet and gentle girl. It was wonderful to be witness to and a small part of this reunion of Avis with her adored mother and brother. Anna was impressively charming as well as grateful for what they had done for Avis over the years. One of the cousins present at that reunion in the fall of 1867 was a girl in her teens, Lizzie Avice Wilkinson. She would marry Rev. Moore and emigrate to Ontario in 1884. In 1939, a widow living in Evanston, Illinois, age ninety-three, she met Margaret Landon. She "remembered clearly the day in 1867 when Anna Leonowens, returning from Siam, arrived at the Wilkinson home in Enniscorthy, Co. Wexford, Ireland, wearing a diamond belt buckle that the King of Siam had given her" (LC, VI C, 1, "Anna and I").

The reunion at the Wilkinsons may have been particularly sweet because it was also piquant—as the prelude to yet another separation between mother and child. This time Anna and Avis would be going away and leaving Louis behind. Louis was his usual irrepressible and irresistible self. The Wilkinsons immediately became fond of him. When the fall term began he was placed as a boarder at the Kingstown School at Dun Laoghaire, County Dublin, run by Rev. William Church Stacpoole, whom Louis's granddaughter would later describe as a man who "believed all little boys were innately bad and were better for an early morning caning." His son, only five at the time, was Henry de Vere Stacpoole, "later to gain special fame for his novel, *The Blue Lagoon*" (Bristowe, 35). Louis had traveled a long way from the Grand Palace of Siam, where everyone loved children. Anna stayed in Enniscorthy long enough to celebrate the children's birthdays on October 25. Then she said good-bye yet again to one of her children and left Enniscorthy on October 28. It was a terrible parting. As Miss King wrote to her, "may you be sustained under the great trial of parting with your son."

It is clear that many of the evenings at Enniscorthy were spent discussing what Anna should do next. Tom's Enniscorthy relatives believed that she was British but had no family of her own to go to. She soon recognized that there was no work in Ireland in the 1860s. No one with any sense immigrated to Ireland. After the devastations of the potato famine, the Irish themselves were leaving as fast as they could. Louis, just eleven and alone for the first time, wrote a sad letter from his new school. "My own darling Mama, I am so glad to write to you that I don't know what to say to my own darling Mama I was so glad to get your dear littile note the words in it felt so sweet to me but I could not help to shed tears." His last sentence was a worried question about her plans and the place he loved so well, "are you going to Bangkok or not?"

The answer, as it turned out, was no. But it was a decision that evolved rather than suddenly being made. Anna did not want to go right back to Siam. Nor did she particularly want Avis to live there. But what were the alternatives? I think Anna came to the conclusion in Ireland that she could not really settle in England. Perhaps it occurred to her that it would be too dangerous to sustain the lie of her birth and family, too easy to be unmasked. Perhaps, after all these years, England and Ireland were a letdown. Perhaps she could not think of a way to make a living (for a "lady," being a governess in England was looked on as a serious loss of status) or simply was not that comfortable there.

Whatever her reasons, she followed the path of many people who came before her and the many more who would come after her. On October 28, when she left Enniscorthy she traveled down the eastern coast of Ireland from County Wexford to County Cork, to Queenstown, the port on the southeast coast of Ireland. Queenstown (now Cobh) was the port from which the great waves of immigrants left Ireland for Canada and the United States. It was the port from which, forty-five years later, the *Titanic* would leave for New York. And it was the port from which in early November Anna and Avis also shipped out to New York. After making the trip from Bangkok and Singapore to Ireland, the United States seemed a short hop away.

The decision was fairly spontaneous. Before she even was sure of her final destination, Anna quickly wrote to Miss King to say that she and Avis would not be passing back through London. Miss King was very attached to Avis and wrote of "so grievous a surprise," of "the sudden wrenching asunder of a bond of personal intercourse between us and your beloved child," and of the distress that "we cannot personally take leave of the beloved child, with whom I parted in July, without any foreboding that I should see her no more, except in the busy intervals of our brief personal intercourse with you" (LC, VI C, 4:2). Anna's stated plan must still have been to return to Bangkok. Miss King ended her letter with the hope that "after her arrival in Bangkok [Avis] will commence and continue a regular correspondence with us."

Anna also wrote to King Mongkut just before her ship left Queenstown. To him also she said she would return. And she asked him for an advance. The king replied to her letter of November 2 when he received it the following February. By then Anna was well past her negotiated six months of leave. But travel and communications were slow enough that there was nothing untoward in this delay. Anna must have been thinking, however vaguely, that after visiting the United States she would pass through London en route back to Siam and perhaps find a loan from the king awaiting her there, in the form of his letter of approval to Mr. Mason, the Siamese consul in London. She was, after all, a woman only in her mid-thirties, reunited with her dear daughter and filled with delight at traveling about for a little while. A voyage across the Atlantic of less than two weeks must have seemed very easy after the distance she had already traveled. She did have good friends to stay with in America. She was delighted at the thought of actually getting to visit the United States, of her and Avis seeing Frank Cobb again after so many years, of meeting his new wife, and of introducing her adored daughter to the Mattoons.

So on November 13, 1867, Anna Leonowens and her thirteen-year-old daughter landed at the port of New York, accidental immigrants to America. Anna never went back to Siam or to Southeast Asia. Instead, without actually intending to at the time, she set out on a new phase in her long life. Still only thirty-five, less than a fortnight shy of thirty-six, she would live another forty-six years, re-creating herself again and again. That winter of 1867–68 in New York she was about to launch herself in several new careers, as a public speaker, a journalist, and an author. For this adventurous woman another adventure, in yet another new country, was about to begin.

Siam had been more than a grand adventure for Anna. Her experiences during that five and a third years in Bangkok and the Grand Palace had radically transformed her. The woman standing on the dock in New York was quite a different person from the woman who had embarked from Singapore with her little boy for a job as a schoolmistress in the Grand Palace of Siam.

Probably the first real change was that she had made peace with her grief over Tom's death and thus made peace with her sense of herself as a woman on her own. During the little over two years she spent in Singapore after Tom's death, from the end of 1859 to March 1862, she was daily aware of his missing presence, of the emptiness of some part of her life. She understood herself as a widow, a person defined by a loss. This was partly because her grief was relatively fresh and she had loved him so much, partly because she had first visited Singapore with Tom, and partly because of the strangeness of being alone and having to look after herself and her children and support herself for the very first time in her life. It was exhilarating, but also frightening and strange.

Much of that changed when she went to Bangkok, a place where Tom had never been, a place where she had never been as a wife. It was, so to speak, an adventure that was all her own. Moreover, she had a secure job there, with a guaranteed salary that did not depend on the erratic payment habits of the parents of small children in Singapore. She did not have to worry about supporting herself and Louis, and she could be proud of the fact that she was earning enough to pay fifty pounds a year to send her daughter to an English boarding school. Finally, in Bangkok and particularly in the Grand Palace where she spent most of her time, Anna was in a culture based not on the concept of monogamy or couples but instead on the concept of separate spheres.

She was surrounded by other mothers for whom, even locked in the inner palace, normalcy was to live their entire lives among other women and without a male partner by their side. One of the unpredictable results of living in a world of polygamy was that Anna's life with only her son felt to her not like the oddity but like the norm.

A second major effect on Anna of her time in the palace in Siam was that she came into her own as an intellectual and a professional. Of course, she had been an intellectual and a professional in Singapore as well. But there her job was to run a small school for children, not much more than a day care center. It was a huge leap in scale to be the teacher to the royal children of the Kingdom of Siam, one of whom was the future king, to teach classes in the Grand Palace, and to be the only such teacher in the Grand Palace. Moreover, she was an occasional secretary and even brief consultant to a king. There was no denying the social and political stature of Anna's job. For the first time in her life, the woman who had grown up a Eurasian girl in rural India moved among people with power—political power and economic power.

And she learned to move among them quite easily. It became clear to Anna that in general she was the intellectual equal of these people, many of whom constituted the most powerful class in Bangkok. King Mongkut was a truly exceptional and admired scholar. But most of the foreign community at least, men such as Mr. Hood and Mr. Knox, were neither as intelligent nor as scholarly as she. Dr. Bradley was brilliant. But his fundamentalist faith too often kept him ignorant and narrow-minded, a limitation of the other American missionaries as well. The foreign women, like the Siamese, tended not to be well educated at all. For Anna, getting to know people who were upper class or had great power or status without necessarily having great ability was an illuminating and, ultimately, a transforming experience. Working within such a context built Anna's confidence and sense of intellectual self-worth. She began to feel that she was their equal.

Anna's years of working in the Grand Palace also radically enlarged her perspective on the world. That enlargement had begun in Singapore, when Americans such as young Frank Cobb talked of issues such as slavery and the American Civil War. In Bangkok the process continued. The woman whose sphere of interest had been restricted in practical terms to contemporary domestic questions and in intellectual terms to ancient literary and religious texts began to see and to care deeply about the larger world. Through her friendships with the women of the inner palace, particularly Sonklin, and her attempts to help her friends a little with the conditions of their lives, Anna became politicized. She started to pay attention to questions of politics and justice, going to Lady Thiang to see how she could help when one of the women or children was in trouble, and writing to the judges to support the justice of Dr. Bradley's defense against M. Aubaret's charges of libel.

When she left Siam, Anna Leonowens had grown well beyond being a racially mixed and lowly born woman concerned with passing as a gently reared and well-educated British lady. That issue was, psychologically at least, pretty well resolved. As Cary Grant explained about abandoning Archie Leach to become Cary Grant, "I pretended to be someone that I wanted to be and I finally became that person . . . or he became me." Thanks to her time in the Grand Palace, Anna now had a lot more on her mind. Not the least of the many influences that had effectively shaped her into the person she had become was King Mongkut himself. His profound and unceasing commitment to scholarship, to knowledge, to learning had an enormous influence on her. Before she went to Siam she had already believed that education was the sacred path to personal development. Thanks to her association with King Mongkut, who lived that principle in so many ways, when Anna left Siam her belief had grown to a certainty, had become one of the central tenets of her life.

Siam was the high point of Anna's life, not because it was the most important thing she ever did—to her, it was not—but because it was the turning point in a process that made her at last into the woman she had all along had the potential to become. The army child who had viewed the world in private terms and rejected her inferior place in the British social and racial hierarchy had matured into a woman with an expanded and inclusive vision of the world, committed to human rights in many forms and places. In November 1867, the woman who arrived in New York had developed most of the significant elements of a personality that would shape the actions of the rest of her life. She was brave and independent, she was a confident intellectual who was also socially at ease, and she was an outspoken crusader both for the value of knowledge and for what she saw as the cause of justice and equality. Mrs. Leonowens was going to be a big hit in the United States.

TWELVE

An American Writer

WHEN ANNA AND HER DAUGHTER LANDED IN NEW YORK, they were not planning to stay. Anna's fragile plan for her future, which she had worked out at the Wilkinsons, was simply to delay making any final plan until the following spring. She was waiting for a reply from King Mongkut sometime in April or May 1868 to her November 1867 letter requesting a salary advance. That was the time when, as her brother-in-law put it, "you may naturally expect to hear from the King, and when you must decide as to your future career" (LC, VI C, 4:2). Even having decided on this delay, Anna's idea all along was to go back to Ireland in late spring of 1868 to see the Wilkinsons and pick up Louis. If Mongkut said yes to advancing her the money, which she thought likely, she could collect the advance from the Siamese consul in London and return to work in Bangkok, having been away about a year.

Meanwhile, Louis could spend a school year in an Irish boarding school and Anna could take a trip to a place she had wanted to visit since at least 1860. With her winter free as she waited to hear back from the king, Anna used the opportunity to jump on a ship to the United States with Avis, rather than just remaining in Ireland. But with Anna a trip was never just a trip. Given her characteristic energy and intensity, she could not simply take a vacation. Anna needed to be doing something she viewed as serious and productive. The trip to America was also an opportunity to try to fulfill a cherished dream. Her true plan, also discussed at the Wilkinsons, was to use her leave of absence from her job to sit quietly somewhere and try her hand as a writer. What she would write about, of course, were her unique and amazing experiences as a teacher inside the Grand Palace of Siam.

In New York City Anna stayed with the Cobbs. Frank was thrilled to see both her and Avis again. Anna quickly became good friends with Frank's wife, Katherine. The couple enthusiastically supported her wish to write, and

Katherine performed what would turn out to be the inestimable service of introducing Anna to Annie Fields (see figure 7). Annie was a writer herself, a minor poet. She was also a literary hostess who entertained many writers and was generous in encouraging other people's careers. Luckily for the many writers who knew her, Annie was married to James T. Fields (see figure 8), another writer and also partner since 1843 in "the premier 'literary' publishing house in America during the middle years of the nineteenth-century," Ticknor and Fields (*Ticknor and Fields, Records: Guide,* Houghton Library, Harvard College Library). Among several name changes, in 1868 the firm became Fields, Osgood and Co. and eventually evolved into Houghton, Mifflin and Co. Annie's social world included such successful writers as Henry Longfellow, Nathaniel Hawthorne, Ralph Emerson, and Harriet Beecher Stowe.

Annie Fields was delighted to meet Anna. She deeply appreciated another intellectual woman, someone cosmopolitan as well as scholarly, warmly emotional as well as serious and smart. She was also fascinated to hear of Anna's amazing professional experiences and joined the voices supporting her dream to write about them. The two became friends and virtually lifelong correspondents. Anna also met Eliza Justice and her husband, William, a Quaker couple in Philadelphia; Mrs. Botta; and Mr. and Mrs. Paine, who summered in Newport. The families were well-off and well connected. Mrs. Botta, the Cobbs, and the Paines in Manhattan, Annie Fields in Boston, Mrs. Justice in Philadelphia, and later the Johnsons and Mrs. Shaw on Staten Island and Mrs. Lawrence in Schenectady would form a small circle of loving friends who gave their long-term support to Anna and her children. Much as she had in Nang Harm, Anna established close friendships with a group of women who loved and admired her as she loved and admired them. Clearly, Anna was going to have the personal connections to become a published author on the American literary scene. All she needed was something to publish.

After just a week or two with the Cobbs, Anna and Avis traveled upstate for a visit with Anna's other good friends from Southeast Asia, the Mattoons. Not well-off at all, they were living in Ballston Spa, a small village just south of Saratoga Springs. Anna was looking for a simple and affordable place to spend that winter, and the Mattoons had the answer. By December Anna and her daughter had settled more or less halfway between the Mattoons and the Cobbs, in a small cottage in Catskill, New York. The rent was almost nothing because it was out of season and the town was empty. There, during that shockingly cold first winter, while her son in Ireland experienced his first snow, the woman from India experienced her first snow and wrote a lot of

FIGURE 7. Mrs. (Annie) Fields. Culver Photos.

FIGURE 8. James T. Fields. Culver Photos.

her first book, *The English Governess at the Siamese Court*. Anna worked very hard. In April 1868, Thomas Wilkinson (who always called her Annie, as her husband had) wrote, "I fear, my dear Annie, you have been working too constantly at your book, and that you have made your holiday a day of labour" (LC, VI C, 4:2). Yet he was proud of her, delighted to hear that Avis was studying while in America so that she could "be learned like her mother."

The subtitle of the book declared it to be *Recollections of Six Years in the Royal Palace at Bangkok*. There is no doubt that what Anna was selling to her American publisher and American audiences was some sort of behind-the-scenes memoir of what life was *really* like in her "experience in the heart of an Asiatic court," as she called it in her dedication to Katherine Cobb. There is also no doubt that Anna had decided to include descriptions critical of King Mongkut and of a familial and political system by which women were locked up for life in the inner palace.

The Wilkinsons were worried about what she was doing, particularly since they knew all about her request for a salary advance from the king. Indeed, Mongkut's response to her request was to be sent to Enniscorthy and forwarded to wherever Anna was staying. As early as the end of January, Anna had heard from Wilkinson senior about the book, beginning with his hope that she had also received a letter from his son Tom. "He feels anxious about your book, and indeed so do I, fearing that it might not be successful, and that its publication might break between you and the King of Siam." Thomas Wilkinson advised her, "I have a lingering idea that your post at Bangkok was more certain and better adapted to your tastes and talents than anything that I can see your way to in America." But he ended, most gently, "my dear Annie, this is only an opinion formed on very slender information, and may be very erroneous."

As it turned out, the king, in a letter that arrived in Enniscorthy the first week of May, replied to her letter of November 2 when he received it the following February. Mongkut was a practical man. He wrote to Anna on February 8, 1868, that he would be happy to give her the two hundred pounds as an advance on her coming salary, as soon as she returned to Bangkok. He wisely observed, "I am desirous of complying with your desire, but fear lest you by any cause would not be able to return to Siam soon" (LC, VI C, 4:6). Imagining she was staying in England, he suggested that she might borrow temporarily from someone in London, then repay the loan with the money he would happily advance her as soon as she reappeared in Bangkok.

By then Anna was far enough along with a manuscript to feel optimistic. It was turning into a beautiful summer in upstate New York, and she was not going to return to Bangkok right away. Nor, even though she was eagerly awaited, was she, for the moment at least, going to return to Enniscorthy. The Wilkinsons expected her back. Mary, Tom's sister, had written affectionately in February, "I hope nothing will prevent you and Avis from coming in the spring" (LC, VI C, 4:2). On May 13, Wilkinson senior thought it likely that "you may embark for Ireland immediately after receiving the [king's] letter." Even as late as June 20, a Wilkinson daughter, Henrietta, wrote to Anna that the family "are all on tip-toe to welcome the travelers and Louis home."

Louis was desperate to see her. The year at Kingstown School had been very hard for him. He had found the lessons difficult and the masters harsh. Certainly, the warm and friendly boy had got on well with the other boys at school. And the Wilkinsons, with whom he spent all holidays, really loved him. His uncle Wilkinson wrote to Anna on January 29, 1868, that Louis "has so won all our affections here that I do not know what we shall do for him when he returns to school." As Selina, one of the five Wilkinson daughters, put it, theirs was "a quiet country home," in a small place, but "there is so much love here that it makes the place quite big to think of" (June 1868). Louis had even made a best friend in Enniscorthy, Willie Mahoney, and his letters are full of their fun.

But school was a different matter. Louis's letters about school were filled with loneliness and distress. During that long first winter he wrote to Anna, "It is very hard for me to be in this prison I awals think of you," "every time I think of you I cant help crying," and "I am your only son I have you only to love" (Feb. 4, 1868). Ten days later, he wrote her a sad child's tale of "how the Masters are so hard on me." He struck a wrong note and the music teacher "began to baul and shout at me and I began to think of you and I count stop the tear from rolling down my cheek." As Louis, at only eleven years old, so eloquently put it, "I wish I was living with you all it is very hard to be in the world when you are young." Selina also wrote eloquently to Anna in March about Louis's anxiety to hear from her. "I do not think the sun shines the same to him the week he does not hear from you."

Louis worried terribly that Anna would go back to Bangkok without him. Remembering in his child's way her part in opposing dreadful M. Aubaret, and trying to insist that she not go back without him, he wrote at the end of April, "You will be in such a dangerous place and I will awals feel so unhappy thinking of you being among all those French peapel who hate you or praps a robber might come." In all these sad letters his plea was touchingly simple, that "I may be with my Mama and be a day boy" (Nov. 12, 1868).

But that summer Anna and Avis stayed in America. And in the fall, on October 1, 1868, King Mongkut of Siam, Rama IV, died. He had been stricken with malaria on a trip to southern Siam in late August to witness a full solar eclipse. His reign, distinguished by its achievements in foreign policy and its advances in the sciences and government administration, had lasted more than twenty-one years. Prince Chulalongkorn was named king. But because he was only fifteen, Siam was to be ruled by a regent until 1873, when the young king reached his majority.

King Mongkut's unexpected death finally ended the possibility of Anna returning to Siam. But even before his death, she had been toying with other possibilities. Mrs. Mattoon had given her a reference to give some lessons in the Parker School for Girls in Brooklyn. And in August or September Anna actually considered going back to India. She definitely decided that Louis would stay in Ireland for his education, with the warm-hearted Wilkinson family happy to be his "home," and he was sent back to Kingstown School for the fall of 1868. Louis wrote on October 10, filled with the brave condescension of a second-year student and a boy about to turn twelve, to announce that "the school has gone down awfully it is nothing to be compaired to what it was last half." He also asked "My own darling Mama" to "please try to come over to Ireland so that we may all see you once more before you go back to India."

Sometime in October, Anna at last made her decision. She liked America. And she knew that there were few opportunities in Ireland. She and Avis would stay. She had already made good friends and would look for a way to make a living. She and Avis went to visit the Cobbs in New York City and then visited the Rev. and Laura Johnson, another missionary family she had known in Bangkok, who lived on Staten Island. She met another woman there, Mrs. Shaw, who soon became one of her small circle of close friends. Anna decided it was the perfect place to start a little school of her own, a practical way to finance her attempt at a writing career. Thomas Wilkinson wrote on December 19, "so glad to hear" about "your prospects and your projects" and "that you are so hopeful." He too thought the school would succeed, commenting that "these things do better in America than in this country."

Thomas Wilkinson had been in charge of all Louis's expenses and bills and sent Anna a little accounting of what she owed him. Thomas Wilkinson became a surrogate father to Louis, not only looking after his accounts but also being the one to supervise the boy's progress at school and to have conferences with Mr. Stacpoole about Louis's "scholastic strides." As Thomas put it, Louis "is growing very much" (he would be a tall man) and "I hope to see intellectual growth keeping pace with his person." He clearly delighted in Louis, a boy "in the best health and spirits," as did the rest of the family. Louis loved the long family vacations at the sea with the Wilkinson girls, "who run about the whole day at the sea like if they were mad." He particularly loved swimming. Thomas Wilkinson reported to Anna that when "Louis came home" for his Christmas vacation in December 1868, he was "blooming" and "he and the girls have just met like parted lovers and are so happy at the reunion" (LC, VI C, 4).

By the end of 1868, it looked as though Anna had successfully settled Louis in Ireland, at school and with the Wilkinson relatives. She focused her attention on making a life for herself and Avis, who was now fourteen, on Staten Island. In the spring of 1869, the little school was paying enough to support Anna and Avis. Anna could go back to her dream of becoming a writer. She wrote and polished the manuscript of her "Recollections" and also taught at the school during the fall of 1869 and spring of 1870. Anna and Avis, in what would become a tradition, spent the summer staying at the vacation homes of some of Anna's wealthy women friends, including time at "Sea Verge," the Paines' summer home in Newport.

The year 1870 was exciting for the Leonowens family. The most emotional event was that Louis, now thirteen, came to the United States that summer. There is no account explaining how or why or even exactly when, just sometime between June and October. Certainly, he did not want to return to Rev. Stacpoole's school. I also suspect that the boarding school expenses were getting to be too much for Anna. And if Louis were not going to school in Ireland, it made no sense for the Wilkinsons to have him full-time when he could live with his mother and sister. In the fall, the small family returned to Staten Island. Anna reopened her school and there is a fleeting mention that Louis, now reunited with them and almost fourteen, had returned to his studies. For Avis the year was marked by a rite of passage from childhood. Just about to turn sixteen, she began her first job. She was an assistant to Miss Comstock at her kindergarten in Manhattan, commuting to work on the Staten Island ferry.

In August 1870, according to Anna's granddaughter, Avis Fyshe, Captain Orton from Singapore wrote proposing to Anna. But Anna's hopes did not include remarrying. The answer was no. The exciting event for her personally in 1870 was that she became a published author. To publish her book Anna had naturally turned to her friend Annie's powerful husband, James Fields. Along with being a partner in a most distinguished publishing company and being the close friend and exclusive American publisher of Charles Dickens, Fields was also the editor of the *Atlantic Monthly*. He had taken over from James Russell Lowell in 1861. Although he retired from publishing and editing in 1870, Fields, warmly encouraged by his wife, provided Anna with her first publication. *The English Governess at the Siamese Court* made its first appearance in four installments in the *Atlantic Monthly,* in April, May, June, and August 1870. The book was published in Boston in the late fall of 1870 by Fields, Osgood & Co. It was also published in Philadelphia by Porter & Coates, and in London by Trubner & Co.

In a pattern that would repeat with Anna's second book in 1873, the American reviews were generally enthusiastic while the British reviews were generally not. The *New York Times* reviewer wrote that *The English Governess* was "well written, and abounds with that rich flavor of the East" and commented on the complex and "peculiar" character of the king (Dec. 10, 1870). A reviewer for the *Overland Monthly and Out West Magazine* called the book "the most remarkable of . . . exposures" of the "private life of the most sacred personages" because "Mrs. Leonowens, in her fresh lively way, tells us of all she saw" (March 1871).

The major American review, and the only one sounding as if the reviewer were familiar with Siam, was in *The Nation.* It emphasized that Anna was unique in having these experiences, that she was "fortunate in her opportunity of authorship" (Mar. 9, 1871). In a balanced evaluation, the reviewer noted that the book had some uninteresting padding and that Anna probably overstated the danger of her work. As to the king, "on the whole, her estimate of his character is not unfair," and when she occupied herself with "the domestic life which no writer but herself has been permitted to observe," she was "very lively and every way admirable."

In England, the major review was in the *Athenaeum,* and the tone was quite different. "We are sorry to confess our disappointment," said the anonymous reviewer, clearly not sorry at all. He then went on to expand on the "inaccuracy of the work," which "renders it not only valueless but dangerously misleading" (Dec. 24, 1870). The criticism was mainly scholarly, faulting Anna's translations from the Siamese ("'Phra-batt' . . . does not mean 'golden-footed,' but simply 'the sacred foot'") in ways that demonstrated the reviewer's own erudition. But the reviewer's main objection, and his greatest anger, was focused on Anna's presentation of the king. He was "a man so full of domestic affection," and yet she "has not hesitated to cast a shadow on his memory, and to stigmatize his conduct as the head of a great family as an abiding disgrace to his name."

The reviewers in England were not the only ones to object to the book. Mr. D. K. Mason, the Siamese consul in London, also must have expressed objections, and he somehow must have expressed them to Tom Wilkinson, Thomas Wilkinson's barrister son, now living in London. They knew each other because mail for Anna from Siam went through Mr. Mason and then through the Wilkinsons. Anna wrote Tom on November 5, 1870, responding to a letter from him, with an outraged defense of her book against Mr. Mason's charges. She was careful to make her first point be that Sir John Bowring, no less, had written a letter of introduction to her London publishers so he was not opposed to her writing, as Mr. Mason must have suggested. Of course, we have no evidence that Bowring knew what Anna's manuscript actually contained.

Anna continued, "I am not surprised that there are members of the Government of Siam who are incensed at the publication of my book." Her explicit claim to Tom was that "from the moment I espoused the cause of the poor slave woman, L'Ore against one of the highest ladies of the palace . . . I was looked upon with distrust and fear by the Siamese Government" (LC, VI C, 4:2). I tend to believe that something like L'Ore's story really did happen when Anna was in Siam, that she accidentally came across a slave woman chained up illegally, for months if not years, by one of the older princesses. Certainly, Anna's version was not even in the book Mason criticized and did not appear in print until 1872. Finally, Anna skewered Mr. Mason as a man who found "light and trivial" such things as "Slavery, Polygamy, Flagellation of women & children, Immolation of slaves, secret poisoning and assassination." In his November 22 response, Tom promised to defend her good name, and "if I see any adverse Mrs. Leonowens review that passes the bounds of fair criticism . . . I shall promptly answer it." He sent his love to Avis and Louis.

The review in the *Athenaeum* of Anna's second book, *The Romance of the Harem,* I suspect authored by the same person who wrote the first, was even more outraged and contemptuous. The reviewer took the opportunity "to point out a few instances of manifest, we might almost say inexcusable, error," going on for several columns to do just that (Feb. 15, 1873). But the second book was a good deal more fabulous, more consciously fictional, than the first, a point that was clear to most American reviewers as it was not to the British. The author of a very brief critique in the *Princeton Review* did call the book "a description of the interior life, customs, forms and usages of an Oriental Court" (April 1873). But the *New York Times* review perceptively observed that *The Romance* "disarms criticism" because "your judgment is charmed to sleep and you willingly give yourself up to the credulous enjoyment of what the skillful author has provided for you" (Feb. 14, 1873). The reviewer in *The Nation* began by correctly observing that *The Romance* was a collection of loosely bound tales, and these tales "deserve the name of romances, so wild and strange are they in incident and atmosphere" (May 15, 1873).

The American reviewer may well have been helped to what seems to me now an obvious insight by the fact that in the nineteenth century in the United States but not in England the term *romance* had a specific cultural and literary meaning, of which Anna would have been perfectly aware. The term had been foregrounded in American literary circles in the early 1850s by Nathaniel Hawthorne, who called his four novels "romances." In what became a famous preface to his novel *The House of the Seven Gables* (1851), Hawthorne wrote that a romance "may present the truth under circumstances, to a great extent, of the writer's own choosing or creation." He had made a similar point in "The Custom-House," an essay that introduced *The Scarlet Letter* (1850), defining the romance as a world between reality and imagination. Hawthorne's argument, one advanced at the time by many other American artists, was that the writer could, and often should, transform the mere facts, should "mingle the Marvellous," in order to present the truth. The American genre within which Anna deliberately placed her second book, and within which its insights need to be evaluated, was not that of realist fiction or of factual memoir, but of truthful romance.

In the fall of 1870, Anna achieved her dream when her first book became a reality. Luckily, she lived in the United States, where the reviews were positive. The moderate success of the book gave her the confidence to begin writing her second book. This time Anna aimed at a more literary effort, drawing on the traditions of both the "romance" theories of Hawthorne and other male writers and the "sentimental" style of Harriet Beecher Stowe and other women novelists. Two installments of the new work appeared in the *Atlantic Monthly* in September and October 1872. *The Romance of the Harem* was published in 1873 (actually, December 1872) by J. R. Osgood and Co. in Boston, who also used the moment to publish a second edition of *The English Governess. Romance* was simultaneously published in Philadelphia by Porter & Coates and in London, as *The Romance of Siamese Harem Life,* by Trubner & Co. That wrongheaded title change would continue in England and have a negative and lasting influence on Anna's reputation as a commentator on Siam. The 1952 edition published by Arthur Barker was titled *Siamese Harem Life,* dropping the crucial term *Romance* and opening the book up to even more harsh attacks on "the inaccuracy of the work."

In spite of such criticisms as those found in the *Athenaeum* review, the publication of her chapters in the *Atlantic* and her first books gave Anna the opportunity to try yet another new career. Suddenly she had the cachet to try her luck on the lecture circuit. In March 1871, a relative of Laura Johnson, Miss Winthrop, reported that in a particularly successful lecture, Anna had grossed $237, "and expenses, such as the rent of the hall, etc. had been only $92" (LC, VI C, 4:2). That kind of profit was rare. But Anna soon saw that paid public lectures were a good deal more profitable than lessons. I am not sure if she was still running her school in the spring of 1871, but if so it would be the last term. The teacher and the writer had moved on to yet a third career.

Starting in 1871, the year she turned forty, Anna found herself for the first time in her life allowed access to public authority for her knowledge. In an age in America when it was still considered daring and unusual for a woman to speak in public, Anna could command an audience. She loved it. And, with her usual intensity, she acted quickly to claim and expand her intellectual authority. She worked hard on *Romance* throughout 1871. And she also turned her efforts to writing more and more lectures, starting with those about Siam and working up a range of subjects far beyond her personal reminiscences. Anna was thrilled to be able to present herself to American audiences as a scholarly authority not only on Siam but also on subjects such as Buddhism and Hinduism. Her scholarly aspirations had been limited by her origins and her sex. But in her tastes and her intellectual pursuits she saw herself very much as a professor manqué.

As he did for many of his authors, James Fields actively encouraged Anna's attempts to establish herself on the lecture circuit. After all, public exposure sold more books. She gave lectures throughout the winter of 1871 and the spring of 1872, including one on April 6 at Cooper Union. Some of her earliest lectures were in Boston, at the Meionaeon, with "an audience large and very select, including a large number of the well known *literati* of Boston." How did that happen? Well, she was preceded to the platform by Mrs. James T. Fields, "with a pleasant word of introduction" *(Boston Journal)*.

James Fields turned Anna over to Mr. B. W. Williams of the American Literary Bureau to manage a full lecture tour in the summer of 1872. Avis went along. Robert Dale Owen, the social reformer and longtime abolitionist who had founded the famous utopian community of New Harmony, Indiana, was a fellow *Atlantic* author and lecturer who had met Anna and Avis and liked them both. He wrote a letter to the *New York Times* pointing out that what the paper had praised "the young King of Siam" for, his forward thinking and commitment to emancipation, was partly due "to the influence of a lady now living unobtrusively among us" (June 25, 1872).

Owen wrote to Avis from Harmony with practical advice on how to survive the "arduous enterprise" of one of these lecture tours. To give an idea of

FIGURE 9. Avis Leonowens Fyshe, picture carte de vista.
Margaret Landon Papers (SC-38), Special Collections,
Wheaton College.

how arduous, in another letter he warned Anna not to accept doing more than seventy-five lectures each tour. Owen's advice included such useful details as "never travel by night . . . except in a sleeping car," and be sure to get "berths near the center of the car." That lecture trip in the summer of 1872 was followed by another during the winter of 1872, with Avis and Louis staying home. By this point Anna had a housekeeper, an Irish woman named Katie Clark, with whom she could leave her two teenagers.

The friendly concern and eagerness to be of help shown by Robert Dale Owen is one example of how Anna was enthusiastically taken up by many of the public figures surrounding Annie and James Fields in postbellum America. Anna became a member of this East Coast literary scene. Most of the people who became Anna's friends were either writers themselves or wealthy people, such as Colonel T. W. Higginson (who financed the Boston Symphony Orchestra), who were committed to supporting the arts. One reason Anna's friends and admirers welcomed her so warmly was that they also tended to share another characteristic: they were socially liberal people and longtime abolitionists who in general believed it was a person's duty to help others and in particular believed that slavery was one of the greatest of human evils.

These people lived and died for their beliefs. Anna arrived in the United States at a very significant historical moment, soon after the Civil War and at the beginning of Reconstruction. In postbellum America the issues, the feelings, and the bitter memories of the war were fresh. Laura Johnson's brother was Theodore Winthrop, "a pre–Civil War novelist and the first officer, on the Northern side" (LC, VI C, 4:3). Mrs. Shaw's son, Robert Gould Shaw, whose memorial now stands in Boston Common, was the first young man to accept a position as "the head of a colored regiment." As an insult, the Southern army threw his body into a pit and piled over him the bodies of the soldiers of his regiment. "All his family considered this very burial the greatest honor that their dear 'Robert' could have done for him" (LC, VI C, 4:2). After the war was a time of social chaos, as Americans like the Shaws and many others were forced to face what the war had cost. People such as William Justice were dedicated to helping the many, many lives the war had destroyed, be they "a 'Germantown beggar' or a colored 'soldier's orphan'" (LC, VI C, 4:2).

As a public speaker, Anna was a great success. She spoke of the horrors of slavery in a country far away. Her talks performed a crucial cultural function, helping to heal those Americans who heard her by reinforcing that their own war had been worthwhile and that they, unlike peoples such as the Siamese, were making true civil progress. Anna not only had unfamiliar materials and a reassuring and inspiring message to an audience recovering from the horror and bitterness of civil war, but she also had a great delivery.

That delivery was no accident. It was a product of Anna's usual enthusiasm for a new project, along with her usual hard work and self-discipline. Anna not only gave lessons but believed in taking them as well. Her granddaughter wrote that Anna often spoke of the many "elocution lessons & the good she derived from them," as she learned to control "her diction, her presence, her dramatic power" (LC, VI C, 4:2).

As the *Boston Times* put it in reviewing her lecture "Asiatic Women" (Jan. 13, 1873), "personal adventure and experiences are always attractive," but also there is "the lady's agreeable and refined manner, combined with a cultured and somewhat dramatic style of delivery." The *Boston Post* also wrote approvingly of the "charming" and "dark-eyed, dark-haired woman, with a musical, though not very powerful voice." Anna lectured in Newport, Rhode Island, and the *News* commented that "there is certainly no one in the field, in America, today, who has material so unique in interest as hers." The *Washington Daily Chronicle* praised her lecture in Lincoln Hall for its "ornate phraseology, and glowing descriptions" (Mar. 8, 1873).

A woman speaker was still a real rarity in postbellum America, particularly one who was erudite as well as eloquent, and who lectured on scholarly topics. Anna gradually worked up seven lectures she could offer to a prospective audience. Her topics were "Siam: Its Courts and Customs," "Asiatic Women, Ancient and Modern," "A Visit to Maha Nagkhon Wat [Ankor Wat]," "Land of the Zend Avesta [history of the early Persians]," "Buddha and Buddhism in Siam," "Brahmanism, Ancient and Modern [Hinduism]," and "Christian Missions to Pagan Lands." She also gave what Annie Fields called her "narrations," dramatic readings of stories loosely based on some of the events and personages of Siam.

In the fall of 1872, Anna had another of her dreams fulfilled when she at last met Harriet Beecher Stowe, the author whose work had inspired her for so long. Through Annie she had already met Mr. Longfellow. Anna paid a visit to Annie at 148 Charles St., Boston, on October 29, and there was Stowe, "who embraced me as if she had known me all her life." That was a great moment. But perhaps an even better one, closer to her heart, was when she received a letter from Sonklin on November 11. "My goodness gracious," wrote Sonklin, "you will not know us any more, we are all so changed, a free-domed people" (LC, VI C, 4:2). King Chulalongkorn had issued an edict to end, albeit gradually, slavery in Siam. Sonklin described people's reactions. "Some of the free like not to leave their master and mistress so they weep for gladness, but most run off like wild deer from shotgun and are for joy like one mad." As for Sonklin, "me and my two sisters are too happy we fear almost to say how happy for fear perhaps it will all vanish." Surely the vivid joy of this letter from a woman of the Inner City can finally put the lie to Western men's assertions either that the women of Nang Harm under King Mongkut were really free to leave or, if not, that they did not mind, accepted the status quo, and had no negative views on the Siamese system of slavery.

With *Romance* being published in December 1872, Anna arranged her speaking tour so as to be in Boston for the momentous occasion. Otherwise it was a lonely holiday time, spent mostly on the road. Avis at eighteen still worked at Miss Comstock's kindergarten. Louis, now sixteen, had stopped school and gotten some kind of a job, since Anna wrote to him on December 15, 1872, to "send me a line from your office daily." But Louis did get into some kind of trouble, by borrowing a lot of money from the father of one of Avis's kindergarten pupils. Anna was distraught. Louis needed to find some way to pay back the money, and in the spring of 1873 he took off for Little Rock, Arkansas, to work a season at the Cairo and Fulton Railroad's Land Department. He wrote charmingly on July 2, "thank God me reformation is complete."

Anna's lecture career was still booming. She now had a new manager, Mr. James Redpath of the Boston Lyceum Bureau, and continued to tour and make money. She and Avis spent some time during the summer at the vacation homes of her friends, but otherwise she continued her speaking engagements for another year, through to the summer of 1874. Louis had come back north in late 1873 and was working in Philadelphia at a steamship company office for six dollars a week. But he was to come home in the fall. Anna was not returning to Staten Island at the end of the summer. She had rented rooms for the winter from some friends in Manhattan, Dr. and Mrs. Barnard of Columbia College, and wrote happily to Annie Fields on August 17 that "Louis will have the best society and many other literary advantages by being there" (F, 5061).

But when, in October 1874, Anna went to give a lecture in Philadelphia, she discovered to her astonishment that her son was gone. She also discovered to her horror that he had left the United States, and borrowed money to do so. Just turned eighteen, Louis wrote from Enniscorthy on November 3, 1874, telling of his hardships on the passage, asking her to understand that "I must do something" more than earn six dollars a week, and begging, "You must *not* when you write say anything against me for it is not fair for I am honestly and truthfully trying a new life." Also, his shoes were so worn that his soles touched the pavement; could she please send one or two pounds.

Anna and Louis would not see each other again for nineteen years, until May 1893. By then he would be very, very rich. But now, Uncle Wilkinson helped the penniless young man to a free passage in steerage as a "common emigrant" to Australia (letter to Anna, Feb. 2, 1875), arriving in June 1875. He stayed until 1881, working at various places, including the Palmer Rise Gold

Fields. Louis made up with his mother and they corresponded for the rest of her life. Unlike Avis, he had never been particularly good at or interested in school and books. This tall young man with the cheerful and open manner much preferred a more active and freer life. In 1881, now almost twenty-five but unable to make a living in Australia, he once again asked Anna for financial help. Because she believed it would be best for him, she said no. It turned out to be the right answer. Louis left Australia and made his way to the one place he had ever really belonged. Fourteen years after he had left, Louis went back to Siam. He went home.

In New York City that winter of 1874, Anna and Avis finally moved from Staten Island for good. Along with Katie Clark, they moved into the rooms at the Barnards' without Louis. Avis, twenty in October, worked at Miss Comstock's and Anna, forty-three at the end of November, kept up an intense winter schedule of lectures. Her travels were extending. She went to the Midwest and spoke at McCormick Hall in Chicago in January. Back in the East in the spring, Anna did a lecture at Swarthmore College in April 1875. For that one she was paid thirty dollars. At this point, Anna had a reasonably financially secure life in New York. Money was tight enough that her rich friends would quietly send extra money to Avis for "your dear Mother." And she depended on them for her vacation visits to their summer homes. But she was certainly getting by.

Anna had successfully created a "little niche as English author lecturer touring America" (LC, VI C, 4:2). Her career, for the moment, was taking care of itself. Her son was off on his own. But what about her daughter? Avis spent a lot of time with her rich Brooklyn girlfriend, Kathleen Ford, who was happy to provide tickets for them both to many of Manhattan's cultural events. And sometime in the winter of 1873–74, Anna and Avis had met Thomas Fyshe. A young Scotsman (born Oct. 3, 1845) nine years older than Avis, he had worked in banks in Scotland, England, and Montreal before moving to New York that winter to try his hand at being a stockbroker. They saw him occasionally throughout 1874 and he was clearly interested in Avis. Then, on May 6, 1875, he took a job at the St. John branch of the Bank of Nova Scotia and moved back to Canada. He wrote pleasant, friendly letters. But that seemed to be that.

During the winter of 1875–76, Anna did another lecture tour, including Albany and a talk at Cooper Union. But the big event was that in February they left Mrs. Barnard's and rented their own apartment in Manhattan, at 701 Sixth Avenue, on the corner of 40th Street. The Cobbs had moved from their home on 23rd Street to an apartment on Sixth Avenue the previous September, needing to economize, and had probably helped Anna find her place. The two families now lived in the same neighborhood. Anna was thrilled with the move, writing of "the delight of being alone together." But the official purpose was to have the space so that Avis, with "a diploma from Miss Haines' institution, where the system of Froebel is thoroughly taught" (LC, VI C, 4:2), could have her very own school. The announcement was made in June 1876 for a "select Kindergarten" opening the following fall. Avis and her mother spent the summer, as usual, at the vacation cottages of their friends.

Anna was at last successful in expanding her career in 1876. She continued to do her lectures. But she also began writing regular articles for a weekly Boston magazine for young people called *Youth's Companion*. She did six of them in 1876, for issues in May, June, July, August, September, and November. She would do eleven more in 1877 and six in 1878. The pay was small, but she saw it as the beginning of a career in magazine journalism.

Meanwhile, the letters from Tom Fyshe to Avis continued. In March 1876 he was writing about true friendship. In May he talked about coming to like the congenial life of Halifax, where he had moved from St. John. And by November, while wishing her luck in her new school, he was writing that he would prefer talking to her in person. Then, in June 1877, just about to leave on a vacation to Scotland (which was suddenly canceled because of the terrible fire in St. John), Tom became brave. On June 19, he declared, "I fell in love with you at first sight" and asked permission to call her "Avis." Her first response was hesitant. But she loved him. In January 1878, Tom came to New York and the two were engaged.

Tom and Avis were married on June 19, 1878, in a church near Anna's apartment. They left immediately for Niagara Falls, and then on July 2 on the R.M.S. *Circassian* to Scotland to meet Tom's family. Avis had closed her school. And Anna too was closing up her life in the United States. Back in February, Tom had written to beg her to live with them, knowing that Avis would be so sad to leave her, loving Anna himself, and asking her to be a Mamma to them both. All three would move to Halifax. It was a perfect solution, and one that would turn out to make them all happy. Immediately after the wedding, Anna packed up the apartment, going to stay with her friend Mrs. Botta until the honeymooners returned.

Frank Cobb stopped by, to gaze "in mute pain on the dismemberment that our dear rooms were undergoing" (LC, VI C, 4:2). He knew, as did Anna, that this was the end of her time in America. She had been in the country a little more than a decade. She had begun as a teacher and had created three new careers for herself: book author, public lecturer, and magazine journalist. She had succeeded in all three and was a well-known public figure in the Northeast. She had also developed a wide circle of acquaintances and friends, some of whom were very close. Now this particular life was almost over. Frank had watched Anna leave Singapore for an unknown world more than sixteen years earlier, when they were both still young. Anna had been only thirty. Now Frank had come to say good-bye to his dear old friend all over again. At the age of forty-six, this vital and resilient woman was leaving once more, for yet another country, yet another adventure.

THIRTEEN

The Canadian Grande Dame

TOM AND AVIS SPENT ALL OF THAT SUMMER of 1878 on their honeymoon. They went home to Tom's family in Scotland. His father, Alex, was a farmer and Tom, along with siblings Sandy, Peter, and Jane, had grown up happily in the country in Easter Balbeggie, near Kirkcaldy. In London, Tom and Avis visited Tom Wilkinson, whom Avis pronounced to be very conservative, and Avis wrote that long lovely letter to Anna about her feelings on seeing her old school and the depth of her love for her mother. Anna had written her in June that "it was a dreadful trial to let you go," but "your happiness is mine, dearest, and I cannot tell you how dear Tom is to me." For her part, Avis wrote of her time with her mother as "years never to be forgotten, so happy and blessed have they been to me."

Feeling joyous but also slightly bereft, Anna kept busy while Avis and Tom were gone. She taught a summer school class in Sanskrit at Amherst for six to eight weeks, from July through August 21, and apparently impressed Professor Boucher, the Sanskrit scholar at Harvard, with her teaching skills. She also visited Barnstable, the coastal town east of Boston where Frank Cobb had moved with Katherine, "our [two] oldest friends on this side of the Atlantic" (LC, VI C, 4:2), and their three children. Then Anna and the newlyweds settled down to make a life in Canada.

Anna arrived in Halifax in September 1878, sailing directly from Boston, and moved into 48 Inglis Street with Avis and Tom. She was beginning what would be her last and, from her point of view, her best identity, that of a Canadian family matriarch. She would live it for the next thirty-six years. During that time, she would raise and for many years be the primary educator of eight children. Still, it would not be her only identity. Again and again throughout the next decades she would take up pieces of the professional persona she had created in the United States. Anna did not just sit in Halifax,

FIGURE 10. Robert Harris (1849–1919), *Portrait of Anna H. Leonowens,* 1905, oil on canvas, 76.2 cm × 60.0 cm. Confederation Centre Art Gallery, Charlottetown, PEI; donated on behalf of the great-great-great-grandchildren of Anna Leonowens: James and Martine Hvezda; Tam, Megan, and Anna Boyar; and Marion and Jamie Fyshe, 1999 (CAG H-8889).

though it was her home base for the next nineteen years. And, of course, she was able to become a highly visible matriarch precisely because her reputation as an author and lecturer in the United States had followed her to Canada.

But the years of worry and struggle were really over. Anna had at last reached a point of "no care, no anxiety for the future" (F, June 2, 1880). Her darling Avis was well married to "a kind brave soul who is your protector and guide, your friend and husband through life." Anna and Avis sat securely within the financial protection of Tom Fyshe, who loved both his wife and the woman who would be a mother to them both. By the time Tom married Avis, he was already well-off, having done very well as a "curb broker in sterling" in New York and now being general manager ("cashier") of the Bank of Nova Scotia. He would go on to become general manager of the Merchant's Bank of Canada in Montreal. A man of great intelligence, good judgment, and "a warm and sympathetic heart," and highly successful in his field, Thomas Fyshe was called by a fellow banker "the best banker Canada has ever seen" (Yorke, *DCB*). He would provide for his family and look after them for the rest of his life. And he would become rich enough to continue to provide for those still living, long after his death.

Halifax was quite a small city in the 1870s, with about thirty thousand people. It was a fishing port, and not particularly pretty in its architecture and layout. In character it was an odd combination—at once semirural, isolated, filled with rugged characters, lacking in facilities, lacking many of the comforts and pleasures of urban culture, and yet socially rigidly hierarchical. The Fyshes, including the famous mother-in-law, were considered among the "best" families and were warmly welcomed into local society. But Anna did not like the place. She noted that "everyone here has been most courteous to us. Still, it is odd to see the airs which the English give themselves here; and the class distinctions which are maintained." Anna did her best to ignore the social hierarchy, having hated class status since her childhood in Poona.

Tom and Avis immediately started a family, and on March 8, 1879, their first child, James Carlyle (Carlyle was Tom's favorite writer), was born. Anna was completely smitten. The birth of James was the beginning of Anna's exceptional love affair with her grandchildren, which would give purpose and meaning to the next three decades of her life and carry her through terrible tragedy. She had to be absent from "dear little Jamie" a year later, in April and May 1880, when she again gave some lectures in Boston and New York. She wrote to Avis that "the strong instinct of the mother out-weighs and over-rules every other sentiment of my life, and this is not mere talk—but a deep truth . . . of my nature." She then went on to describe in particularly distinctive terms her tenderness for Jamie. "It is sweet, sweeter than the most passionate love of one's youth, this love of a grandmother for her grandchild" (LC, VI C, 4:2).

This sweet love would soon enough become the driving force that dictated Anna's choices in life. But not yet. In the early 1880s she was still partly in her previous identity, as a professional educator, author, and speaker. She was offered a job as a teacher in the Berkeley School for boys, on Madison Avenue between 38th and 39th streets, with a five-year contract. She began work in the fall of 1880, boarding for the school year with a German family who spoke no English because, with her characteristic fervor for education, she saw this time in New York as an opportunity to learn as well as teach. Her goal was to become fluent in German. Anna had a successful year at the Berkeley School, the director telling her that the parents "one & all were most enthusiastic about my teaching" (LC, VI C, 4:2). But she missed her family too much and decided to give up the remaining four years of her contract. Avis's second child, Anna Harriet, was born May 11, 1881, and by May 30 Anna was back in Halifax to meet her little namesake.

Anna also had a professional reason for leaving her job. She had once again begun to write for *Youth's Companion,* publishing three articles in 1880. In the spring of 1881, *Youth's Companion* offered her a dream assignment, a trip to Russia, with the journey chronicled in a series of articles in the magazine. The czar of Russia, Alexander II, was killed by a bomb thrown by a Polish nihilist on March 13, 1881. Though Alexander was a moderate reformer who had freed the serfs, he had also harshly suppressed the Poles. They hated him. Even many Russians were dissatisfied with him and wanted faster, more radical reforms. The question many outsiders wanted answered was what the state of Russia was like after the assassination. Were the people really ready for revolution? Or did Alexander III have the nation under control?

For Anna it was another grand adventure. Now almost fifty, she set off in mid-June 1881, through London, Berlin, and East Prussia, entering Russia through Wierzbulow. She traveled all across Russia, visiting Yaroslaf, St. Petersburg, Archangel, Moscow, Ninji, and Kazan, traveling by train and by "wretched little boat." She was the first "Western" woman to make the trip by herself and was "never for a moment lost sight of; gendarmes, spies, police officers, went in & out." She had a fine time, surprising Tartars by bargaining with them in Hindustani for rugs, and visiting churches, mosques, and Muslim schools. Anna occasionally saw what she called "one of the saddest sights I have ever seen." This was a "cage-like wagon guarded by soldiers on horseback, and bound by iron bands, full of human beings on their way to Siberia." The prisoners were young men and women, "exiled for their 'nihilistic' views." She became convinced that "unless some very important reforms are conceded by the Government, there will be in Russia a sudden and violent revolution of the most fearful character, for the greater part of the people are savages still." Anna was gone for four months, returning in October to Halifax.

The period 1881–1882 was a particularly pivotal time for Anna and the people she held dear. James Fields died in 1881 and Mr. Shaw in 1882. The winter of 1881, Frank Cobb, who had truly grown up, won election as a representative to the Massachusetts state house. Also in 1881, after Anna, as she wrote to Avis, made the difficult decision not to bail out Louis by sending him the money to come home but to "let him work out his own independence," Louis took a step toward growing up as well. He gave up on Australia and went back to Siam, where King Chulalongkorn was delighted to see him and promptly appointed him grand master of the horse, "with a salary of eight hundred pounds a year." His new job was to buy horses from Australia to increase the king's cavalry. Although Anna was sorry he had left Australia, the move to Siam would be the making of her son, personally as well as financially. At last Louis was back in the one place where he belonged.

For her part, Anna also faced a pivotal moment in 1882. She was flattered in April, on what was becoming her annual spring lecture tour to the United States, to get an offer from *Youth's Companion* to become one of the magazine's editors. Here was validation at last. She was deeply tempted, understanding that this job would give her professional stability in her journalism career. But the offer placed her professional desires in direct conflict with her personal desires. And because it was an offer that forced her to choose, it turned out to clarify her own direction for the next years. She found herself unable even to consider living in Boston while Avis, Tom, and her grandchildren were in Halifax.

Faced with such a clear choice between family and public career, at fifty-two years old Anna suddenly realized that "my future great work was already begun." Her writing and speaking had to be relegated to an avocation. Her real vocation was to educate her grandchildren. She would stay in Halifax. Her decision was made. It was another turning point in her long life. It was the beginning of the last long major movement of that life, a movement in which Anna would dedicate herself almost completely to her family, to helping Avis and Tom and to raising what would ultimately be her eight grandchildren living under their roof.

FIGURE II. Louis Leonowens. Margaret Landon Papers
(SC-38), Special Collections, Wheaton College.

Anna always found Halifax to be narrow, dull, and staid. She wrote Laura
Johnson in October 1882 "that I felt, when in the midst of a grand party of
all the grandees here, like giving a wild war whoop, and running amuck like
the wild Malays, not because I wanted to kill anyone so much, as because I
was burning to do something desperate, to stir up the cold vapid formalism

and the empty minutiae of a still more empty life" (LC, VI C, 4:2, 29b). Nor was she relieved later that she had controlled the impulse. In keeping with her belief that one should follow one's beliefs, Anna felt that she had done the opposite. She had failed to be true to what she knew was right. She had gone along with the stuffed shirts and acquiesced to their stuffiness. She reported, "I did nothing and have felt humiliated ever since."

But doing nothing was hardly a fair description of Anna's response to Halifax. She condemned this place "where the people know nothing and care less about anything beyond their own little world, and a very little one at that," and told Laura "how much more precious is the thought of that larger and richer life we share at times with you and yours." But she also got busy as a force for change. Anna turned her formidable attention and her enormous energies for educating herself and the world around her to the task of making a good life for the Fyshes and herself. At the public level, she committed herself to making Halifax a more educated place. She set about doing something about the paucity of culture by starting the Pioneer Book Club as a monthly reading and discussion group, and later also started the Shakespeare Club.

For Anna the lesson of living in stultifying Halifax, full of its mean-spirited do's and don'ts, after the stimulations of the great metropolitan centers of her past—Bombay, Singapore, Bangkok, and New York—echoed eerily the lessons of her own childhood. It also echoed the lessons of Tom Fyshe's childhood. For both of them, the way out of a small world was a thorough education. Comparing her years in New York to her present time in Halifax, Anna wrote Laura that "it is an inexpressible blessing to me that there is a new world, a world of real existence, of real ideas, of real individualities, of aggressive thought and aggressive form of government."

Precisely because in Halifax Anna felt "tied up and bandaged from head to foot," she was especially determined that her role was to teach her grandchildren about this "world of real existence, of real ideas," and to provide them with the credentials they would need to enter it. In terms of her family, Anna's commitment was absolute. When she said she would educate Avis and Tom's children, she really meant it. As she had been rescued from a limited life by knowledge, so too would be the generations of her family who came after. She dedicated most of the next twenty-five years of her life to making sure of just that.

In the spring of 1883, the Fyshe family moved to a "nice old fashioned, rambling cottage" called Sunnyside, with grounds that "reach some two miles into the woods" outside Halifax. They settled in to a domestic existence, albeit with some important excursions, for the next fourteen years. A third child, Thomas Maxwell, was born September 7, 1883. One of the Wilkinson girls, Lizzie Avice, now Mrs. Harry Moore, moved to Ontario in 1884, but did not get to Halifax. That spring Anna did another lecture tour and visited her good friends in Boston, Philadelphia, New York, and Staten Island.

Anna had found time between her return from Russia and settling at Sunnyside to write a third book. In May 1884, she dropped off the finished manuscript at Porter & Coates in Philadelphia, which would be the sole American publisher of the book later that year. It would come out in London under Trubner & Co. This book was different from the first two in that it was not based on her time in Siam. *Life and Travel in India: Being Recollections of a Journey before the Days of Railroads* purported to be a memoir of Anna's travel experiences as a proper young lady in India when she was sent out there from England to join her mother and stepfather as a girl of fifteen. It invoked all the usual lies about Anna's upper-class origins and upbringing, complete with coy accounts of her dainty shock at encountering India and descriptions of the life of the wealthiest British in India.

Life and Travel was in fact a tribute to the places and the peoples of Anna's homeland, though cast in the framework of the extensive genre of British women's travel literature. What is unusual about Anna's use of the conventions of that genre is that her descriptions were so often positive. One section of the book offered a long paean to the Western Ghats and the Deccan Plateau, noting that "no artist, however gifted, no pencil, however matchless, can catch and transfer to canvas the entrancing beauties of the views as seen from the top of the Bohr Ghauts" (213). Anna's praise was not reserved only for the scenery. In the same section, she commented on the good nature of some naked Hindu children at play and on the religious seriousness of the Brahmin guides.

Then there was Poona, which, Anna assured her readers, was a picturesque town full of fascinating history and streets "far more Oriental" than even Bombay. She offered an account of the many people who thronged the streets:

> The sedate and white-robed Brahmin; the handsome Hindoo; the refined and delicate Hindoo woman in her flowing graceful saree and red sandals (for in this city Mohammedan influence has not yet reached the point which it has in other parts of India, and the women are not cooped up in harems but are everywhere in the streets, temples, and bazaars); the pompously-dressed Musulman, Arab, and Mahratta horsemen completely armed, prancing along

on their splendid chargers; . . . emaciated devotees, fakers, and mendicants of all denominations, some wholly nude, others clothed in the skins of wild beasts, and yet others covered with dust and paint and ashes of cow-ordure; fat lazy-looking Brahmanee bulls; Jews, Parsees, native Portuguese Christians, and occasionally a British Mahratta sepoy in his neat undress Uniform. (219–20)

Anna even threw in the "additional fascination" of elephants in the streets.

Anna was explicit in mentioning some of the places important to her while she was growing up in Poona. She praised the Sanskrit College, which produced "men of very great learning" who could "hold their own" with "some of the greatest scholars in England, France, or Germany" (225). She admired the "European portion" of the city, with its "handsome barracks for the European soldiers, bungalows for their commanding officers, a hospital, a lunatic asylum, a pretty little church with reading-room and library adjoining" (226). Anna concluded by describing a drive in "Poonah at night." It seemed, she wrote, "like passing through some fairy scene filled with the thousand and one pictures of the Arabian Nights" (227). Anna did her best for the beloved city of her childhood, writing a virtual hymn to its charms. This is what you could see, she seemed to say to her Western audience, if you would only look.

Life and Travel also reconstructed the life of the British upper class in Bombay, all the while presenting it as Anna's own past. She claimed to have lived with her new British officer husband in the "Aviary," a lovely villa in the exclusive Malabar Hills with "numerous servants" (43). There she claimed to have attended those elegant dinner parties the wealthy British in India were so fond of. But as she imagined one dinner she was supposed to have attended, she could not quite keep her imagination in check. She could not help also picturing the servants at the dinner, with their "dark, restless eyes watching every turn, motion and expression of our faces." No one else seemed to notice "those dark, silent, stationary figures any more than if they had been hewn out of stone." But Anna, quite unlike lady travelers really from England in their published accounts of actually visiting India, did. She specifically imagined that the dinner conversation was about the "exaltation of British power and British supremacy," and how best to govern India. And in case we missed the point of juxtaposing in this passage the noisy, unaware British diners with the silent, alert Indians, she offered an authorial comment to make it clear. She felt, she wrote, that "it was a very solemn affair for the Briton to be in India luxuriating on her soil and on her spoils" (35).

That startling moment in the narrative reflected Anna's lifelong dislike of imperialism and commitment to the rights of local peoples. Her sympathies were always with those she saw as compelled, whether by force or tradition, to render their lives subservient to others: the natives in India and Canada, the slaves in America, the women of Nang Harm in Siam, and the serfs and imprisoned radicals in Russia. It is easy enough to guess that her early life as lower class and mixed race had given Anna a strong sense of the injustices of social, economic, and racial categories. We need also to see that when Anna grew up, her early insights enlarged into a much stronger and more general commitment to justice and equality, in actions as well as in ideas. For her the key to measuring a person's value was not class or race or nationality or gender but what Martin Luther King in the twentieth century would so eloquently call "the content of their character."

After Anna delivered her manuscript in May 1884, she did not return straight home, because she had learned that Prince Krita, Sonklin's son, now Prince Nares and minister of foreign affairs, was about to visit New York. Anna wrote Avis a glowing account of the reunion in a Fifth Avenue hotel on May 19. They had not seen each other for seventeen years. Krita "embraced me just as he used to do when a little boy. I was quite overcome with joy." Anna was thrilled that her dear old friend's son was doing so well. Krita told her a great deal about his mother and also about Louis, whom he said was "doing good work and making himself useful to the King in every way" and was now fluent in reading as well as speaking Siamese. He also told her that Siam was much changed, modernized, with "prostration, slavery, imprisonment of wife or child for the husband or father's debts" all abolished. It was a wonderful and loving moment for them both, invoking for Anna the best feelings of her time in Siam and reminding her that her years there had provided warm memories for others as well as for herself.

During the next four years, from 1884 to 1888, Anna dedicated herself to life at Sunnyside, teaching James and Anna at home in a little school, helping to run the household, and looking after Max. On April 22, 1886, a fourth child, Avis Selina, was born. Anna found herself, as she put it to Avis away on a vacation, "very busy with this large house and farm, three little children, cows, horses, & domestics," "busy from morning to night." These were happy years. As she wrote Annie Fields, the children were "blooming like ripe peaches" (F, 4/10/85). But Anna did not just stay home. She made occasional trips to lecture and visit her dear friends in the United States and kept up with her own correspondence and writing. She wrote four articles for a Boston magazine, *Wide Awake,* which became the basis for her fourth book.

FIGURE 12. *Mrs. Anna H. Leonowens, Montreal, QC, 1903.* William Notman & Son, 1903; silver salts on glass, gelatin dry plate process; 17.8 cm×12.7 cm; purchase from Associated Screen News Ltd., II-148671. Notman Photographic Archives, McCord Museum, Montreal.

Aptly titled *Our Asiatic Cousins* in order to emphasize her belief in the equal status of all people and their fundamental relatedness, it was published in Boston in 1889 by D. Lothrop.

Anna also attended to the larger world. In Halifax, along with keeping the reading clubs flourishing, she was one of the founders of the Victoria School of Art and Design, still there today as the Nova Scotia College of Art and Design. And she continued to be politically engaged as well. When the rebel Riel was captured and all Halifax seemed to be rejoicing, Anna's acerbic comment was that "from all I can gather, . . . he has been fighting for the natural rights of the Indians and their descendants, which have been hitherto entirely ignored" (LC, VI C, 4:2).

Anna's thinking during these years seems to have become even more pervasively committed to the notion of social and economic equality. She was hopeful that she lived in the time of a "new phase of human history." Moving toward socialism, she believed that private property should be done away with, and instead land should be owned by the government as a representative of all the people. Her wide travels, her lives in various countries, her own background, all seemed to offer her prolific instances of the ways private ownership led to exploitation of the many and enrichment of the few. In the situations of the natives in India and Canada, the debt slaves in Siam, the serfs in Russia, Anna could not but see the ways injustice and inequality were tied to the economic system of capitalism.

Anna wrote Annie Fields that "'The Labour Problem' is still one of deepest interest to us at Sunnyside" (F, 2/6/1887), referring to her horror that "land, railroads, and industries are to a great extent controlled by a few." She wrote again on March 20, talking of the "ever full and overflowing" country life. "And below it all our hearts beat with deepest sympathy with the great labour question. When will man do justice to his fellow man?" Anna did not find an optimistic answer to that question. She wrote Annie again on December 12, 1888, "I cannot help feeling very blue over the great question just now," that of nations, particularly the United States, moving away from the concept of private property. A year later, on December 12, 1889, Anna was still discussing this upsetting topic, writing to Annie of the "poor hunger-tossed toiling classes" and hoping for a "great but thorough reform."

In the spring of 1888, the woman about whom a Halifax man is said to have remarked, "what a passion that woman had for education!" began yet another adventure. Anna, Tom, and Avis had been increasingly concerned about schools for the children. Deciding that nothing in Halifax would do, they began to cast about for what would. Boarding schools were expensive, and Anna and Avis agreed that separation was unbearable anyway. That left day schools. With impressive aplomb, they decided to go for the best, in a place where living expenses were quite affordable. In the spring of 1888, Avis and Anna and the four Fyshe children, along with a fifth child, Edith Thomson, packed up and moved to Germany. Tom was "losing the whole family for an indefinite period" (Dow, 99). Anna was fifty-seven, and off to yet another new country.

They rented a nice apartment in Cassel (since 1926, Kassel), a centrally located city on the Fulda River, in the state of Hesse-Nassau. Cassel was an ancient settlement, which was almost totally destroyed in a British bombing raid in 1943. Anna lived there when it was still a beautiful old town. She and Avis settled in and enrolled the two older children in school. Max and little Avis were too young to attend. They settled down happily in this interesting world. Avis went back when she could to visit Tom, and he came over for visits as well. Avis did plan to return to Halifax in the spring of 1890, and the idea was that she would leave Anna and the children to stay on just one more year (F, 12/10/1889). But Anna and the children lived in Cassel from 1888 to 1893, a total of five years, just about as long as she had been in Bangkok.

On the way home, there was a great moment for her. Anna met Louis in London, getting to see her beloved son again at last. They had been apart for nineteen years, and Louis had been back in Siam for twelve. He had metamorphosed from the lost teenager who had fled the United States in 1874. He was thirty-six, a successful businessman, and grief-stricken. Louis had married Caroline Knox, daughter of Prang, a Siamese lady, and Thomas Knox, in 1884. He and Carrie had a teak mansion in the northern town of Raheng and another in Bangkok. Louis became rich supplying teak for the Borneo Company. Sarah Cheek (Dr. Bradley's daughter) wrote Anna that Carrie was "a good wife who is a great help to him and a very nice lady" (Bristowe, 73). They had two children, Thomas George Knox, born March 3, 1888, and Anna Harriet, born November 1, 1890. But Caroline had kidney problems and died May 17, 1893. Louis was very close to his children, but was also convinced that Anna would be best for them. She took them back to Canada. When they sailed, Louis was sobbing as George had to be restrained from climbing over the rails to come back to him (Bristowe, 87). Louis went back to Bangkok, to drink and buy the Oriental Hotel. He sold what Anna called "that incubus of a hotel" five years later in 1898, and in 1899 he married Reta Maclaughlan, of unclear origins (perhaps her name was Katie Butler, and she was probably part Siamese), and began a new happy life in Lampang, Chiengmai, and Bangkok.

The Fyshe family was reunited once again in Halifax by the summer of 1893, along with the two Leonowens children. Also, sometime before the summer of 1896, Tom and Avis had two more children, Kathleen Roberta and their youngest, Francis (Frank). The household at Sunnyside now included eight children. But Anna was comfortable with large numbers. She and Tom and Avis set about the daunting task of educating them all, morally as well as intellectually. Avis and Tom's first daughter and Anna's namesake, Anna Fyshe, published a brief memoir of her grandmother in *Chatelaine* magazine in January 1962, "Anna and I," and addressed Anna's beliefs. She described Anna as "liberal in a world-embracing sense. . . . She taught us that Britain had no moral right to control India, a nation capable of governing itself, nor the right to send missionaries to convert Buddhists and Hindus to Christianity. It would seem to me that Anna Leonowens was a real citizen of the world. She acknowledged no national ties. I never heard her say, 'We British'—it was always 'the British'" (LC, VI C, 4:2, 64). Anna's granddaughter went on to say that for Anna "there existed no racial discrimination. Life in the Far East had taught her tolerance and respect for other nations."

Anna Fyshe did not realize the specific way in which that last statement was true, the ways in which Anna's social and political education came from looking up, not looking down. But her memoir does provide a small window into Anna's ideas. Anna Fyshe emphasized that "Grandmama was not religious in the sense of being a churchgoer; in fact she hardly ever took us to church except to listen to a Bach cantata" (63). She explained that Anna "knew too much of the ideals and beliefs of Oriental religions to place Christianity above other faiths."

Along with Anna's refusal to claim that other faiths were necessarily inferior to Christianity came a profound discomfort with those making such claims. Anna was firmly against proselytizing. "Often she spoke with resentment about missionaries in India trying to convince deeply religious Hindus or Buddhists that Christianity was the only hope of salvation." Anna referred to this herself after her dear friend and ex-missionary Laura Johnson died. As she gently put it to Annie Fields, "there were some points of difference between mine and dear Laura's spiritual outlook" (F, 4/12/1889).

The *Chatelaine* article did somewhat idealize Anna. But Anna Fyshe also offered a fairly rounded view of Anna's personality, emphasizing the real drawbacks of growing up under the influence of Anna's "dedication to the development of the specific gifts of her grandchildren." She described her father and grandmother as "an extraordinary team, though distinctly strenuous to live with," and noted that "our sweet mother" led a serene life "entirely governed by Grandmama's wishes." She recalled that "we children were of such overwhelming importance" that "there was a complete lack of humor in this attitude toward us," and that "we were never allowed to go to other children's houses or parties." Instead, they studied, even in the summers, between four and eight hours a day.

Anna Fyshe's article drew a portrait of Anna during the years in Canada as a socially and politically free-thinking woman, a reformer in her beliefs, and also full of "restless, dynamic energy." She was distinctive looking, and "everyone turned to her when she entered a room," because "there was something regal about her that commanded attention." She was very serious in her conversation, and "her deep-set brown eyes regarded one with intense searching earnestness." She was somewhat tall and wore long dresses, and her wavy grey hair was parted in the middle and "coiled into a pretzel on the top of her head." Anna was never idle, and other people described her as making butter, darning socks, taking the eight children for holidays at the seaside, and learning Italian in her spare time because she had always wanted to.

Anna Fyshe's memoir is invaluable in offering a unique firsthand account of Anna by a person who spent her first twenty years living with her. It also offers what I think is an important clue to the mystery of Anna's phenomenal and virtually single-handed metamorphosis in her youth from a poor army brat to an exceptionally well-educated young woman. How did she make that first leap? Anna Fyshe remembered that Anna was always "reading, writing letters, studying or translating from one into another of the many languages she knew." But "most amazing of all was her extraordinary memory. She could give a clear synopsis of a book she had read thirty or forty years earlier" (LC, VI C, 4:4, 63).

Suddenly we have a glimpse of a teenage girl in Poona, living in a small but highly cosmopolitan city, her low class rendering her fairly free of social constraints and gifted with a photographic memory, who loved books and could devour them and retain their contents. Her memory gave her a facility with words, spoken as well as written. No wonder it was easy for her to learn to read and speak so many languages. No wonder she learned so quickly and so thoroughly that, even for a poor, mixed-race girl, knowledge could bring social and economic freedom and an entrance into a wider world. And no wonder she spent so much of the rest of her life eagerly traveling to and settling in some of the fascinating places in that wider world.

Back in Halifax in 1893, Anna was sixty-one years old. But she still had a lot to do. Along with household work and tutoring the children, she joined

FIGURE 13. Anna Leonowens in old age.
Margaret Landon Papers (SC-38),
Special Collections, Wheaton College.

the Halifax Local Council of Women and in 1895 became president of the newly founded Women's Suffrage Association. Clearly, Anna was not going to let the international women's movement pass her by. Always committed to justice, she fought for the vote, becoming what Lois Yorke referred to as the "most visible and articulate spokesperson" for Halifax feminists during this period *(DCB)*. But her energies as lecturer and author did not simply go to the fight for suffrage. True to her own long-term concerns, she was personally horrified by the dreadful "treatment of female prisoners" (F, 10/24/1896) in the local jails and worked hard to create separate prison cells for women in Halifax.

Then her attention turned back to needs at home. James had started Harvard in September 1896, a success story. Anna Fyshe graduated from Halifax Ladies College in 1897 with a medal for scholarship. And Tom had accepted a wonderful offer to be the general manager of the Merchant's Bank of Canada. The whole family was moving to Montreal. Before the move, in June 1897, the National Council of Women of Canada met in Halifax, and Anna was the highly visible representative of the Halifax branch. Her eloquent and impassioned speeches were a hallmark of her political presence. Promptly after the meetings, Anna and her granddaughter Anna Fyshe, ages sixty-five and sixteen, took off for Germany. They lived there for the next four years. Anna was a pianist, and her grandmother wanted only the best training for her. The rest of the family, now down to six children with Anna gone and James at Harvard, said good-bye to Halifax and settled at 70 McTavish Street in Montreal. Most of them would attend McGill.

Anna and her grandchild went first to London to visit with the Tom Wilkinsons. There, in a wonderful moment for Anna, she had a reunion meeting on August 19 with King Chulalongkorn, who happened to be visiting England. They had not seen each other in thirty years. It was a meeting distinguished by its warm feelings and its civility. Anna Fyshe was present and later wrote that the king "expressed great sorrow that she had pictured his father as a 'wicked old man' in her books. He said 'You made all the world laugh at him, Mem. Why did you do it?' 'Because I had to write the truth,' was the answer" (LC, VI C, 4:3).

Is this account accurate? It is surely slanted in favor of Anna. But it is also surely accurate in recounting that the king challenged Anna about her portrayal of his father. I think we can be certain that Anna felt affection for her old student and that King Chulalongkorn felt affection for his old tutor and the mother of his friend Louis, and yet that, early in the interview, he directly criticized her for sketching his father as she did. At the least, her portrayal of

Siam twenty-five years earlier as so backward must have been politically as well as personally mortifying to him, and must have reverberated in the diplomatic attitudes of Western countries to Siam.

On the other hand, a central reason why Chulalongkorn was a great king was that he saw his country's limitations and had dedicated his reign to modernizing Siam, in its social institutions as well as in practical terms. He was himself a fierce opponent of slavery and one of the most serious critics of Siam's traditional ways. And he had fought hard in his country to change those ways. Much of what Anna deplored, Chulalongkorn also deplored. As an honorable man, he would have long since acknowledged to himself the truth of at least a part of what Anna had written, though feeling also the unfairness of her disrespect to his father in writing as she did. And, of course, Chulalongkorn was a deeply courteous man. The reunion, on both their parts, was almost certainly warm and friendly, and full of talk of Anna's old friends and of how much Siam had changed in the past thirty years. The next day the king sent Anna a gift of one hundred pounds. She wrote back to thank him and to emphasize the "great and unexpected happiness" of seeing him again. For both of them, it was a cordial good-bye.

Anna and Anna settled at 11 Grassi Strasse in Leipzig for the next four years, until the summer of 1901. Young Anna studied piano at the Conservatory and by 1900 had reached the point of being able to give concerts. Her grandmother took three years of advanced Sanskrit classes at Leipzig University with Dr. Ernest Hindrich. Both Annas loved Leipzig, and Anna Fyshe became German in all but nationality. She would return to Leipzig in 1904 after a failed engagement to Laura Johnson's grandson, Templeton. Her father forbade the engagement because the boy "is not earning enough to keep himself," and Anna described him as "a good natured fellow but without a spark of intellect" (F, 1/10/1904). Anna Fyshe then stayed in Germany until she called the Nazis "murderers and gangsters" in 1934 and had to flee, abandoning her second husband, Dr. Schultze. Divorced, she lived all over, including Italy, France, and Bermuda, dying in Berlin on September 1, 1967.

Anna and Anna returned to Canada, but now to Montreal, in the summer of 1901. Almost seventy, Anna took up her Canadian life again, helping Avis with the children, giving public lectures, and visiting the United States to see old friends. James had graduated from Harvard and was in medical school at McGill. Life seemed smooth. Then, in May 1902, her beloved Avis died of food poisoning after a dinner in Toronto with Tom. Avis was forty-seven. Anna wrote to Annie, "She was my all in all" (F, 5/21/1902) and, "The one being who gave my heart its impetus, who made the world dear, and life worth living, is gone, leaving everywhere such a fearful blank" (F, 11/4/1902). Anna's grief was overwhelming, and every member of the family was "left stranded, desolate and broken hearted."

But there were the children. James and Anna were grown. Max was off studying engineering. But the others, Avis, Kathleen, and Frank, along with George and Anna Leonowens, were still at home. Tom buried his grief at the bank and Anna, though the "governing motive of my inner life is gone" (F, 12/28/1904), found herself at age seventy-one in primary charge of five teenagers. She rallied, of course, and made sure they all attended McGill. Still, much of the joy had permanently left Anna's life. Her daughter had been in many ways her dearest love.

There were high points outside of raising children in the years that followed. Anna continued her public involvements, becoming an executive of the Montreal Women's Art Society and a supporter of the Montreal Foundling and Baby Hospital (she became president of the board in 1906). Wonderfully, Louis brought Reta to visit in the summer of 1904. It had been eleven years since he had dropped off George and Anna with their grandmother in London. Anna wrote Annie Fields, now living with Sarah Orne Jewitt, that "George and Anna are growing into interesting young people" (F, 1/10/1904). Reta stayed on for the winter. She needed an operation and also wanted to get to know Louis's family, while he set up the Louis Thomas Leonowens Company, headquartered in London.

Louis and Reta visited Canada once more, in late 1906 or 1907, now keeping homes in both England and Bangkok, with Louis more and more the proper English gentleman. Anna commented to Annie that George and Anna, nineteen and sixteen, were both "unmistakably foreign looking" (F, 1/5/1907). On the Fyshe side, James had long felt the lure of Siam from his grandmother's tales, and he moved to Bangkok as a doctor around 1905 or 1906. He married his college sweetheart, Julia Mattice (Zulu), in Bangkok and honeymooned on the king's yacht. They came back to Canada with their little son, Thomas Gregory, around 1910 or 1911.

Sometime in the spring of 1908, disaster came to the Fyshe household yet again. Thomas Fyshe had a serious stroke. Anna, as always, coped. But she was seventy-six, and having trouble with her eyes. Tom was in a wheelchair and had a nurse, but Anna did what she could to revive him from the stroke. Along with her attention to her family, Anna was still caring about the larger world as well, still writing to Annie about the "evils of large land ownership and wealth in the hands of the few" (F, 1/5/1909).

On November 26, 1911, Tom died, and it seemed that Anna's remaining energy for life died with him. He died on Anna's birthday. She was eighty years old. At some moment that fall, I do not know exactly when but I believe shortly after Tom died, Anna had a stroke herself. It left her blind and mostly confined to bed. It was a particularly terrible fate for a woman who had always burned for action. But Anna lived for another three years. That was long enough for her educational task to be complete. In 1914, the youngest of the eight children in the Fyshe household, Anna Leonowens, graduated from McGill.

After graduation young Anna went for several months to London to stay with her father and Reta. She would come home and marry Richard Monahan and adopt a daughter, Isabella. George Leonowens also married and had two sons, the elder of whom, Louis, married Sylvia Peterson, a Norwegian, and started a coffee plantation in Guatemala. Max Fyshe became an engineer in Calgary, married Olive Bayne, and had a son, Thomas, and a daughter, Olive. Anna Fyshe had two daughters with Ernst Schultze, Anna and Irene. Kathleen Fyshe married Ronald Redpath and had three children, Ronald, Alice, and John. Frank Fyshe died in World War I. And Avis never married. She was subject to epileptic seizures. It was Avis who took over after her grandmother's stroke, looking after her until her death on January 19, 1915. Anna was eighty-three years old. Her daughter was long dead, and her son would die in London in 1919 at only fifty-two, in the terrible flu epidemic after the World War.

Anna's last years were dreary and sad. She had lost many joys, including that of reading. And it must have weighed her spirit to see the beginning of World War I. But this tireless and intense woman had become the matriarch of an extended and productive family. And she had known eight decades full of life. Anna had lived in India in the first half of the nineteenth century, during the great transition phase of the Honourable Company. She had been in Singapore during its time of economic expansion, in Siam during the period when its monarch met and engaged the West, in the northeastern United States as the country rebuilt itself into a new nation after the Civil War, in Russia in the unsettled years leading up to the revolution, in Germany as it processed the great political ideas of socialism, and in Canada as that nation moved into the modern times of the twentieth century. She had made her home in many of the exciting cities of the world, in Bombay, Singapore, Bangkok, New York, and even Perth, Leipzig, and Montreal. She had been interested in, had cared about, and had been intellectually engaged in the issues of every one of those places and historical moments. Whatever her limitations or imagination in rewriting the facts, of both her own background and her experiences in Siam, she had truly thought about her world and she had acted on her thoughts. In re-creating herself, Anna had opened up for herself the richest engagement with the possibilities of her life. She had actively embraced those possibilities, with energy, brilliance, and verve. Not many of us could do, or could be, more.

FOURTEEN

"Shall We Dance?"

Anna and U.S.-Thai Relations

A situation has developed which is frightening,
especially so to historians, namely, that a musical film
based on a novel, which was made for commercial
purposes, should have been able to alter history in the
minds of hundreds of millions of people.

PRINCE CHULA
Chakrabongse, Lords of Life

ALTHOUGH ANNA DID ACHIEVE SOME FAME during her lifetime, she did not really "live," with all the media pizzazz attached to that term, until she had been dead for some thirty years. Anna came back to life in May 1944 as the heroine of Margaret Landon's runaway bestseller, *Anna and the King.* Her resurrection has turned out to be phenomenal, in both its impact and its longevity. That resurrection is going on even now. At the beginning of this millennium yet another actress—this time, Jodi Foster—was seduced by the chance to play Anna, almost one hundred years after Anna's death and well over fifty years since Margaret Landon's book about Anna's life first thrilled the American public.

Anna would have been delighted with her resurrection as the well-born and gently bred English lady of Margaret Landon's book. Landon's Anna was the very gentlewoman whom Anna, so long ago in Singapore, had envisioned and then declared herself to be. Margaret read Anna's books and was entranced by what she saw as the nobility of Anna's experiences. Margaret then invented an identity and a life for Anna that, to Margaret's surprise, transformed this long-dead woman into a major icon of twentieth-century American culture. Landon's fictional character beautifully justified and even gave accreditation to Anna's lifetime of passing.

FIGURE 14. Margaret Landon, ca. 1931. Margaret Landon Papers (SC-38), Special Collections, Wheaton College.

Anna would have been less delighted with some of the values Margaret had resurrected her in order to defend. It is one of the small ironies of history that Anna was brought back from the dead by a woman who was the spiritual descendant of the American missionary ladies whom Anna had known, and found to be so limited in their proselytizing beliefs, in the 1860s in

Bangkok. Margaret Landon could almost be described as Anna's opposite. She was of Scandinavian origins and had a sheltered upbringing in the American Midwest, a woman of unimpeachable moral principles with the Christian certainty of a missionary—literally. Born Margaret Mortenson on September 7, 1903, in the small farm community of Somers, Wisconsin, she grew up in Evanston, Illinois, where her father worked for Curtis Publishing. Margaret dreamed of going east, to study at Vassar College and become a writer. But her Norwegian and Danish Methodist parents would not even consider Northwestern University, right there in Evanston, never mind such a hotbed of free-thinking women as Vassar. They sent her to a small Christian college northwest of Chicago. A major purpose of Wheaton College was, and is, to train young dedicated Christians to become missionaries to convert the heathen around the world.

At Wheaton, Margaret met Kenneth Perry Landon, a smart and ambitious young man from Meadville, Pennsylvania, who transferred to Wheaton from the University of Cincinnati in 1922, after a year spent studying to be an engineer like his older brother and realizing that he did not like it. Ken did like Wheaton, telling his children "of meeting this gorgeous coed with long blond hair in Greek Smith's office [the registrar] and thinking, 'you know, this place ain't so bad'" (LC, 1 B, 8/30/1993). From then on the two were a couple. Ken graduated in 1924, ahead of Margaret, but the separation did nothing to cool their affection. Ken spent the next three years studying for a bachelor of theology degree at Princeton Theological Seminary. Margaret finished at Wheaton and married Ken on June 16, 1926.

Ken's immediate professional choice was the obvious one. He was ordained in the First Presbyterian Church in Meadville. But part of what had brought Margaret and Ken together was a shared hunger for adventure and a fascination with the larger world. They decided to apply to the Presbyterian Board of Foreign Missions for a post in the Middle East. They were accepted, but with what would prove to be an enormously fortuitous shift in destination. In May 1927, when Margaret was only twenty-three years old and pregnant, they sailed from San Francisco to Siam. The couple served two four-year terms there. The first term, from 1927 to 1931, began with a year of language training in Bangkok. Their first assignment was Nakon Sritamarat, a small town in southern Thailand. The second term was also in southern Thailand, in Trang, where Margaret ran a girls' school.

The pattern of the four-year terms was simple. Margaret stayed home in the small towns in which their missions were located, looking after her own children and teaching. Ken was assigned "the most difficult work, touring

FIGURE 15. Kenneth Landon, ca. 1931. Margaret Landon Papers (SC-38), Special Collections, Wheaton College.

evangelism" (LC, VI C, "Anna and I"), traveling throughout southern Siam by car, by elephant, by boat, and on foot. He was frequently gone for weeks at a time. Ken was the model missionary, unquestioningly believing that to be a Christian meant to know the one true way to salvation and therefore to have an obligation to proselytize. He wrote to Margaret from Bandon of God's message to Ezekiel to tell his word plainly, reminding her that "if we don't give the message then God demands their blood at our hands." He "flooded" the region with books of Luke and wrote to Margaret that his preaching "pulled down idols and set before them a spiritual way of salvation" (LC, I B, 2/3/1929).

Margaret and Ken's work in Siam was part of a long, and generally not admirable, history of attempts to impose Western religious beliefs on Eastern peoples. The Presbyterian Board alone had been sending missions to "go forth to war" in Siam since 1840 (Ken writing to Margaret, Aug. 25, 1929). The Landons in the twentieth century continued the American missionary tradition of the Bradleys, the Mattoons, and the Johnsons in the nineteenth century. Indeed, the Mattoons had been sent by the same Presbyterian Board that sent the Landons. In the intervening years the board had sent out many other Americans, including the McGilvarys, Samuel McFarland, Dr. and Mrs. Dunlop, and Lott and Jessie Hartzell (Jessie was actually Canadian). The Landons were the latest in this long line of determined Christian soldiers who never doubted that Christianity was the true religion and that Christ himself "became a missionary from a home of ease in heaven" (LC, 1 B, letter to Margaret, July 23, 1932).

All these American missionaries, Ken and Margaret Landon quite as much as their nineteenth-century and earlier twentieth-century predecessors, fervently believed in the inferiority of Eastern religions. Christianity was the truth and all others, including Buddhism, were false. Their letters and memoirs are full of comments about the Siamese as heathens or, at least as often and more benignly, about them as children, needing to be led, whom Ken referred to as "the common people . . . held by the simple Bible stories" (LC, 1 B, Jan. 21, 1929). Many missionaries loved Siam and found many aspects of Siamese culture uplifting and noble. Yet they shared a blind certainty that, as servants of the Christian god and the Presbyterian Mission Board, their way was the best way. Proselytizing required, as a fundamental principle, the belief that they were the ones who held the truth.

In general, American missionaries did not do well at converting the Siamese. Though the missionaries actually paid their converts, those whom Jessie Hartzell worriedly referred to as "rice Christians" (xvi), they had few takers. Siam was a stable culture with a long and distinguished religious tradition in Thai Buddhism. In the twentieth century as in the nineteenth, the missionaries never seemed to accept the point King Mongkut made so clearly in an early letter to Anna, that "the followers of Buddha are mostly aware of the powerfulness of truth and virtue as well as the followers of Christ" (LC, VI C, 4).

On the other hand, the missionary contribution in Siam was positive and profound. Most of the Americans were medical missionaries, like Dr. Dan Bradley. They became fluent in the local languages, and they worked hard to provide health care and to teach Western hygiene concepts to the local population. The board had also charged them to found schools and teach children, girls as well as boys, to read and write in the local languages. The American missionaries were an integral and often productive part of the process of changing the cultural landscape of Siam over the second half of the nineteenth century and on into the twentieth.

It was absolutely traditional that while Ken was a traveling preacher Margaret stayed home and ran a little Christian school. For his part, Ken did have some little success with his eight years of conversion efforts, though not with Siamese Buddhists. After the time of the American missions in the nineteenth century, great numbers of poor Chinese laborers immigrated to Siam looking for work. Ken did convert some of these more recent settlers. It became a sort of proselytizing specialty with him. Ultimately he set up six small Christian missions with Chinese members in Siam.

In 1932, after the first four-year term, the Foreign Missions board granted the young couple a year's furlough. Ken used that year to get a master's degree at the University of Chicago. Their second term as missionaries in Thailand was from 1933 to 1937, followed by a second one-year furlough, during which Ken, with breathtaking intensity, completed all the work toward a doctorate in theology at the University of Chicago. While Ken wrote his dissertation, Margaret looked after their three children and found the time to take evening courses at the Medill School of Journalism at Northwestern University.

Sometime during that second term, probably at least 1933, Margaret took the train from Trang across southern Siam ninety miles to Nakon Sritamarat to visit Mr. and Mrs. Bruce McDaniel, a missionary doctor and nurse. Here is her account in "Anna and I":

One morning as they were about to leave for the leper asylum that they had founded Dr. McDaniel reached into his bookcase with its three sections and locked doors. Searching with his hand behind a row of dun-colored books, he brought out a book with a brown cover. The title was *The English Governess at the Siamese Court,* by Anna Harriette Leonowens.

As he handed it to me, he said, "Now here's something you ought to read. The Siamese government did everything in its power to keep it from being published. I've been told they even tried to buy up the whole edition to prevent its distribution. In fact, there's been so much feeling against the book that I still keep my copy out of sight, just to be on the safe side and not offend my Siamese friends."

With that, he and Mrs. McDaniel left on their morning rounds, and I sat down on their veranda, opened the faded covers and began at the first line. Almost at once the present dissolved, and I moved back into a glittering world out of the *Arabian Nights,* a world that had passed forever, even in Siam. I literally knew nothing until the McDaniels pried me from between its covers at noon. (11)

Dr. McDaniel then offered her another of Leonowens's books, *The Romance of the Harem,* which Margaret also "devoured."

Margaret never forgot reading the story "that hot morning on the McDaniel's veranda." She told her audiences that she found the book not only "wildly exciting" but also "completely real." She saw no discrepancy between her sense of "real" and her sense of being in a "glittering world out of the *Arabian Nights.*" The familiar clichés recounting the imperial myth of the white man's burden are unmistakable in her account. There are the noble and hardworking missionaries, off to their "leper asylum," the repressive Siamese authorities who did "everything" in their power to block publication (does this refer to Mr. Mason at the Siamese Embassy in London complaining to Anna's nephew?), the book of truth disguised in a "brown cover" and hidden "to be on the safe side," yet brought out to expose the real Siam to an open-minded audience, all cast in an East/West dichotomy between the Siamese trying to bury the truth and the Americans bravely bringing it to light.

In 1938, at the end of their second furlough, the Landons resigned from the mission. It was time to try a different path. With a doctorate from a distinguished university, Ken went looking for a new future. He thought he had found it as an assistant professor at Earlham College in Richmond, Indiana. Starting in September 1939, Ken spent two pleasant years teaching philosophy and religion, lecturing, studying, and publishing, while Margaret raised the children in the role of a faculty wife and started writing her first book.

Quite by accident, in 1938 she had been delighted to find a used copy of *The Romance of the Harem* at the Economy Bookstore in Chicago and two months later a copy of *The English Governess* at the Marshall Field & Company sale. At last she had her own copies of Anna's fascinating books. Then in 1939 "an even more amazing thing happened." At a luncheon for ministers in Evanston, Ken was approached by Dean Grattan Moore of St. Luke's Cathedral. Dean Moore told Ken, "Our family has had a long-time interest in Siam. My mother had a very dear friend, the wife of a cousin really, who once lived in Siam. Mother often talks about Aunt Annie and the letters she used to write from Siam" (LC, "Anna and I," 15). Ken had stumbled across someone who had actually known Anna.

When Ken and Margaret went to visit Dean Moore's mother, she turned out to be Lizzie Avice, one of the Wilkinson daughters, who married Reverend Moore and immigrated to Ontario in the 1880s. Lizzie never saw Anna in Canada. But though she was ninety-three in 1939, she told the Landons that she "remembered vividly the day in 1867 when Anna Leonowens had appeared in the family home in Enniscorthy, Ireland, wearing a diamond belt buckle that the King of Siam had given her" (16). Lizzie Moore also recollected that, as Margaret put it, "in that quiet Irish home Anna had seemed to flash and glitter" and the Wilkinsons "had hung on her tales."

The next step in "this incredible turn of events" by which "we met the only people in the United States related to the Leonowens family" was just as amazing. The Moores had kept in touch with their distant relatives, the Fyshes in Montreal. And one of them was coming to visit. In August 1939, Avis Fyshe, Anna's granddaughter, arrived in Evanston to stay with the Moores. She spent a day with Margaret. Avis had been trying to write a biography of her fabulous grandmother. For years she had gathered family letters and other information, and now she had actually begun to write. But it was not going well. At their second meeting, Avis wondered if Margaret would like the typed draft of a biography she herself had already written (well over two hundred pages), which included family letters and, oh yes, a little autobiography that Anna herself had written. And with that she produced "a thick red envelope and a cardboard box containing material she had collected on her grandmother." It was a would-be biographer's dream. Without having done much of anything, Margaret was handed a world of family information about Anna Leonowens, not to mention having the full help of Anna's closest living relative.

All during the Landon family's peaceful existence in their Midwest college world, the larger world outside them was engaged in a terrifying and expanding war. As with the rest of America, their sheltered life could not last. In August 1941, a phone call came from Washington, DC. The United States was not yet officially in World War II, because the Japanese had not yet attacked Pearl Harbor. But they had moved into French Indochina, and some American administrators, rightly predicting the future, were worried about what the Japanese would do next. A new agency called the Office of Coordinator of Information, or OCI (soon to be renamed the OSS and then, after the war, the CIA), was being put together in Washington to gather information about what was happening and might happen in Asia. Colonel William "Wild Bill" Donovan was in charge. He wanted Ken to come for "three weeks" to help. The group was so new that Ken was the fourth employee (LC, "Margaret Landon," eulogy).

The strange fact was that Ken's background turned out to qualify him uniquely for a career he had never prepared for or even considered. From the perspective of Washington bureaucrats, Ken's linguistic and missionary experience for eight years in Thailand, his advanced degrees, and his two books (*Siam in Transition* in 1939 and *The Chinese in Thailand* in 1941) made him an "expert" on Southeast Asia. The government had historically ignored the region as irrelevant to American concerns, although Ulysses S. Grant made a goodwill visit to Bangkok in 1879. Siam did join the Allies in World War I, so a grateful President Wilson granted them full diplomatic status (Sogn, 64). In 1920, officially acknowledging Siamese sovereignty, America gave up its extraterritoriality rights in Siam.

But in early 1941, the U.S. government was suddenly hungry for "experts" on the region. As Kip, Margaret's and Ken's fourth child, said in his eulogy, "this was one of the great turning points in Dad's life, the beginning of his glory years in government" (LC, "Kenneth Landon"). Ken began his third, his longest, and his most influential career, from 1941 to 1965, from 1942 on as one of the top advisors in the Far East section of the State Department.

During the late 1930s and early 1940s, Margaret, herself extraordinarily energetic and self-disciplined, was raising four children and writing her first book, the fictionalized biography of Anna. She began it that fall of 1939 in Richmond, Indiana, and continued throughout the early years of World War II and the family's permanent move to Washington, DC, in September 1942. Happily, there were old consular records and Siamese books in the Library of Congress. Margaret began looking for a publisher during the winter of 1941–42, with only a section done. The first three publishers turned it down. Doubleday noted that the book "was too academically written" and "would have no interest for the American public" (LC, "Anna and I," 19). My favorite was the publisher who suggested Margaret "change the locale to China" because "Pearl Buck had made China acceptable" (LC, VI C, 1:1, 3). Margaret's project was rescued by coincidence and Ken. At the founding dinner of the East-West Association, at the Mayflower Hotel in February 1942, "Miss Elsie Weil, managing editor of Asia Magazine, for whom Kenneth had written articles on Siam, was at the same table with Richard J. Walsh, Senior, publisher and editor-in-chief of the John Day Company, Miss Weil's employer." As Margaret put it, "before the evening was over, Kenneth had succeeded in arousing their interest in my book about Anna."

Margaret sent a partially completed manuscript to Mr. Walsh that fall. Miss Weil told her the sequel. "The first reader was a young woman just out of college who scrawled across the manuscript, 'Nothing but a Sunday School story. Send it back.'" But Miss Weil "retrieved it and personally persuaded Mr. Walsh to read it by saying, 'Dick, I believe in this book'" (LC, "Anna and I," 20). After cutting the whole first section of the manuscript on Anna's life before Siam, John Day published *Anna and the King of Siam* in May 1944, and Doubleday published a Literary Guild (book club) edition.

The book, which Margaret explicitly labeled "fictional in form," was a huge success, going into many printings and being published in at least fifteen foreign editions. Apart from the literary value of the book, there are some fairly obvious reasons for its popularity. For American audiences, still lost in the horrors and anxieties of World War II, not geographically sophisticated yet loathing Japan and suspicious of the "East," Margaret's story offered a reassuring respite. The reviews were uniformly clear in treating the book as history rather than fiction and as a tale of West (meaning English and, implicitly, American, *not* European) vanquishing East. The *Atlantic* emphasized that Anna was "heaven-sent" and had "complete integrity" in the face of the "enervating atmosphere of the court." Of course, she triumphed, and the reviewer remarks on the king's "almost childlike penitence" (12/1944). The theme of civilized West versus savage and barbaric but childlike East is repeated again and again in the reviews, in the *New York Herald Tribune* (6/29/1944), the *Boston Daily Globe* (7/13/1944), the *Philadelphia Inquirer* (7/2/1944), the *New York Times* (7/1/1944), and many others.

There have been innumerable adaptations. I mention only the most important three. The movie *Anna and the King of Siam,* produced by Darryl Zanuck and Twentieth-Century Fox and starring Irene Dunne and Rex Harrison, premiered June 20, 1946. It remained fairly close to the book. *Variety* announced that the gross was "tremendous" (Aug. 28), topping one million dollars in the movie's first eight weeks at Radio City Music Hall, and it was selected as one of three Hollywood entries at Cannes. Following the American book reviews, the American movie reviews spoke enthusiastically of Anna as a "plucky rebel" and of "occidental independence in an oriental oligarchy" (*Newsweek,* 6/24/1946). The *New Yorker* reviewer made a similar point, with a bit of irony: "eventually he succumbs to her ideas, and the Siamese become part of the modern world, God help them" (Aug. 6, 1946). As with Anna's own books the previous century, American praise was countered by British scorn. The *Standard* reviewer emphasized what should have been an obvious truth, that "the film can make no claim whatever to being an historical picture" (3/1/1947).

Then came the musical play. *The King and I,* by Rodgers and Hammerstein, starring Gertrude Lawrence and Yul Brynner, opened at the St. James Theatre in New York on March 29, 1951. The musical had major changes from Margaret's book and, in fact, she had sold all her rights to the production, had no say in it, and, to her chagrin, was not even invited to opening night. Margaret, who had been hoping "for a second South Pacific," at first found reading the play "empty" (LC, 1 B, 1/9/1951).

Rodgers and Hammerstein had added several key elements. Their delightfully choreographed sequence in which Anna is introduced to the king's children visualized for American audiences Landon's implicit presentation of the Siamese as both childlike and sweet. Also, they included lyrics, particularly the unforgettable "Shall We Dance," which cleverly insisted on a romantic tension between the king and Anna not present in the dialogue, implying "a heterosexual romance of unconsummated trans-racial love" (Klein, 195). Third, their play-within-a-play sequence, borrowed from *Uncle Tom's Cabin*, Americanized the story of this "English" lady's achievement, so that the issue of slavery was presented not as a shameful time in American history but as something that the civilized United States, from the American Harriet Beecher Stowe by way of the English woman Anna Leonowens, had been teaching barbaric Siam. Finally, the play fulfilled American fantasies of the exotic and erotic East by offering a fabulous visual presentation of the court of Siam and life in a royal harem. Credit was due to the costumes made of real Thai silk from the looms of Jim Thompson in Bangkok. Jim was an ex–OSS chief–turned-businessman who had roomed for a bit with Ken in Thailand after the war (Neher, 46).

The plot changes and the visual delights all combined to create a portrait of Siam and its people as backward and barbaric but nevertheless attractive and charming. They were not really enemies, just in need of Western guidance. They were eminently teachable and to be viewed as too childlike, even in their temper, to be any kind of national threat. American theater audiences could not get enough of this version of themselves and of Siam. In May 1956 the musical play opened as a movie from Twentieth-Century Fox, starring Deborah Kerr and Yul Brynner. The movie musical expanded the Rodgers and Hammerstein version into a national phenomenon. Through the book to the first film to the musical play and film, Margaret became, to her real astonishment, internationally famous. And so did Anna. Perhaps most significantly, the Landon/Rodgers and Hammerstein portrait of Siam sailed unforgettably into American culture and consciousness.

At the same time that Margaret and the media's representation of Siam was shaping unofficial American attitudes, Ken's verbal and written position papers at the CIA were shaping official American policies to Thailand. Ken's first assignment for Donovan was to write a report on Thailand's relations with the Japanese. After a year with Donovan and some time with the Board of Economic Warfare, Ken moved to the State Department as an international relations officer for Southeast Asian affairs. Ken described his role in a letter to Margaret as "the American authority on Thailand" (LC, 1 B, Aug.

27, 1941), and he was considered "the man largely responsible for Thai affairs in the State Department" (Neher, 38). His official role was research and analysis rather than policymaking, but his analyses of the Thais did shape policy.

Ken's political attitude to American-Thai relations during his years at State was a practical variation of his proselytizing attitude during his missionary years. He believed that the Thais needed and to a great extent truly wanted to be guided by the West in general and the United States in particular, which had an obligation to tell them what to do. As Anna had instructed the king and the royal court so long ago, so America would instruct Thailand in the twentieth century. For Ken, the Chakri dynasty's continuing interest in modernizing Thailand, beginning with King Mongkut, meant that the traditional Thai elite were pro-Western. On this last point he was mostly right. On the one hand, he was committed to providing the kind of guidance to the Thais that would lead Thailand to its place under the wing of the United States. On the other hand, he was also committed to defending Thailand; to explaining to and, when necessary, strongly advising his superiors at the State Department that an optimistic paternalism was the appropriate approach to dealing with the Thais.

Ken's unwavering vision of Thailand as pro-Western and his commitment to a benevolent and paternal approach to international relations had its first major challenge in the early years of the war. A military coup had ended the absolute power of the Chakri dynasty in 1932 and Thailand was now governed by its prime minister, Phibun. He disliked the encroaching power of the British and the Americans and plausibly enough believed in regional strength as opposed to toadying to the Western colonial powers that had long plagued the region. Along with many other Thais, Phibun sympathized with the Japanese in World War II. The Japanese moved into Thailand early in the war, in an unopposed takeover that the British and Americans did nothing to stop. Pressed by Japan, on January 25, 1942, Thailand took an official stand and declared war on the Allied powers, including the United States.

Semi Pramoj, the head of the Thai legation in Washington, took the extraordinary step of refusing officially to deliver the Declaration of War to the U.S. government. Ken Landon stepped in to support his decision and became the intermediary between Pramoj and the U.S. government. Ken insisted that the declaration was not really what the Thai people wanted, arguing persuasively both in public and in private that it should be read as a product of Japanese threats and that there was certainly an underground resistance in Thailand that reflected "true" Thai feelings (Neher, 20). Margaret would later get into the act, writing an article for *Asia* magazine in 1944, "Thailand under the Japanese," which also supported the Pramoj/Landon position. The State Department went along with Ken's view and secretly sent a group of what were called "Free Thai" forces into Thailand to find the resistance and get accurate information out. The group was composed of forty Thai students who underwent some intensive OSS training with Ken and Colonel Preston Goodfellow (Sogn, 304). The British sent in their own "Free Thai" team. Basing his narrative on OSS reports, E. Bruce Reynolds noted that many members of both groups were arrested and spent the rest of the war in jail (330).

The truth seems to be that while Thailand was, indeed, an occupied country, the Thais were actually divided in their sympathies. Some, including those from families in a financial position to have traveled abroad, supported the Allies. But a great many Thais were weary of a long history of Western, particularly British and French, condescension and interference, and actively supported Japan. Still, in the United States, Landon had carried his point. Pesky details such as Declarations of War notwithstanding, the American image of the Thais as a freedom-loving people who ultimately looked to the United States to support them had carried the day. The men at the State Department saw themselves as "guardians" of Thai interests (Reynolds, 341).

Ken's second major challenge came just after the war. In December 1945, the State Department sent him to Bangkok with Charles Yost, the man appointed to head the American legation. The two had a round of formal public dinners and private conversations with prominent Thais, including the king and many members of the royal family, and Hugh Bird, British political advisor. Ken "tangled with" Bird, who "pontificated" that the "Thai were on the wrong side" and dismissed Ken's mention of "the Siamese underground" as "nothing." Bird thought that Thailand needed to be brought "down to the economic level of the neighboring countries" (LC, 1 B, letters to Margaret, Nov. 15 and 24, 1945). The British had taken the Thai Declaration of War seriously, saw Thailand as a vanquished enemy, and had never bought the Landon version of Thais as somehow merely childlike and just bullied by the Japanese.

Landon and Yost became convinced that the "punitive policy" being demanded by the British would pervasively damage the Thai economy for decades to come. They actively pressured the American undersecretary of state to insist that the British back down on their ultimatums to the Thais and, directed by the State Department, advised the Thais to delay signing their treaty with the British. Again, Ken was successful in his arguments. The

British, harangued by the Americans, criticized in American newspapers for their harshness, pressed by President Roosevelt, dropped their punitive terms. The moderate Singapore Agreement between Thailand and Britain was signed on January 1, 1946.

Ken Landon remained "the fulcrum figure in Thai-American relations in the late 1940s," a medium for American businessmen trading with or investing in Thailand (Neher, 14). The economic power the English had tried to force on the Thais, Thailand gave willingly to America. Many American businessmen in Thailand, Jim Thompson being but one example, got their start as OSS agents and were friends or acquaintances of Ken (Neher, 47). And in matters economic as well as political, Ken continued as Thailand's active friend in the State Department.

After World War II, greatly facilitated by Ken Landon, the United States and Thailand developed what Daniel Fineman has named "A Special Relationship." Of course, Ken's influence was made possible in large part by factors and circumstances that went far beyond his own practical Christian perspective. Thailand for its part had a military government, which saw an emerging communist China as a serious regional threat. As Ken put it, they "were scared stiff" (LC, 1 B, letter to Margaret, Jan. 25, 1946). The United States agreed that an increasingly powerful China was a growing threat and was committed to developing an "open door" policy with Thailand. That small country, with lots of American public aid ("the primary thrust of America's aid effort [being] security") and lots of American private investment, would stand as a prodemocracy, pro-Western nation in Southeast Asia (Randolph, 26). If necessary, it could be virtually a U.S. base. As Bill Donovan, ambassador to Thailand until the end of 1954, explained in an article in *Fortune* titled "Our Stake in Thailand" in July 1955, "in the cold war struggle for Southeast Asia, the independent kingdom of Thailand . . . is the free world's strongest bastion in Southeast Asia" (quoted by Randolph, 27).

In 1954, the Geneva Conference had divided Vietnam into North and South, a move clearly understood in the region as a communist victory. Encouraged by the State Department, meaning, of course, familiar figures such as Ken Landon and Bill Donovan as well as many others now involved in Southeast Asia affairs, the U.S. response was the 1954 Manila Pact. The pact committed the United States generally to peace in Southeast Asia and created the South East Asia Treaty Organization, SEATO. In a diplomatic move that would have made King Mongkut proud, Thailand had turned to its present-day protector, the United States, to lend its strength against this newest threat to Thai independence.

Siam's policy toward the West, virtually unchanged since even before King Mongkut's time, was to find a balance of power that would protect it from the aggressions of its near and far neighbors. In the nineteenth century the balance was between England and France, and in the twentieth century between the United States and the Vietnamese communist movement. Thus it was quite of a piece with the traditional way of doing things when in 1963 Thailand signed the Special Logistics Agreement Thailand. SLAT allowed the United States, eager for Asian allies in its escalating fight in Vietnam, to build and improve the Thai infrastructure in exchange for using Thailand as a base to fight its war. That included an agreement for U.S. servicemen to take rest and recreation in Thailand, a move that made sense to Americans, who had grown up on Hollywood images of Siam as a land of lovely and docile women, polygamy, and harems.

American public and political sympathy has remained with the Thais, frequently revitalized by reissues of Margaret's 1944 *Anna and the King* and reruns of the 1946 film in which Rex Harrison, though an "oriental despot," charmed American audiences and was handily put in his place by Irene Dunne. But it has been Rodgers and Hammerstein's versions, in 1951 and 1956, that have had by far the most impact on American audiences. Through the musical play and movie, the image of the Siamese as childish, backward, sometimes barbaric, but ultimately exotic, charming, in awe of Western values, and therefore willing to be educated has become entrenched in American popular culture. There have been literally countless revivals of the play, in every state and in numerous countries, as well as a steady stream of reruns of the movie. It is almost impossible to grow up in America without being introduced to the Landon/Hollywood version of Siam. The paternalistic perspective on Thailand that Ken Landon brought to Washington has long since been taken up and supported by many others at the State Department and has guided U.S. relations with Thailand ever since. It may be that "the heritage of beneficent US/Thai relations continues to this day" (Sogn, 539). But as King Mongkut always understood about his relations with the English, it is a heritage based on self-protection, one in which Thailand is always at the mercy of its potentially dangerous "protector."

Kenneth and Margaret Landon both died in 1993, he in August and she in December. Their individual achievements are profound and impressive. Their marriage was an adventurous and productive union. It was also a union of enormous and up to now unacknowledged cultural and political impact. Together, this husband and wife controlled or significantly directed American attitudes to Thailand for several crucial decades of the twentieth century, from the early years of World War II up through the beginnings of American involvement in Vietnam. The Landons as a couple were possibly the most influential arbiters of U.S.-Thai relations in the middle years of the twentieth century. Their shared perspective directed much of both official international policies and American public opinion. From World War II on, this dynamic duo shaped American attitudes and actions toward the Thais, he officially as the groundbreaking "expert" on Thailand inside the OSS and she unofficially as the author of the popular book that, through the lens of Anna's "fictionalized biography," introduced Thailand, which is to say, Margaret and Ken's vision of Thailand, to the American people.

Anna herself would not have shared their vision. Behind the familiar images of Margaret's Anna shocked by the barbarity of bare chests, of Rex Harrison in his ridiculous eye makeup, and Yul Brynner repeating "etcetera, etcetera," and behind the Vietnam news footage of American soldiers enjoying R and R with Thai girls in the bars of Bangkok, stands a different way of seeing Thailand. To catch a glimpse of it we have first to see Anna Leonowens as someone other than the well-bred lady from England, genteel purveyor of Western cultural and moral superiority. We need to see her as the army child from India and the intelligent, self-made woman who struggled all her life in the causes of education, tolerance, and cultural and national equality.

Even though she was long dead at the time, Anna bears some responsibility for the condescending and paternalistic views of Siam perpetrated by the Landons and Hollywood, because of her own fictionalizing about both her time in Siam and her racial and class identity. Anna herself was, after all, the origin of her self-image as a genteel British lady teaching the Siamese a better way. It was Anna's lies that allowed Margaret's successful re-creation of her as a kind of unofficial cultural ambassador from the West.

Still, Anna's ambitions were never merely personal, though that is also true of the Landons. But if Margaret and Ken wanted to "save" other people, to help them, and benevolently to guide them along the right path, Anna wanted to educate them in order to allow them the responsibility for making their own paths. That general purpose had long been at the heart of her educational commitment. Her critiques of Siam were not about how the West should treat the East. They were about how men should treat women, about the immense potential women have if only allowed to develop it freely, and about the equalities that should exist between people everywhere as a natural and spiritual right. Anna's own complex heritage, and her ability to value it, would have made her scornful of the simple hierarchies the American media has invoked about her and about Siam. While she might have been able to imagine herself as a cultural icon, she would not have imagined, would not have wanted to imagine, the political and cultural uses for that icon. We have, to borrow a phrase from Henry James, made a convenience of her.

Anna wrote a letter to Annie Fields in 1885, during the years when she was particularly horrified by the imbalances of land ownership, in which she discussed her dawning hopes for "a new phase of human history." By that she meant a time when different classes, races, religions, and nations saw and treated each other as equally worthy of respect. It would be a time when land and material goods were not owned by the few and kept from the many, when white upper-class and middle-class Christians, be they European, British, or American, would not see themselves as superior to others, and when a country's domestic and international policies would reflect and nurture that sense of respect. That "new phase" has not come to pass. But, at least for this moment, we might stop to admire the extraordinary woman who had the vision to believe that it could.

The Magnificent Charter: How the British Got to India

A Company which carries a sword in one hand, and a ledger in the other, which maintains armies and retails tea, is a contradiction, . . . if it traded with success, would be a prodigy.

Quoted by Peers, 18

In December 1600, in what would prove to be one of the most influential acts in the economic history of Europe, Queen Elizabeth I granted a royal charter to a group of London businessmen. The charter was effectively a license, granting them monopoly control of any kind of trading between England and all the lands from the Cape of Good Hope as far east as Cape Horn. What may strike us now in the early twenty-first century is the enormity of the monopoly they were granted. But early modern merchants saw their enterprise quite differently. They had pressed for such a monopoly because they saw that their own fortunes (as well as England's financial future as, of necessity, an island of traders) lay in setting up and supporting orderly international trade practices. Their goal in pressing for a charter was not monopoly but government oversight. Government authority meant in essence the right to license, which is to say, the right to continuing decisions about who could lay claim to being officially involved in the trade as a "representative" of the Company and what the rules of that representation were.

The idea behind the charter was simple. In terms of international trading practices in the sixteenth century, there had been little profit for the English. In the new markets opening up for Europeans in the East, the English merchants were being shut out. One reason they were failing to compete was that they had been sailing in the wrong direction, and walking in the wrong direction as well, as they repeatedly tried to go east overland. They had wasted their resources for several decades in what turned out to be the geographically foolish commitment to finding a northern land and sea route to China. By 1600, the Portuguese, the Spanish, and the Dutch, who would have their own government-chartered company in 1602, were successfully sending ships to the East, while the English had yet to figure out how to navigate the route. The English were losing the race for the riches of the Eastern trade.

The Londoners had tried, of course. Two trading companies, the Muscovy in the 1550s and the Levant in the 1580s, both committed to combining land and sea routes to bring goods from the East, had been established but had not proved profitable. At least twice British merchants sent small private fleets, wisely attempting to copy the routes of the Dutch. Both ventures ended in disaster, with the ships arriving in the East but never returning. They just vanished, with all their cargoes (Lawson, 14). It was very discouraging to potential investors as well as to merchants. There had been one sterling success. In the 1570s, Sir Francis Drake had sailed the globe for three years in his ship, *Golden Hind,* attacking Spanish galleons and taking their cargoes. He collected such a phenomenal amount of booty that he made fortunes for his backers, which included the Crown. John Maynard Keynes noted that Queen Elizabeth made so much profit that she "paid off out of the proceeds the whole of her foreign debt" and still had more left for new projects (Schweinitz, 43).

But delightful as Drake's success was to his private London backers, to the British government, and to the admiring British public, it remained a limited option. The future of trade could hardly be based on one adventurous captain or on a trading method that was somewhere between nationalistic privateering and plain robbery. Not everyone could just turn pirate. What was needed was a steadier and more predictable approach, one that might actually involve trade. Many London merchants came to believe that what they had not been able to accomplish individually or even in small groups they could do as a differently combined force. Educated as well as galled by Dutch successes, they accepted at last that what they also needed was an all-water route south around the Cape. Instead of each business having to fund its own few ships, a larger group effort supported by the Crown could increase fleet size and would-be investors' confidence. The merchants would be able to finance larger, and therefore safer, fleets to chart a route east by the method of pooling the "risk in the form of joint stock to support a trading venture" (Lawson, 21).

In economic terms, the plan was aimed at nothing less than changing the way investment capitalism worked in the London mercantile community. Unlike the previous trading companies, set up to offer individual projects, all the projects of the company would be funded by many investors. People could invest in "stock" in the company itself. Clearly, the ideas behind this modern investment practice were nationalistic as well as economic, a matter of investing in the future of England.

There were many incentives for foreigners who agreed to do business with the new Company. They could be guaranteed a wide range of merchants and shipowners to take up their goods. As much as the English, they would profit from the benefits of a continuing and regulated trade relationship. The stockholder system guaranteed that the Company would send out trading voyages in the future as well as the present. Perhaps foremost among the benefits would be that these trading partners would gain the protection of a large organization outside themselves that would hold the individual merchants and shipowners with whom they did business accountable for their trade practices. At the very least, they would know where to send their complaints.

The Company turned out to be a sound business idea. And, for a while, it worked. Sending large fleets out meant that they actually got back. Many merchants and traders operating so far from London made enormous profits—much of which they simply kept for themselves as the result of "private" deals—through being licensed by the Company as its trade representatives. But most of those profits also went to making the East India Company a solid business, with a reputation for being one of the most desirable investment opportunities in England.

Nor were all of the traders who got rich freelancing on the side while licensed by the Company British. Late in the seventeenth century, the American-born Yale brothers, Thomas representing the Company in Siam and Elihu as governor of Madras, used their company positions to make enormous fortunes. Thomas operated as a trader in Siam, making successful private trade deals. Elihu used his position and influence in India to invest privately what Thomas gathered up. The profit gathering of these brothers, in an age when private profit gathering was accepted, was so excessive that the Company ultimately censured and fired them both for misusing their positions to acquire personal wealth, though Thomas bore the brunt of the censure. Elihu, at his death, left part of his takings to his old school, His Majesty's College of Connecticut. In 1718, the grateful school trustees marked their donor with a "posthumous respectability" when they renamed the school Yale College in his honor (Keay, 201).

The charter, and the East India Company (EIC) it created, initially set up for fifteen years, was periodically reconsidered and renewed, often with some modifications of its terms, by a majority vote in Parliament. Even from the beginning, the charter included what would turn out to be some particularly notable and, in hindsight, perhaps even astonishing terms. At the time they looked like nothing more than practical legislative attempts to combat the competitive disadvantage the British found themselves in at the beginning of the seventeenth century. First, the charter officially allowed that this "Company of Merchants of London trading into the East Indies" and the traders they licensed might well need to control actual territory in foreign locations. They would need ports for docks or land for trading stations (called factories, because they were managed by company agents called factors), warehouses, and offices.

Second, since the primary goal of this extensive licensing was to promote and ensure regulated and peaceful trade for English businesses, the charter allowed that the group could arm themselves—for the purposes of defense only, of course. They could arm their ships and their employees and make their own laws (such as did not violate the laws of England). In other words, the Company had the blanket permission of its sovereign to fight against whomever it might consider a threat to its business.

The Company's extraordinary rights did not stop here. By the charter renewals of 1661 and 1669, the right to carry arms was recognized explicitly as now meaning the right to recruit a private army and to exercise martial law. The reasoning, again, was simple. These merchants were entitled to protect their increasingly valuable businesses, their ships, and their goods. Thus, in 1600, as a kind of commitment to promoting law and order, to upholding respectable and honorable ways for Englishmen to do business in foreign lands and find strength and profit from uniting against unscrupulous traders among the Dutch, the Portuguese, and the French, and to establishing an internationally competitive and respected British firm, the Company began.

It all sounded so sensible, so moderate and reasonable. It was merely a practical matter to give government sanction to the creation of a corporation that could own territory, have an army, and make its own laws. English merchants joining together could be a force to be reckoned with around the world. From the Crown's perspective also, this was good business. The Company would enrich the Crown. And how convenient it must have appeared that the cost of this national setting out would be paid by private enterprise. Indeed, the cost of containing the various foreign disruptions of and threats to British shipping interests and British international power, as well as keeping British trading practices reputable, would be borne by the shipping interests themselves rather than by the state.

But with all her practical wisdom, Queen Elizabeth could never have imagined the monstrosity her charter made possible. Two and a half centuries after being granted its first charter of trading rights, the EIC had created what must have been the largest Eastern empire the world has ever seen. A firm of merchants had turned itself by government permission into a private kingdom far larger than the largest nations in the world. Its offices, at the East India House on Leadenhall Street in London, were a national and also an international landmark, home of "the Grandest Society of Merchants in the Universe" (Philips, 1). Less grandiloquently but more dangerously, India House was the center of control of territories that extended from the entire subcontinent of India all the way to Hong Kong.

A vast empire was not the only monstrous creation of the EIC. Thanks to the allowances of that infamous charter and its renewals, the Company also created a vast body of soldiers to sustain and often to expand that empire. From the beginning, trade for the English meant armed trade. And business was a matter of war. The Indian subcontinent had already been conquered by foreign invaders at least a century before the British merchants got there. At the opening of the seventeenth century, the northern parts of India were ruled by the emperor, a descendant of Emperor Babur, himself a descendant of Genghis Khan. One hundred years before Queen Elizabeth granted her charter, Babur had "placed my foot in the stirrup of resolution and my hand on the reins of confidence in god," and swept down with his army from the northeast to conquer India (Heathcote, *Military in British India,* 11).

During the first decade of the 1600s, Babur's descendant was the Moghul emperor, Jehangir, whose son would build the Taj Mahal as a mausoleum for a particularly beloved wife. Jehangir ruled India somewhat distantly. Like his father, he had granted exclusive trade agreements to the Portuguese. It took several sea battles in which English ships of the Company beat back Portuguese armies before the emperor took this other European group seriously and granted permission for the English at last to be allowed to land and start to trade. The lesson for the Company of these early trading experiences was clear. The English were not landing in new markets but in ports where the competition was already well settled. Setting up trade was going to be a matter of force.

And how were the Company's servants to tell who their enemies were, as they pushed their way into port after port? Were the enemies their European competitors or the local princes and administrators who were already bound to written trade agreements with those competitors? Again and again, ships licensed by the Company landed after sea battles with the Portuguese and with their guns trained on a port. Whether as a historical accident of specific situations or as a deliberate policy of aggression, or some combination of the two, the Company's chartered mandate of peaceful and negotiated trading agreements was a farce. Those agreements "only succeeded because of its armaments" (Lawson, 28). The right to defend was understood from the beginning as a license to attack.

In spite of the continuous skirmishes to force trade, at the end of the seventeenth century, already one hundred years after the Company's creation, its army remained a paltry affair. Its entire soldiery could still be described as "a few companies of ill-led Europeans retained for the local defence of a few coastal trading stations" (Heathcote, *Military in British India*, 36). The Company relied heavily on the British Navy's ships. But the Company wanted to expand, to move on into the interior, past the enabling reach of British naval guns, to see what there was to buy or to take. And the French were powerful competitors. We tend to forget that the British did not simply walk in and take India. The fight between countries in Europe for control of what were believed as an article of faith to be the vast riches of India went on from the sixteenth century up through almost the middle of the eighteenth. Moreover, the entire history of the European presence in India, from the fifteenth to the twentieth century, is also a history of resistance wars. But history, or at least the official version of history, belongs to the victors. European historians have often not attended to the fact that Indian rulers fought repeatedly against British takeovers.

The question in the 1760s was how to reorganize the Indian Army. The Company came up with a beautiful and insidious plan. In a startling insight into the economic possibilities of an imperial business enterprise, the Company grasped that it did not have to use its profits to pay for its enforcers. No, indeed. The Company's army could be paid for by revenues either collected from the territories that this army had conquered or provided by local rulers as the cost of maintaining troops for the ruler's "protection." The benign rhetoric of this plan was that the Company would just take over tax collection in the various Indian states where it had a presence, in the name of the indigenous ruler of that state. In twentieth-century America this was called a protection racket. This new form of affording an army had major potential. Theoretically, an army so financed could just keep growing, limited only by the revenues of the territories from which the army could collect the money to pay for itself. Shortages of funding could be solved by more takeovers of more places where rulers were declared to need the Company's "help" in collecting taxes. It was an elegant plan. By the end of the 1770s the simple trading company had metamorphosed into a fledgling territorial empire.

The decision, made in London by the Company's directors, to create a standing army paid for locally amounted to an invitation to aggression on the part of the Company's commanders in India. It was virtually a carte blanche to take more and more territories, impose taxes on more and more places, and "protect" more and more local rulers. And the invitation was accepted. It is notable how quickly "the old trading imperatives of the British had been exchanged for autocracy by force of arms and racial condescension" (Lawson, 159). In 1760, the Company had an army of 18,000 men (Lawson, 134). Not quite forty years later, "the army of the East India Company was 73,000 strong" (Singh, 15). In 1805, the army consisted of 154,500 men, and double that, 300,000, by 1820 (Lawson, 134, 152). By the middle of the nineteenth century, less than ninety years after the beginning of its expansion, the Company's Indian Army consisted of some 352,000 men (Mollo, 87).

But the Company's financial problem was that the amount of revenues company officials at home and in India believed could be collected from local rulers and their peoples was hugely overblown. The "exotic East" was not that rich after all. By the beginning of the nineteenth century the "resources that this military machine consumed ensured that the Company could never be profitable" again (Lawson, 147). The more territory the army took to pay for itself, the more it cost to maintain it. In spite of the Company's dreams, the revenues generated by the army never caught up with its expenses. But the army just kept growing, having taken on a life of its own.

By the later decades of the eighteenth century there were two major military forces in Great Britain. One was public and the other private, and each had its own recruitment stations, cadets and training academies, officers and regulations. The British Army or Royal Army belonged to the Crown. The EIC had its own enormous private Indian Army, including infantry, cavalry, artillery and lascars (to maintain the guns), a corps of engineers, and even a small navy, all of them separate from and independent of the British Army. Still, the Indian Army was by law required to be, when requested, at the service of the Crown, and its regiments were routinely borrowed in place of or in addition to British Army regiments in England's aggressive wars around the world. One of its nicknames was "the fire brigade" (Lawson, 145). The Indian Army also fought countless wars in the Company's march to control—and collect taxes from—more and more places and peoples. "The list of wars and expeditions for the years 1813–56 represents an unrelenting advance of military interests under the guise of Company trade and revenue needs" (Lawson, 146).

One of the first of the Company's licensed traders was Sir Thomas Roe, who was sent to the Moghul court in 1615 to negotiate a trade agreement for the Company. He warned the company directors back home in London that they were embarking on a dangerous path with this acquisition. "Lett this be received as a rule that if you will profitt, seek it at sea and in quiett trade for . . . it is an errour to affect garrisons and land wars in India" (Schweinitz, 78). No one listened to Roe. The land grabbing and the increasing losses as potential profits were eaten up by the expense of military aggression characterize the history of the Company. Over two centuries, the Company's army would fight land wars in India, Burma, the Malay Peninsula, the Straits Settlements, and the East Indies, all the way to Hong Kong. Both privately and as a frequently employed weapon of the Crown, the Company's army would become responsible for the destruction of peace and the invasion and takeover of peoples and property across half the globe.

By the beginning of the eighteenth century, the official title of the Company was "The United Company of Merchants of England Trading to the East Indies." The contradictions involved in what this mercantile company had metamorphosed into by the beginning of the nineteenth century are wittily skewered by C. N. Parkinson. He notes that, given the Company's title,

> There would be nothing manifestly reckless in concluding that India House sheltered a body of English merchants trading with India. Nevertheless, such a conclusion would be wrong: the men within were not merchants, and they were not trading with India. One might add, a little unkindly, that they were not always united, and that they were not all Englishmen [the bosses were often Scots and the common soldiers, apart from the natives, as often Irish]. How was the East India Company controlled? By the Government. What was its object? To collect taxes [i.e., revenue]. How was its object attained? By means of a large standing army. What were its employees? Soldiers, mostly; the rest, Civil Servants. Where did it trade to? China. (Keay, 450–51).

What the Company imported to China—though not, of course, from England but rather grown and processed by farmers in India and sold by the Company—was opium. The Company's role was not the middle man, the trader, but rather the agricultural producer.

The opium was grown in India and auctioned in Calcutta. The bales were then carried east on the ships of free traders, to be smuggled into China and sold there illegally (Keay, 455), much as heroin and cocaine are smuggled into the United States today. China protested repeatedly, of course, and by the 1840s finally went to war to stop the smuggling of this dangerous drug into the country. China lost the first Opium War because of the superior firepower of the ships of the Royal Navy. The British terms in the 1842 Treaty of Nanking were to force China to agree to making the opium trade legal, to open up trading ports to the British, and to turn over Hong Kong. This small island right off the coast was perfectly situated for warehouses for opium.

In August 1858, just a few decades shy of three centuries after this monster of a private war machine was first officially created, the charter was officially withdrawn by the government of England through the passing of what was known as the India Act of 1858. This historic moment was the last blow in a process of killing this corporation that had been going on for almost a century. Parliament had already withdrawn monopoly trading rights to absolutely everything except the tea trade with Canton by 1813. From then on "it was private traders that ran fast and loose over the subcontinent" (Lawson, 142). Even the Company's charter for the tea trade was lost in 1833, tea having become much too huge and profitable a market for the already financially weakened Company to keep to itself through staving off its eager competitors. In 1833, the Company officially "lost the right to carry on trade in India or anywhere else," though it still managed the growth and sale of opium, simply as an agricultural activity (Heathcote, *Military in British India,* 72).

The Company had been in financial trouble since the second half of the eighteenth century and had needed on occasion to be bailed out by the government. Its debts were caused a good deal by the enormous expenses involved in maintaining its armies and carrying on wars that were supposed to pay for themselves. But in spite of the Company's mistaken budget projections, its perennial insolvency was not to be the cause of its downfall. The Indian Rebellion of 1857, which the Company and the British insisted on referring to as the "Mutiny," was the final ignominious moment for the Company and the army that had taken so much from so many. The rebellion began in Bengal and started with sepoys in the Native Infantry regiments. But the rebellion was more than military, spreading throughout 1857 to many of the local peoples, who saw themselves as having another significant opportunity to rebel against the oppressions of British occupation. The rebellion failed, crushed by the end of 1857, but not before the rebels had killed some British women and children and the British had responded by killing tens of thousands (Bayly, 194) of local peoples with a startling violence and cruelty. For the peoples of both India and Great Britain, the "Mutiny" was a watershed in their long and troubled relations, probably the single most horrifying event in the history of the British takeover of India.

Given how many sons and brothers and fathers and cousins had served in the Indian Army over three centuries, by the 1850s the British public's attachment to the Indian Army and the Company it worked for extended throughout British society. Though the Company had long since stopped being a good financial investment, it had remained a good social investment. But in spite of jobs and careers for all those young men in want of a future, in spite of the resulting sentimental attachments at home to the very idea of the Company, and in spite of the substantial political clout on the part of the members and supporters of the Indian Army in and out of Parliament, support for the Company was swept away by the British public's shock and outrage at the "Mutiny" of those whom the British had long portrayed as their "own" loyal native soldiers in India.

The extent of the British public's shock at this "Mutiny" and its inability even to understand that it was actually a rebellion, and by no means the first one, either, are measures of how completely the British had used the myth of Indian loyalty to cover up and erase the ugly facts of their presence in India. "The fidelity of the Native Army of India was an established article of faith. . . . Commanded by officers whom he trusted and loved, though of another colour and another creed, there was nothing, it was said, which he would not endure" (Schweinitz, 136). And if the sepoys were not instances of noble fidelity, the British also lost their roles in this particular imperial fable. They were no longer credible as the beloved "sahibs" of their own myths. The falseness of the imperial narrative of good intentions, mutually beneficial trade, and heroic actions was laid bare for all to see at last.

The truth much of the upper-class British public had seen in the rebellion was that many of "their" Indians hated them and had long wished to be free. The 1857 rebellion stripped away the veil of illusion that had obscured the true history of the British presence in India with a happy narrative of mutual acceptance and willing prosperity. At the very center of that illusory narrative had been the East India Company. The British could no longer represent their presence in India through that beloved and traditional seagoing image of "The United Company of Merchants of England Trading to the East Indies." They could no longer portray themselves as essentially "traders," just keeping order for the sake of good business and with the gratitude and blessing of the local inhabitants. The image that had covered the reality of their occupation of India for so long simply vanished.

The truth that so many Englishmen had for so long avoided having to look at was that the British did not trade with India. They occupied India, by force, as nothing better than unwanted foreigners. And without the Company's cultural role of providing the mercantile image that covered over the ugly truth of Britain as military conqueror, there was no political or ideological need left for the Company at all. In fact, the very existence of the East India Company now functioned as an extremely unpleasant reminder of how mistaken the British public's vision of its activities in India had been. Parliament could hardly wait to dissolve it for good.

Not that the British were so shocked by the "Mutiny" as to give up India. They just kept it under a different rubric. By the terms of the India Act of 1858, everything that the East India Company had—the military and naval forces, the lands, the contracts with indigenous leaders ceding rights to the Company—was passed to the control of the British government. At long last, with the help of the rebellion and the public backlash it generated, the vote in Parliament went against keeping any vestige of the hoary institution the Company had become.

The immediate practical result of the dissolution of the Company and the national takeover of its assets was that the government took over not only a subcontinent but a military force already in place to control and administer it. At last, the Crown was able to seize control of the elusive behemoth known as the Indian Army.

That army was now not only under the command of the British Army but, as quickly as possible, merged into it. With all that experience completely under its command, the British government could feel that if ruling India was now a mandate, successfully ruling India was a manageable task. And rule they did. The age of the British Raj, the Indian Empire, had officially begun. On January 1, 1877, Queen Victoria was crowned "Empress of India."

The Women of British India

One must travel to understand Englishness.

GIKANDI, *89*

Long before the first British merchant, Captain Hawkins, reached the Indian west coast at Surat in 1607, the Portuguese were there. The Portuguese soon faced the central social problem that a century and a half later would haunt the next imperial wave of English intruders as well. It was impossible to maintain an army over long periods, to have enough men to hold a city, a region, and even a subcontinent, without women. The king of Portugal, after first experimenting with importing women from home, adopted the obvious solution. The soldiers were commanded to look for liaisons among the indigenous population, a method officially declared to meet with government approval whether the soldiers married the women or not, as long as the offspring of these unions were baptized as Christians (meaning Catholics).

Starting with Captain Hawkins, the English followed the Portuguese example. Hawkins married a person who would come to be called, in one of the many racial euphemisms generated by the British presence in India, a "country-born" girl. His wife, presented to him by the Moghul emperor, Jehangir, was the daughter of one of the emperor's generals, an Armenian, through a union with a local woman (Rodrigues, 127). Captain Hawkins's wife is a perfect example of the kinds of women many British men of status in India did marry. First, most often they were women who were themselves "mixed race," as the offspring of previous unions between Indians and foreigners (usually the Portuguese, but also the Dutch, the French, and many others). Second, at least in the seventeenth century, they were women of good family, bringing as part of their value some sort of political or economic alliance.

The British did not leap immediately into the business of mixed-race marriages. First, like the Portuguese, they tried the import route. But what with passage and room and board, it turned out to be a costly proposition. Moreover, the volunteers were "scandalous to our nation, religion and government" (S. M. Edwardes, *Gazetteer of Bombay City and Island,* 2:62). Just how "low" these women were, even given the near-catastrophic shortage of British women, is seen by a notice placed by the local theater in the *Calcutta Gazette* of February 23, 1797. "A certain person who made her appearance on the first night of the performance is desired to take notice that in future she will not be permitted to remain in the house should she be so ill-advised as to repeat her visit" (Bhatia, 23).

Of the British women in India, most, of course, were of the sort who would not be thrown out of the theater. The problem was simply that until about the third decade of the nineteenth century they were so few. And those few were almost all already married. Wives were of two kinds. There were the very upper echelons, wives of the top officers or of the leading investors or merchants in the civil service, virtually always in India only temporarily. The others were the women who settled in India with their soldier husbands.

After the wives, there was a second, almost infinitesimal, group, the unmarried females sent out to India to find a husband. These included the girls who set out for India single but were already engaged and traveling to meet their fiancés and the girls who became engaged or even married before they landed. A very few were still available when they got off the ship. These young hopefuls were the subject of a malicious poem by Thomas Hood.

> By Pa and ma I'm daily told
> To marry now's the time,
> For though I'm very far from old,
> I'm rather in my prime.
> They say while we have any sun
> We ought to make our hay—
> And India has so hot a one
> I'm going to Bombay. (Bhatia, 32)

Very rarely, the daughters or sisters or cousins sent to India were "old maids" who had failed to snag a husband at home, but almost all were young, anywhere from twelve to sixteen.

Given the extreme shortage of British girls, marriage at thirteen in India was considered optimum, at sixteen already on the edge of too late. In this feverish marriage market, to be seventeen and unmarried was to have an unusually serious flaw. The general attitude was that there was nothing to wait for and every reason to hurry. The intense sun, the frequent diseases, most commonly dysentery, and the general physical difficulties of the life aged women quickly. A planter's wife tearfully reported that her daughter, returning from a trip to England, could only say, "Oh Mother, how ugly you are!" (Bhatia, 30). Unmarried girls, not to mention the men who were courting them, could become ill or die at any moment. Carpe diem was definitely the theme of the marriage mart in British Bombay.

On the other hand, if you were young and British it was easy to look healthy. Health included not only youth but fair skin and, most desired of all, rosy cheeks. As to the rest of a girl's self-presentation, no signs of wealth or mannered elegance were necessary. "A modest garb and mien were all that were required" (Rodrigues, 183). Sophia Goldbourne wrote home that "the attention and court paid me was astonishing. My smile was meaning and my articulation melody" (Bhatia, 32). It was a heady, and extremely short-lived, experience for these unsophisticated teenage girls. In the 1790s and the first two decades of the nineteenth century, a few eligible girls arrived on every ship. They were immediately rushed at: dances were given in their honor and marriages offered, often before a dance began. They were the subjects of extensive gossip. As two sisters wrote of their experiences, "everybody in India knows exactly the number of proposals each young lady has received the day after they were made, and even the exact words used on the occasion" (Bhatia, 22).

The goal of this marriage game was to receive as many proposals as possible so as to choose the best one. That would be from the man who could combine some personal attractiveness with the most possible money. It would be easy to sneer at this, but unfair. Much more than greed was at stake. These girls, young and immature and ignorant as they were, carried a heavy burden of family responsibility. They were sent precisely to find someone to support them, and preferably give financial help to their relatives, particularly siblings, for the rest of their lives. As a friend wrote to the governor of Madras about a young lady named Anne Miller, she sailed for "your parts to make her fortune; her father is a Vigntner an honest man but has many children" (Kincaid, 164). In England at least as much as in India, these women were at the service of their families and dependent on men economically for their survival. They had only one thing of value in this market to sell in exchange for their keep: their youth.

These young women had a duty to aim for someone whose financial assets were greater than the cost of keeping them. They had to figure in the cost of their potential husbands dying as well. A soldier's wife learned a lot about what was called the "splendid misery of life in a red coat," a life reflected in this popular poem:

> I had his children—one, two, three,
> One week I had them safe and sound,
> The next beneath this mangoe tree
> By him in Barracks burying ground. (Bhatia, 24)

The death statistics were at least as frightening for their spouses and children as for the wives.

Apart from the extremely few women deemed unmarriageable and the very few young, fresh, single girls from England, the third group of available British women in India were the widows, often enough still no more than fourteen or fifteen. Even with a baby or two, they were likely to remarry quickly. Men thought nothing of marrying a widow with children, provided she were young enough still to look healthy, in part because, given the very high death rates for the young, odds were the children would not be a financial burden for long. Only the older widows, in their twenties and above, with children to feed or to send home and pay for, were in serious financial jeopardy. And without a man for financial support, they would literally soon be dead.

The men who had first pick of the English girls were the older civil servants of the East India Company, the men with the largest savings or even fortunes. "The merchants and officials were old enough to be sentimental over fresh English complexions and rich enough to be admired" (Rodrigues, 183). They were the best choice, already rich and, on attaining senior status, likely to retire and go home. Unfortunately, many of the single or widowed men who had amassed fortunes tended to take their fortunes back to England to get wives there.

After this first group came the younger or less rich, but still well-off, merchants and the senior military officers. The drawbacks were obvious. Both these groups had much longer to serve in India, so they had much less chance of surviving to return home. Even as survivors, they represented the option of living in India for a long time, a hard choice for teenage girls separated from their own families. But they often had youth and charm on their side, to persuade these barely pubescent girls to choose against security and for romance.

The attention of the girls virtually never went past this second group. No other men could even get near them. As a young lieutenant in the 1830s recalled, "if an unfortunate ensign, or lieutenant, dining at a friend's table, challenges the lady of a rich civilian to a glass of wine, or asks his daughter's hand to a quadrille, his doing so is put down to an act of bold affrontery" (Hervey, *A Soldier of the Company,* 67). A few lieutenants, a very, very few, did marry. About their only chance was a marriage that had been arranged back home. As for the "other ranks," the enlisted men, their possibilities for having British wives also depended on their being able to bring wives and families from back home. It was inconceivable that a single British woman in India would marry an enlisted man. Yet there developed in India one other source of possible marriage material for enlisted men. This was the daughters of the enlisted men who brought their wives and perhaps their families to India or produced families once they were there. There would be fierce competition to charm the daughters of fellow soldiers in any of the ranks.

The acute shortage of British women (a staggering ratio of about fifty women to a thousand men at the beginning of the nineteenth century in Bombay) was not the only obstacle to marrying in the Company's service. That shortage, after all, was no accident, but part of the Company's mercantile plan. The Company had a harsh quota system for marriage in all ranks. Officers required the permission of the commanding officer for "Leave to Marry," which was severely limited. Permission was virtually never given to younger officers. For enlisted men, the Company allowed a maximum of ten men per battalion (per one hundred men) to be married and have their wives with them. In practice it was no more than six. That is six out of a hundred, and even fewer once we factor in the death rates. Since the first stint was for fifteen years, with the choice to reenlist after that in five-year segments, young men who signed up were committing themselves to remaining single for fifteen to twenty years. That seemed easy to boys at sixteen. It looked a lot bleaker at twenty, twenty-five, and thirty.

For the wives and families of the "other ranks," life in India was a matter of extreme poverty. But so were their lives in Britain. If they were left behind when their husbands went to India, as almost all were, their lives were even simpler: with relatives who were themselves too poor to feed a returning adult, without any welfare system or even laws (before 1834) requiring their husbands to support them, and with parishes notorious for refusing to take them in, they starved (Trustram, 51). There are many accounts of East Indiamen sailing away leaving wives of soldiers on the dock, screaming and sobbing as they faced permanent abandonment and financial ruin. With their husbands leaving forever, divorce illegal, and family support not required of soldiers (who had no money anyway), these women lost the only honorable form of supporting themselves, which was through a man. Thus yet another of the many disincentives in recruiting East India Company soldiers was that young women would not marry them. To do so meant almost certain abandonment, probable prostitution, and death. That's a lot for a man to ask.

For lower-class women in India, the wives of the enlisted men, life was about as hard as it had been back home, but probably no worse. But for the middle class and the very few members of the upper class, life in India was better. They had servants who did all the housekeeping, shopping, and cooking. Their laundry was sent out, and there were ayahs to look after the children. In fact, part of the problem for these girls becoming women was how few tasks they were allowed.

> Her day began at five, with a horse ride up to seven in the morning; then a breakfast called "chota hazari" and dressing for visitors who might call between ten and one o'clock in the afternoon, followed by tiffin or lunch. After this a restful siesta, another bath to freshen up and a change of dress to meet the other memsahibs at an interesting gossip session, over a cup of tea. Home again to dress and go out to a party and the whole routine to be repeated the next day. (Rodrigues, 184)

Middle- as well as upper-class women's lives were mainly social.

In 1770 the first tavern opened in Bombay, and by 1800 there was a public assembly hall. There were several dances a week, starting at nine and often going until five A.M. Like the men, the women smoked the hookah and cheroots and also drank what visitors from home constantly reported with horror as vast quantities of beer and wine. Food filled the day, with tiffin often including "every part of a calf on the table at once, nearly half a Bengal sheep, several large dishes of fish, a kid's tongue, fowls, and a long train of etceteras" (Rodrigues, 182). Women suffered from terrible boredom, illnesses, and children's deaths.

The acute scarcity of European women was not a permanent feature of British company life. A radical change began in 1813, when Parliament came out with its new charter renewal for the Company. It opened British India to hundreds of independent shipping firms and merchants, who were not subject to the rules of the East India Company. It also canceled the requirement for company permission to travel to India. This business change was also an immense social change. It destroyed at last the Company's long-cherished policy of blocking British and European women from coming to "their" India. There was an influx of what came to be called the "nonofficial British," hordes of independent traders and women, including the wives, children, and other relatives of these new independent businessmen who could thumb their noses at the restrictions against marriage and women relatives of male employees of the East India Company. Without its monopoly status, the Company was just another private business, one viewed as having particularly harsh rules about its employees' family lives.

The second momentous change in the 1813 Charter Renewal Act was that for the first time British Christian missionaries were allowed into India. The Company had lobbied successfully since 1600 to keep them out, arguing that Christian proselytizing was contrary to the business principles of trade among equals that were the foundation of the Company. From a business point of view, missionaries served only to alienate foreigners and to interfere with the Company's own business arrangements with those foreigners. The Company was right, of course. Still, it is remarkable how long the Company succeeded in keeping the Church of England at bay. With the arrival of Protestant missionaries, along with all the other nonofficials, the tenor of British social life in India would change. And more than just drinking and hookahs would be put aside.

But before that moment, the Company had followed the Portuguese example and supported the obvious solution to the lack of British women. Their employees were to take up with local women. Intermingling with the natives was encouraged as a means of strengthening the Company's hold on the country they more and more occupied. The church was right all along in its suspicions about company morality. The policies that blocked married men from soldiering in India were not antifamily. The Honourable Company was, first of all, a business, and legislating sex just turned out to be a necessary aspect of making money. Company directors recognized that morality as it was defined back in Britain did not fit the economics of profit making in India.

Intermingling with local women had a variety of forms. Marriage was often not the choice of the lowest ranks. There were alliances between the very poor and the very poor, a matter of doing the laundry and sharing a bed for a tent shelter and rice. The woman's family often shared the tent as well. One soldier tells of getting a "wife" for a few months while stationed in Ceylon, desperate for clean cooking "for the sake of his bowels" (McGuffie, 120). The Indian women who lived for a while with ordinary soldiers were often servants with sex thrown in. It was to some extent a question of survival on both sides. None of the parties—the women, their relatives, or the soldier—would have seen much point to taking on the problems and expense of trying for an official and permanent union.

For men above the rank and file, either a mistress or a wife was an option. British visitors commented with some surprise on the mixed quality of Bombay society. In the late 1820s, Bessie Fenton confided to her journal her mortification at discovering that a cousin of hers in the Company's civil service in Calcutta was married to a half-caste, a "natural daughter of" an Englishman. Bessie was shocked, for "we had not the *most remote idea,* and felt very unwilling to be the medium of conveying it to his family, knowing the surprise and disappointment they must feel" (69). Bessie's final point about her cousin's wife reveals her true discomfort: "I had not supposed I had a single connection in the country of that colour which seemed so unfashionable." She referred approvingly to a colonel in one of the Company's European regiments who "will not allow a soldier to marry a native woman, but laments he cannot prevent the officers *disgracing* themselves."

But Bessie Fenton's attitude was not the norm. Captain Williamson, writing of the scarcity of British women in 1810, when Billy Glascott arrived, claimed that "the entire number of European women did not exceed two hundred and fifty" (1:453). Captain Williamson's *East India Vade-Mecum,* a massive two-volume guidebook for the upper classes on traveling to and living in India, discusses in elaborate detail how much a mistress costs (sixty pounds per annum), who she is (nine out of ten are Muslims, the tenth mixed-race Portuguese), and precisely what clothes and jewelry will have to be bought for her. Williamson is perhaps most eloquent in his long discussion of the status of these mistresses. He is at pains to argue that women of the country who are "under the protection" of a European man and regularly consider themselves to be married actually are married, and cannot be considered as prostitutes or concubines. He insists that "a tolerated extension" of the binding licenses required "according to the Mahomedan law" means that both "received opinions, and local peculiarities" direct that there are "traits exempting individuals from being confounded among that mass of prostitution" (1:452).

Tolerance is not at the heart of Williamson's argument for relations with locals. Practicality is. For him, "The case speaks for itself." First, there is the lack of European women. Second, there is the lack of "means" (1:453). Williamson puts the cost of supporting a British woman—in penurious circumstances—at a minimum of three hundred pounds a year, a minimum of six hundred with children, both figures well beyond the salaries of any but the topmost employees of the East India Company. After 1813 and the opening of India, British "morality" would trounce practicality. When a second "revised" edition of the guide was published in 1825, after Captain Williamson's death, the entire section on relations with local women had been excised.

The intermingling system had meant that for people domiciled in India just before and after 1800, to be a "natural daughter" of an Englishman meant not to be a bastard but to be a kind of European. And intermarriage was quite an accepted thing. As Mrs. Postans, who toured India in 1838, described it so succinctly, in the old days "officers married Indo-Britons" (227) and "Bombay officers . . . did not feel it dishonourable to marry Indian women" (208). Nor did the officers of the other two presidencies.

The company plan went beyond allowing, nay, encouraging, mere sexual encounters or cohabitations between company men and local women. The Company was counting on children. Beginning as early as 1684, the directors in London gave explicit instructions on this subject. They allowed, first, that "the soldiers' [British] wives shall come to their Husbands, if they can find means to satisfy, or pay the owners for their passages." This permission, with its financial qualifier, was useful only to the highest levels of company employees. For the rest, the Company gave these directions to its representatives in India: "For such soldiers as are single men, if you could prudently induce them to marry Gentues [locals], in imitation of ye dutch polliticks, and raise from them a stock of protestant mestizees" (Cumming, 148). The advantages of taking up with a "country-born" included a recruitment incentive and a way to keep costs low. The Company could pay little and not offer family allowances, home leaves, or pensions, penny-pinching policies particularly beloved by the directors and repugnant to their employees, if the men followed in Indian ways. Eating curry and rice really was cheaper than trying for potatoes with steak and kidney pie.

There would also be less agitation about the slowness of promotions with the pay raises necessary to allow soldiers to afford the European-style households that British women were believed to find so necessary to their existence in India. And interracial relations significantly lessened the pressure on the Company to accept financial responsibility for the usually destitute widows and orphaned children of all those dead soldiers. The directors also saw familial interconnections with the locals as a direct benefit to trade, establishing social connections and a network of obligations and information. It was to be a kind of extended infiltration policy, with free language lessons besides.

Then there was that "stock of protestant mestizees." The idea was so simple. The Company would "grow," as it were, its own future employees, a "biological residue" of its policies (Dutt, 27). The children were required to be baptized as Christians, and specifically as Protestants, to counteract all that Catholicism the Portuguese had brought. Catholicism was considered foreign, treasonous, anti-British. The children would grow up locally, fluent in English as well as in local languages, grateful to the Company and waiting to serve it as soon as it cared to scoop them up. Local familiarity with India along with a built-in loyalty to the British, easy recruitment, and no transportation expenses: it was an irresistible combination for solving the Company's employment problems. Intermingling would be, from the Company's point of view, a match made in economic heaven.

The Company went a long way to make it happen. Rich merchants and traders and some of the Company's leading officers all took local wives, often from families with some kind of political or social status. They sent their sons to be educated in England, and those sons returned in their own right with good appointments in the Company. The directors also encouraged breeding among the lower levels of their employees by spending money on the idea. During the late seventeenth and early eighteenth centuries, the Company actually paid women who had children by company men. The rate was eight to nine shillings per baby, at the time of their christening in the Protestant religion, with strong encouragement to have more (Dutt, 28).

The official sanction and social dignity attached to these cross-cultural encounters eroded during the late eighteenth century and had vanished by the middle of the nineteenth century. For complex reasons, including a rising racism toward peoples in British colonial possessions, but perhaps most immediately the directors' need to have more plum assignments to bestow on young men in British families in exchange for political support in Parliament, the Company decided to abandon the whole "go local" policy. They were through giving mixed-race people (then called Eurasians) the benefits of being British. In what at the time was a shocking reversal of historical precedent, between 1786 and 1795 the directors made three infamous rulings. They first banned Eurasian children of company fathers from higher education in England (required for upper-level company positions), then banned all Eurasians from being hired by the Company, and finally made the ban retroactive and fired all such people already working for the Company. It was a purge.

The late-eighteenth-century purge of Eurasians from the payroll of the Company radically transformed relations between company men and local women. Important local families lost their incentive to marry their daughters to company employees. The children of such unions were fated to exist in some kind of employment purgatory, never to qualify for either native or European positions. The East India Company, in the dual roles of both private employer and government ruler, had permanently withdrawn its approval from interracial relations and its economic support from the children of those relations.

Billy Glascott lived in Bombay during precisely that blackest interim period between the 1790s and the 1830s, when the East India Company had explicitly turned its back on the mixed-race people whose existence its policies had helped create. But official policies do not completely make reality. The problem for the Company's British employees, both civil and military, which had led to promoting relations with locals in the first place—the sheer lack of British women in India—remained. Moreover, a substantial community of mixed-race, English-speaking people, including their marriageable daughters, now existed in India. Two centuries of interrelations did not just vanish when the Company turned its face away. The Anglo-Indians' history and fortunes were intertwined with the Company, as was their social life. They were linked in loyalty, at the very least because of family backgrounds in which fathers or uncles or grandfathers or great-grandfathers, and usually brothers and male cousins too, had been company men. They were linked in culture, since their "manners, habits and affections would be English" (Abel, 13). And they were linked in religion, since the Company had long required that the mixed-race children of its employees be baptized as (Church of England) Christians.

Barring Anglo-Indians from jobs began what would be an uneven legal history for Anglo-Indians under company and British government rule. During major wars, they would be called back to serve with the Company, under penalty of being charged with treason if they did not, only to be fired again as the wars ended and so did the extra appointments. In 1830, a delegation from these Eurasians, named then

East Indians, presented a petition to Parliament. In 1833, the Company again officially allowed persons of any race to hold appointments. After that, Anglo-Indians, because their mother language was English, were hired for midlevel appointments as clerks in government services: the railroads and telegraph and customs offices.

Anglo-Indians had a visible social presence as part of British life all through the eighteenth and nineteenth centuries in Bombay. But the official sanction and social dignity attached to these cross-cultural sexual encounters in the seventeenth century had eroded by the eighteenth century and vanished by the mid-nineteenth century, in both British and Indian attitudes. In the first half of the twentieth century, in the context of ongoing struggles for independence, racial stereotypes reigned. From the British side, we heard that "Physically the Eurasians are slight and weak. They are naturally indolent" (quoted in Gist and Wright, 45). The European assumption was that "there is nothing that the Anglo-Indian deplores more than his dark skin. He would give anything in the world to see his daughter married to a low vulgar European and to be ill-treated afterwards than see her marry one of her own kind" (Gaikwad, 44). And from a nationalistic Indian pamphlet from Bombay in 1946, when the question was what to do with these people who were neither British nor Indian: "Let them go back to where they have always wanted to be: in the arms of white soldiers and licking the jack boots of imperialism. . . . [They are] traitors to the very core of their halfcaste hearts" (Gist and Wright, 44).

In 1911 came the legal creation of a third "race," though referred to as the Community, with a capital C. After three hundred years of using terms such as *half-caste, Luso-Indian, Eurasian, Indo-Briton, East-Indian,* and *country-born,* the British viceroy of India finally acceded to the pressures from Anglo-Indian groups. He officially created the Anglo-Indians as a race through the act of legally granting them the name *Anglo-Indian.* The 1935 India Act spelled out, and the 1949 Constitution affirmed, that Anglo-Indians were to be guaranteed an existence as a third race through a quota system that operated in education, in employment, and—most important in an independent India from 1949 on—in seats in the legislative assembly. These quotas would end by 1960, but in the private sector the Anglo-Indian Community, in its social organizations, private schools, journals, and newspapers, continued to exist for at least another twenty years.

Although the Anglo-Indian Community apparently still exists as a cultural group in India, its special legal status has long since vanished. To a great extent its twin fates have been exodus—as an estimated fifty thousand Anglo-Indians left India after Independence—and assimilation (Gist and Wright, 20). Its colonial history as a race—tied to the history of the East India Company's efforts first to dominate and then to rule the Indian subcontinent—is over.

SELECT BIBLIOGRAPHY

BIBLIOGRAPHIC ABBREVIATIONS USED IN THE TEXT

F   James Thomas Fields Papers, Huntington Library
LC   Margaret and Kenneth Landon Papers, Buswell
           Memorial Library, Wheaton College

UNPUBLISHED AND ARCHIVAL SOURCES

Anna Leonowens Letters. New York City Public Library, New York.

Bonneau, Marlene. "Anna of Montreal." Typescript of McCord Museum lecture, April 3, 2001, Montreal.

Bradley, Dan Beach. "Abstract of the Journal of Rev. Dan Beach Bradley, M.D., Medical Missionary in Siam, 1835–1873. Transcribed MS. by Dan F. Bradley." Wason/Echols Collection, Cornell University, Ithaca, NY.

Colonial Secretary's Office Records, 1854–1857. State Records Office, Perth, Western Australia.

Devon Non-Parochial Registers, Hatherleigh Parish Registers, Census of 1841. Devon Record Office, Exeter, England.

East India Company Records. Oriental and India Office Collection (now Asia, Pacific, and Africa Collections), British Library, London.

Government Archives, State of Mumbai. Elphinstone College, Mumbai, India.

Great Britain, Foreign Office in Siam. Correspondence, 1867–1948. Microfilm. Kew, Richmond, Surrey: Public Record Office, 1984.

The Inquirer: A Western Australian Journal of Politics and Literature. 1853–1857. Microfilm. Battye Library, State Library of Western Australia, Perth.

James Thomas Fields Papers. Huntington Library, San Marino, CA.

John C. Shaw Private Papers. Chiengmai, Thailand.

Kepner, Susan Filop. "Anna and the Context of Siam." Unpublished paper. University of California, Berkeley, May 1995.

Kislenko, Arne. "Bamboo in the Wind: United States Foreign Policy and Thailand during the Kennedy and Johnson Administrations, 1961–69." Ph.D. diss., University of Toronto, 2000.

Koompirochana, Vikrom. "Siam in British Foreign Policy, 1855–1938: The Acquisition and Relinquishment of British Extraterritorial Rights." Ph.D. diss., Michigan State University, 1972.

Lilley, Ian, and Martin Gibbs. "An Archeological Study of the Lynton Convict Hiring Depot." Unpublished paper, 1993. Battye Library, State Library of Western Australia, Perth.

Lloyds Register of Shipping. Guildhall Library, London.

Margaret and Kenneth Landon Papers. Buswell Memorial Library, Wheaton College, Wheaton, IL.

McFarland Collection. University of California, Berkeley.

Mechanics' Institute Minutes, 1853–1856. Perth Literary Institute Records, Battye Library, State Library of Western Australia, Perth.

Neher, Arlene Becker. "Prelude to Alliance: The Expansion of American Economic Interest in Thailand during the 1940s." Ph.D. diss., Northern Illinois University, 1980.

Parish Registers. St. Thomas Cathedral, Bombay (reviewed for me by a church official).

Photograph Album of Siam. Division of Rare and Manuscript Collections, Cornell University, Ithaca, NY.

Rundle, D. C. "The History of Port Gregory." Unpublished and undated paper. Battye Library, State Library of Western Australia, Perth.

Singapore Straits Times. 1850–1868. Microfilm. National Library of Singapore.

Singapore Straits Times. 1852–1868. Microfilm. Wason/Echols Collection, Cornell University, Ithaca, NY.

Sogn, Richard Randolph. "Successful Journey: A History of United States–Thai Relations, 1932–1945." Ph.D. diss., University of Michigan, 1990.

Soonthornrojana, Adulyasak. "Thai-American Relations 1945–1955: The Road to U.S. Commitment." M.A. thesis, University of Akron, 1982.

Subwattana, Thaveesilp. "The United States and Thailand, 1833–1940." Ph.D. diss., Illinois State University, 1987.

United States Consulate in Bangkok. *Records, 1856–1912.* Washington: National Archives and Records Service, 1960. Microfilm.

Western Australia Registry of Births. Registrar General, Perth.

PUBLISHED SOURCES

Abel, Evelyn. *The Anglo-Indian Community: Survival in India.* Delhi: Chanakya Publications, 1988.

Albuquerque, Teresa. *Bombay, a History.* New Delhi: Rashna, 1922.

Aldrich, Richard J. *The Key to the South: Britain, the United States, and Thailand during the Approach of the Pacific War, 1929–1942.* Kuala Lumpur: Oxford University Press, 1993.

Alexander, M. Jacqui, and Chandra Talpade Mohanty, eds. *Feminist Geneologies, Colonial Legacies, Democratic Futures.* New York: Routledge, 1997.

Allen, Charles, ed. *Plain Tales from the Raj.* New York: Holt, Rinehart and Winston, 1975.

Altink, Sietske. *Stolen Lives: Trading Women into Sex and Slavery.* Binghamton, N.Y.: Haworth Press, 1996.

Anderson, Philip. *The English in Western India; Being the Early History of the Factory at Surat, of Bombay, and the Subordinate Factories on the Western Coast.* Bombay: Smith, Taylor, 1854.

Anglo-India: Social, Moral and Political; Being a Collection of Papers from the Asiatic Journal. London: W. H. Allen, 1938.

Anon. "A Comparative View of the Plans of Education of Dr. Bell and Mr. Lancaster, and Remarks on Dr. Bell's Madras School." *Quarterly Review* 6 (October 1811): 264–275.

Anon. "The East India Community." *Calcutta Review* 9 (January–June 1849): 73–90.

Anon. *Life in Bombay, and the Neighboring Outstations.* London: Richard Bentley, 1852.

Anthony, Frank. *Britain's Betrayal in India: The Story of the Anglo-Indian Community.* Bombay: Allied Publishers, 1969.

Archer, Mildred. *Early Views of India: The Picturesque Journeys of Thomas and William Daniell, 1786–1794.* London: Thames and Hudson, 1980.

Arnold, D. "European Orphans and Vagrants in India in the Nineteenth Century." *Journal of Imperial and Commonwealth History* 7, no. 2 (1979): 104–127.

Arnold, David. *Colonizing the Body: State Medicine and Epidemic Disease in Nineteenth-Century India.* Berkeley and Los Angeles: University of California Press, 1993.

Ashcroft, Bill, Gareth Griffiths, and Helen Tiffin. *The Post-Colonial Studies Reader.* London: Routledge, 1995.

Asiatic Society of Bombay. *Bombay.* Bombay: Tata Press, n.d.

Augustin, Andrea, and Andrew Williamson. *The Oriental Bangkok.* Vienna: n.p., 2000.

Backscheider, Paula R. *Reflections on Biography.* London: Oxford University Press, 1999.

Bacon, George B. *Siam: The Land of the White Elephant as It Was and Is.* 1893. Reprint, Bangkok: Orchid Press, 2000.

Bain, Mary Albertus. *Ancient Landmarks: A Social and Economic History of the Victoria District of Western Australia, 1839–1894.* Nedlands, Western Australia: University of Western Australia Press, 1975.

Baker, Alan R. H., and Gideon Biger. *Ideology and Landscape in Historical Perspective: Essays on the Meanings of Some Places in the Past.* New York: Cambridge University Press, 1992.

Ballhatchet, K. *Race, Sex and Class under the Raj:Imperial Attitudes and Policies and Their Critics, 1793–1905.* London: Weidenfeld and Nicholson, 1980.

———. *Social Policy and Social Change in Western India, 1817–30.* London: Oxford University Press, 1957.

Bamfield, Veronica. *On the Strength: The Story of the British Army Wife.* London: Charles Knight & Company, 1974.

Bamrungsuk, Surachart. *United States Foreign Policy and Thai Military Rule, 1947–1977.* Bangkok: Editions Duangkamol, 1988.

Bancroft, N. W. *From Recruit to Staff Sergeant.* 1885. Reprint, Essex, Eng.: Ian Henry Publications, 1979.

Baron, Archie. *An Indian Affair.* London: Pan Macmillan, 2001.

Bastin, John, comp. *Travellers' Singapore: An Anthology.* Kuala Lumpur: Oxford University Press, 1994.

Battaglia, Debbora. *Rhetorics of Self-Making.* Berkeley and Los Angeles: University of California Press, 1995.

Baxter, Ian A. *A Brief Guide to Biographical Sources,* 3rd ed. London: British Library Board, 2004.

Bayly, C. A. *Indian Society and the Making of the British Empire.* Cambridge: Cambridge University Press, 1990.

Beauvoir, Marquis de. *A Week in Siam in January 1867.* 1870. Reprint, Bangkok: Siam Society, 1986.

Beekman, E. M. *Troubled Pleasures: Dutch Colonial Literature from the East Indies, 1600–1950.* Oxford: Clarendon Press, 1996.

Bhatia, H. S., ed. *European Women in India, Their Life and Adventures.* New Delhi: Deep & Deep Publications, 1979.

Bird, Isabella. *The Golden Chersonese and the Way Thither.* 1883. Reprint, London: Century Publishing, 1983.

Bishop, Ryan, and Lillian S. Robinson. *Night Market: Sex Cultures and the Thai Economic Miracle.* New York: Routledge, 1998.

Blagden, Edward. *A Cadetship in the Honourable East Company's Service, 1805.* Ed. Florence Mostyn Gamlen. Oxford: Oxford University Press, 1931.

Bock, Carl. *Temples and Elephants, Travels in Siam in 1881–1882.* 1884. Reprint, Singapore: Oxford University Press, 1986.

Bohls, Elizabeth A. *Women Travel Writers and the Language of Aesthetics, 1716–1818.* Cambridge: Cambridge University Press, 1995.

Bombay Calendar and General Directory (annual). Bombay: Bombay Educational Society Press, Bombay Government Gazette.

Bourne, F. W. *The Bible Christians: Their Origin and History (1815–1900).* London: Bible Christian Book Room, 1905.

Bowring, John. *The Kingdom and People of Siam.* 2 vols. 1857. Reprint, Kuala Lumpur: Oxford University Press, 1969.

Bradley, Dan Beach. *The Bangkok Calendar.* Bangkok: American Missionary Association, 1859–1865.

Bradley, William, David Morrell, David Szanton, and Stephen Young. *Thailand, Domino by Default? The 1976 Coup and Implications for U.S. Policy.* Athens, OH: Center for International Studies, Ohio University, 1978.

Bradley, William L. *Siam Then: The Foreign Colony in Bangkok before and after Anna.* Pasadena, CA: William Carey Library, 1981.

Braga-Blake, Myrna, ed. *Singapore Eurasians, Memories and Hopes.* Singapore: Eurasian Association, 1992.

Bristowe, W. S. *Louis and the King of Siam.* New York: Thai-American Publishers, 1976.

Bryant, Gerald. "Officers of the East India Company's Army in the Days of Clive and Hastings." *Journal of Imperial and Commonwealth History* 6, no. 3 (May 1978): 203–227.

Buckley, Charles Burton. *An Anecdotal History of Old Times in Singapore, 1819–1867.* Singapore: Oxford University Press, 1984.

Burbidge, F. W. *The Gardens of the Sun: A Naturalist's Journal of Borneo and the Sulu Archipelago.* 1880. Reprint, Singapore: Oxford University Press, 1991.

Burton, David. *The Raj at Table: A Culinary History of the British in India.* Boston: Faber and Faber, 1993.

Byrd, Cecil K. *Early Printing in the Straits Settlements, 1806–1858.* Singapore: National Library, 1970.

Caddy, Florence. *To Siam and Malaya in the Duke of Sutherland's Yacht, "Sans Peur."* 1889. Reprint, Singapore: Oxford University Press, 1992.

Cadell, P. *History of the Bombay Army.* London: Longmans, Green & Co., 1938.

Callahan, Raymond. *The East India Company and Army Reform, 1783–1798.* Cambridge, MA: Harvard University Press, 1972.

Callcott, Maria. *Journal of a Residence in India.* Edinburgh: A. Constable, 1813.

Campa, Roman de la, E. Ann Kaplan, and Michael Sprinker, eds. *Late Imperial Culture.* New York: Verso, 1995.

Carey, W. H. *The Good Old Days of Honorable John Company.* 1882. Reprint, Calcutta: Quins Book Company, 1964.

Chakrabongse, Chula. *Lords of Life: The Paternal Monarchy of Bangkok, 1782–1932.* London: Alvin Redman, 1960.

Chalou, George C., ed. *The Secrets War: The Office of Strategic Services in World War II.* Washington, DC: National Archives and Records Administration, 1992.

Chandan, Amarjit. *Indians in Britain.* New Delhi: Sterling Publishers, 1986.

Chard, Chloe, and Helen Laydon, eds. *Transports: Travel, Pleasure and Imaginative Geography, 1600–1830.* New Haven, CT: Yale University Press, 1996.

Chaudhuri, K. N., ed. *The Economic Development of India under the East India Company 1814–58.* Cambridge: Cambridge University Press, 1971.

Clark, John Heaviside. *The European in India*. London: Edward Orme, 1813.

Collen, Edwin. *The Indian Army: A Sketch of Its History and Organization*. Oxford: n.p., 1907.

Cort, Mary Lovina. *Siam: or, The Heart of Further India*. New York: Anson D. F. Randolph & Company, 1886.

Cotton, Evan. *East Indiamen: The East India Company's Maritime Service*. Ed. Charles Fawcett. London: Batchworth Press, 1949.

Crawford, Ian, Ann Delroy, and Lynne Stevenson. *A History of the Commissariat Freemantle, 1851–1981*. Perth: Western Australian Museum, 1981.

Crockford's Clerical Directory for 1860. London: Crockford's Clerical Journal and Directory Offices, 1860.

Cumming, John. *Political India, 1832–1932: A Co-operative Survey of a Century*. Oxford: Oxford University Press, 1932.

Darton, F. J. Harvey, ed. *The Life and Times of Mrs. Sherwood (1775–1851), From the Diaries of Captain and Mrs. Sherwood*. London: Wells Gardner, Darton & Co., 1910.

Davies, Rupert A., Raymond George, and Gordon Rupp, eds. *A History of the Methodist Church in Great Britain*, vol. 2. London: Epsworth Press, 1978.

Dersin, Denise. *What Life Was Like in the Jewel in the Crown*. Richmond, VA: Time Life, 1999.

Diddee, Jaymala, and Samita Gupta. *Pune, Queen of the Deccan*. Pune: Elephant Design, 2000.

Douglas, James. *Bombay and Western India: A Series of Stray Papers*. 1893. Reprint, London: K. K. Book Distributors, 1985.

Dow, Leslie Smith. *Anna Leonowens: A Life beyond* The King and I. Lawrencetown Beach, Nova Scotia: Pottersfield Press, 1991.

D'Souza, Austin A. *Anglo-Indian Education: A Study of Its Origins and Growth in Bengal up to 1960*. Delhi: Oxford University Press, 1976.

Dutt, Kantala Lahiri. *In Search of a Homeland: Anglo-Indians and McCluskiegunge*. Calcutta: Minerva Associates, 1990.

The East-India Register and Directory. London: Kingsbury, Parbury and Allen, 1808–1853.

Eden, Emily. *Up the Country*. Oxford: Oxford University Press, 1937.

Edney, Matthew H. *Mapping an Empire: The Geographical Construction of British India, 1765–1843*. Chicago: University of Chicago Press, 1997.

Edwardes, Michael. *Bound to Exile: The Victorians in India*. New York: Praeger Publishers, 1970.

———. *Glorious Sahibs: The Romantic as Empire Builder, 1799–1838*. London: Eyre & Spottiswodde, 1968.

———. *The Nabobs at Home*. London: Constable, 1991.

Edwardes, S. M. *Gazetteer of Bombay City and Island*. 3 vols. Bombay: Times Press, 1909–1910.

Edwards, Thomas. "Eurasians and Poor Europeans in India." *Calcutta Review* 72 (1881): 38–56.

Elliott, David. *Thailand: Origins of Military Rule.* London: Zed Press, 1978.

Elwood, Mrs. *Narrative of a Journey Overland from England by the Continent of Europe, Egypt and the Red Sea, to India.* London: Henry Colburn, 1830.

Erickson, Rica. *The Bicentennial Dictionary of Western Australians pre–1829–1888,* vol. 3. Nedlands: University of Western Australia Press, 1988.

Ernst, W. *Mad Tales from the Raj: The European Insane in British India, 1800–1858.* London: Routledge, 1991.

Falkland, Viscountess. *Chow-Chow.* London: 1857.

Fay, Eliza. *Original Letters from India.* Ed. E. M. Forster. 1925. Reprint, London: Hogarth Press, 1986.

Feltus, George Haws, ed. *Abstract of the Journal of Rev. Dan Beach Bradley, M.D.* Published by Dan F. Bradley. Cleveland: Pilgrim Church, 1936.

Fenton, Bessie. *The Journal of Mrs. Fenton: A Narrative of Her Life in India, the Isle of France (Mauritius) and Tasmania during the Years 1826–1830.* London: Edward Arnold, 1901.

Fineman, Daniel. *A Special Relationship: The United States and Military Government in Thailand, 1947–1958.* Honolulu: University of Hawai'i Press, 1997.

Fisher, Michael H. *The First Indian Author in English: Dean Mahomed (1759–1851) in India, Ireland, and England.* Delhi: Oxford University Press, 1996.

———. *Indirect Rule in India: Residents and the Residency System, 1764–1858.* New Delhi: Oxford University Press, 1991.

Forbes, James. *Oriental Memoirs: A Narrative of Seventeen Years Residence in India.* London: Richard Bentley, 1834.

France, Peter, and William St. Clair, eds. *Mapping Lives: The Uses of Biography.* London: Oxford University Press, 2002.

Frankenberg, Ruth. *White Women, Race Matters: The Social Construction of Whiteness.* Minneapolis: University of Minnesota Press, 1993.

Frankfurter, O. "King Mongkut." *Journal of the Siam Society* 1 (1904): 191–206.

Frederick, Bonnie, and Susan H. McLeod, eds. *Women and the Journey: The Female Travel Experience.* Pullman: Washington State University Press, 1993.

Frere, Mary. *Old Deccan Days, or, Hindoo Fairy Legends Current in Southern India.* London: J. Murray, 1868.

Furber, Holden. *Bombay Presidency in the Mid-Eighteenth Century.* London: Asia Publishing House, 1965.

———. *John Company at Work: A Study of European Expansion in India in the Late Eighteenth Century.* Cambridge, MA: Harvard University Press, 1948.

Gaikwad, V. R. *The Anglo-Indians: A Study in the Problems and Processes Involved in Emotional and Cultural Integration.* Bombay: Asia Publishing House, 1967.

Ghose, Indira. *Women Travellers in Colonial India: The Power of the Female Gaze.* Delhi: Oxford University Press, 1998.

Ghosh, Suresh Chandra. *The Social Condition of the British Community in Bengal, 1757–1800.* Leiden: E. J. Brill, 1970.

Gikandi, Simon. *Maps of Englishness: Writing Identity in the Culture of Colonialism.* New York: Columbia University Press, 1996.

Ginsberg, Elaine K., ed. *Passing and the Fictions of Identity.* Durham, NC: Duke University Press, 1996.

Gist, Noel P., and Roy Dean Wright. *Marginality and Identity; Anglo-Indians as a Racially-Mixed Minority in India.* Leiden: E. J. Brill, 1970.

Glascott, Cradock. *The Best Method of Putting an End to the American War.* London: J. W. Pasham, 1776.

Gosling, Betsy. *Old Luang Prabang.* Kuala Lumpur: Oxford University Press, 1996.

Grant, C. *Anglo-Indian Domestic Life.* 1862. Reprint, Calcutta: Bibhash Gupta, 1984.

Grewal, Inderpal. *Home and Harem: Nation, Gender, Empire, and the Cultures of Travel.* Durham, NC: Duke University Press, 1996.

Griswold, A. B. "King Mongkut in Perspective." *Journal of the Siam Society* 45, part 1 (April 1957): 1–41.

———. *King Mongkut of Siam.* New York: Asia Society, 1961.

Guha, Ranajit. *Dominance without Hegemony: History and Power in Colonial India.* Cambridge, MA: Harvard University Press, 1997.

Gullick, J. M. *Adventures and Encounters: Europeans in Southeast Asia.* Kuala Lumpur: Oxford University Press, 1995.

Gullick, John. *Adventurous Women in South-East Asia: Six Lives.* Kuala Lumpur: Oxford University Press, 1995.

Gupta, Pratul C. *The Last Peshwa and the English Commissioners.* Calcutta: S. C. Sarker and Sons, 1944.

Harfield, Alan. *British and Indian Armies in the East Indies, 1685–1935.* Chippenham: Picton Publishing, 1984.

Harris. *Recollections of Rifleman Harris.* Ed. Henry Curling. 1848. Reprint, Hamden, CT: Archon Books, 1970.

Hartzell, Jessie McKinnon. *Mission to Siam: The Memoirs of Jessie MacKinnon Hartzell.* Ed. Joan Acocella. Honolulu: University of Hawai'i Press, 2001.

Hatherleigh Millennium Committee. *The Story of Hatherleigh.* Bromley, Kent: Typlan, 1981.

Hawes, C. J. *Poor Relations: The Making of a Eurasian Community in British India, 1773–1833.* Surrey: Curzon Press, 1996.

Heathcote, T. A. *The Indian Army: The Garrison of British Imperial India, 1822–1922.* London: David & Charles, 1974.

———. *The Military in British India: The Development of British Land Forces in South Asia, 1600–1947.* Manchester: Manchester University Press, 1995.

Hempton, David. *Methodism and Politics in British Society, 1750–1850.* Stanford, CA: Stanford University Press, 1984.

Hervey, Albert. *A Soldier of the Company: Life of an Indian Ensign, 1833–43.* Ed. Charles Allen. London: Michael Joseph, 1988.

Hervey, H. J. A. *The European in India.* London: S. Paul & Co., 1913.

Hickey, William. *Memoirs of William Hickey.* Ed. Alfred Spencer. 4 vols. 1925. Reprint, London: Routledge, 1975.

Hillier, Mrs. Charles B. "A Pair of Siamese Kings." *Household Words,* April 24, 1858, 447–451.

———. "At Home in Siam." *Household Words,* November 21, 1857, 481–88.

Holland, Cecelia. *The Story of Anna and the King.* New York: HarperCollins, 1999.

Hong, Lysa. "Of Consorts and Harlots in Thai Popular History." *Journal of Asian Studies* 57, no. 2 (May 1998): 333–353.

———. "Palace Women at the Margins of Social Change: An Aspect of the Politics of Social History in the Reign of King Chulalongkorn." *Journal of Southeast Asian Studies* 30, no. 2 (September 1999): 310–324.

Hoyt, Sarah Hayes. *Old Malacca.* Kuala Lumpur: Oxford University Press, 1996.

Jayapal, Maya. *Old Singapore.* Singapore: Oxford University Press, 1992.

Jeffrey, Leslie Ann. *Sex and Borders: Gender, National Identity, and Prostitution Policy in Thailand.* Honolulu: University of Hawai'i Press, 2002.

Jumsai, M. L. Manich. *History of Anglo-Thai Relations.* Bangkok: Chalermnit, 2000.

Kaplan, Caren. *Questions of Travel: Postmodern Discourses of Displacement.* Durham, NC: Duke University Press, 1996.

Keay, John. *The Honourable Company: A History of the English East India Company.* New York: Macmillan, 1991.

Kepner, Susan Fulop. "Anna (and Margaret) and the King of Siam." *Crossroads: An Interdisciplinary Journal of Southeast Asian Studies* 10, no. 2 (1997): 1–32.

———, ed. *The Lioness in Bloom: Modern Thai Fiction about Women.* Berkeley and Los Angeles: University of California Press, 1996.

Kindersley, Arthur Fasken. *A Handbook of the Bombay Government Records.* Bombay: Government Central Press, 1921.

Kinkaid, Dennis. *British Social Life in India, 1608–1937.* 1938. Reprint, London: Routledge, 1973.

Klausner, William J. *Reflections on Thai Culture.* Bangkok: Siam Society, 2000.

———. *Transforming Thai Culture.* Bangkok: Siam Society, 2004.

Klein, Christina. *Cold War Orientalism: Asia in the Middlebrow Imagination, 1945–1961.* Berkeley and Los Angeles: University of California Press, 2003.

Knight, Ruth Adams. *The Treasured One: The Story of Rudivoravan, Princess of Siam.* New York: E. P. Dutton, 1957.

Kolff, D. H. A. *Naukar, Rajput and Sepoy: The Ethno History of the Military Labour Market of Hindustan, 1450–1850.* Cambridge: Cambridge University Press, 1990.

Kopf, David. "Orientalism and the Indian Educated Elite." In *Education and the Colonial Experience,* ed. Philip Altbach and Gail Kelly, 117–135. 2nd ed. New Brunswick, NJ: Transaction Books, 1984.

Kukrit Pramoj, M. R., and M. R. Seni Pramoj, eds. *A King of Siam Speaks.* Bangkok: Siam Society, 1987.

———. *Si Phaendin, Four Reigns.* Trans. Tulachandra. 2 vols. Bangkok: Duang Kamol, 1981.

Kumar, Ravindar. *Western India in the Nineteenth Century: A Study of the Social Life of Maharashtra.* London: Routledge, 1968.

Landon, Kenneth P. *The Chinese in Thailand.* 1941. Reprint, New York: Russell & Russell, 1973.

———. "Ladies Wear Skirts." *Asia* 42 (January 1942): 25–26.

———. "Monks of New Thailand." *Asia* 40 (March 1940): 129–132.

———. *Siam in Transition: A Brief Survey of Cultural Trends in the Five Years since the Revolution of 1932.* 1939. Reprint, New York: Greenwood Press, 1968.

———. "Siam Rides the Tiger." *Asia* 39 (January 1939): 43–45.

———. "Siam's Fighting Premier." *Asia* 39 (April 1939): 221–224.

———. "The Thai against the French." *Asia* 41 (March 1941): 172–174.

———. "Thailand." *Annals of the American Academy of Political and Social Science* 206 (March 1943): 112–119.

———. "Thailand for the Thai." *Asia* 39 (October 1938): 557–559.

———. "Thailand's Struggle for National Security." *Far Eastern Quarterly* 4 (November 1944): 4–9.

Landon, Margaret. *Anna and the King of Siam.* New York: John Day Company, 1944.

———. "Thailand under the Japanese." *Asia* 44 (September 1944): 389–393.

Lane, John. *In Praise of Devon: A Guide to Its People, Places and Character.* Totnes, Devon: Green Books, 1998.

Lawrence, C. *Schools for Europeans in India.* Calcutta: Calcutta Press, 1973.

Lawson. Philip. *The East India Company: A History.* London: Longman, 1993.

Lee, Edwin. *The British as Rulers Governing Multiracial Singapore, 1867–1914.* Singapore: Singapore University Press, 1991.

Lefroy, J. H. *Report on the Regimental and Garrison Schools of the Army and on Military Libraries and Reading Rooms.* London: HMSO, 1859.

Leonowens, Anna Harriette. *The English Governess at the Siamese Court; Being Recollections of Six Years at the Royal Palace in Bangkok.* Boston: Fields, Osgood, & Co., 1870.

———. *Life and Travel in India: Being Recollections of a Journey before the Days of Railroads.* Philadelphia: Porter & Coates, 1884.

———. *Our Asiatic Cousins.* Boston: D. Lothrop, 1889.

———. *The Romance of the Harem.* Ed. Susan Morgan. Charlottesville: University Press of Virginia, 1991.

Lewis, E. B. "Recollections of a Visit to Bangkok, the Capital of Siam, in the Year 1862." *Bentley's Miscellany,* December 1867, 625–634.

Lewis, Reina. *Gendering Orientalism: Race, Femininity and Representation.* London: Routledge, 1996.

Lim, P. Pui Huen. *Singapore, Malaysian and Brunei Newspapers: An International Union List.* Singapore: Institute of Southeast Asian Studies, 1992.

Loos, Tamara. "Sex in the Inner City: The Fidelity between Sex and Politics in Siam." *Journal of Asian Studies* 64, no. 4 (November 2005): 881–909.

———. *Subject Siam: Family Law and Colonial Modernity in Thailand.* Ithaca, NY: Cornell University Press, 2006.

Low, Ursula. *Fifty Years of John Company.* London: John Murray, 1936.

Mackenzie, Helen. *Life in the Mission, the Camp and the Zenana (or Six Years in India).* New York: Redfield, 1853.

MacMillan, Margaret. *Women of the Raj.* London: Thames & Hudson, 1988.

MacMullen, J. *Camp and Barrack Room: or, the British Army as It Is.* London: Chapman and Hall, 1846.

MacNaughton, John. *Mrs. Leonowens.* Montreal: Gazette Printing Company, 1915.

Maher, Reginald. *These Are the Anglo-Indians.* Calcutta: Swallow Press, 1962.

Mahmood, Syed. *A History of English Education in India: Its Rise, Development, Progress, Present Condition and Prospects.* Delhi: Idarah-I Adabiyat-I Delli, 1895.

———. *A History of English Education in India, 1781–1893.* 1895. Reprint, Delhi: Aligarh College Press, 1981.

Mainwaring, Arthur. *Crown and Company: The Historical Records of the 2nd. Batt. Royal Dublin Fusiliers.* London: Arthur L. Humphreys, 1946.

Makepeace, Walter, Gilbert E. Brooke, and Roland St. J. Braddell, eds. *One Hundred Years of Singapore.* 2 vols. Singapore: Oxford University Press, 1991.

Malabari, Behramji. *The Indian Eye on English Life.* London: A. Constable, 1893.

Marcus, G. J. *The Age of Nelson: The Royal Navy, 1793–1815.* New York: Viking Press, 1971.

———. *Heart of Oak: A Survey of British Sea Power in the Georgian Era.* London: Oxford University Press, 1975.

Marcus, Laura. *Auto/biographical Discourses: Theory, Criticism, Practice.* Manchester: Manchester University Press, 1994.

Martin, John M. "Pages from a Manuscript History of Hatherleigh." *Reports and Transactions of the Devonshire Association for the Advancement of Science, Literature, and Art* 41 (1909): 356–359.

Masani, Zareer. *Indian Tales of the Raj.* Berkeley and Los Angeles: University of California Press, 1987.

Mayhew, Arthur Innes. *Education in the Colonial Empire.* London: Longmans, Green, 1938.

McDonald, N. A., ed. *The Bangkok Recorder, a Semi-Monthly Journal.* Bangkok: American Missionary Association, 1865–1866.

McGilvary, Daniel. *A Half Century among the Siamese and the Lao: An Autobiography.* 1912. Reprint, Bangkok: White Lotus Press, 2002.

McGuffie, T. H. *Rank and File: The Common Soldier at Peace and War, 1642–1914.* London: Hutchinson, 1964.

Menezes, S. L. *Fidelity and Honour: The Indian Army from the Seventeenth to the Twenty-First Century.* New Delhi: Viking, 1993.

Mills, L. A. *British Malaya, 1834–67.* Kuala Lumpur: Oxford University Press, 1966.

Mills, Sara. *Discourses of Difference: An Analysis of Women's Travel Writings and Colonialism.* London: Routledge and Kegan Paul, 1991.

Minney, R. J. *Fanny and the Regent of Siam.* London: Collins, 1962.

Moffat, Abbot Low. *Mongkut, the King of Siam.* Ithaca, NY: Cornell University Press, 1961.

Moledina, M. H. *History of Poona Cantonment, 1818–1953.* Poona: M. N. Merchant, 1953.

Mollo, Boris. *The Indian Army.* 1981. Reprint, Poole, Dorset: New Orchard, 1986.

Morgan, Susan. *Place Matters: Gendered Geography in Victorian Women's Travel Books about Southeast Asia.* New Brunswick, NJ: Rutgers University Press, 1996.

Mui, Hoh-cheung, and Lorna H. Mui. *The Management of Monopoly: A Study of the English East India Company's Conduct of Its Tea Trade, 1784–1833.* Vancouver: University of British Columbia Press, 1984.

Mungkandi, Wiwat, and William Warren, eds. *A Century and a Half of Thai-American Relations.* Bangkok: Chulalongkorn University Press, 1982.

Nartsupha, Chatthip, and Suthy Prasartset, eds. *Socio-Economic Institutions and Cultural Change in Siam, 1851–1910: A Documentary Survey.* Singapore: Institute of Southeast Asian Studies, 1977.

Norman, Henry. *People and Politics of the Far East.* London: T. F. Unwin, 1900.

Odzer, Cleo. *Patpong Sisters: An American Woman's View of the Bangkok Sex World.* New York: Blue Moon Books, 1994.

Paget, Mrs. Leopold (Georgiana Theodosia Fitzmoor-Halsey). *Camp and Cantonment: A Journal of Life in India in 1857–1859.* London: Longman, 1865.

Partridge, Jan. "The Establishment of Mechanic's Institutes in Western Australia: A Case Study of the Swan River Mechanics Institute." In *Instruction and Amusement: Papers for the Sixth Australian Library History Forum, Monash University, 1 November 1995,* ed. B. J. McMullin, 3–39. Melbourne: Ancora Press, 1996.

Peers, Douglas M. *Between Mars and Mammon: Colonial Armies and the Garrison State in India, 1819–1835.* London: I. B. Tauris Publishers, 1995.

Peleggi, Maurizio. *Lords of Things: The Fashioning of the Siamese Monarchy's Modern Image.* Honolulu: University of Hawai'i Press, 2002.

Pemble, John, ed. *Miss Fane in India.* Gloucester: Alan Sutton, 1985.

Philips, C. H. *The East India Company, 1784–1834.* Manchester: Manchester University Press, 1940.

Picard, Michel, and Robert E. Wood, eds. *Tourism, Ethnicity, and the State in Asian and Pacific Societies.* Honolulu: University of Hawai'i Press, 1997.

Postans, Mrs. Thomas (Marianne Young). *Western India in 1838.* London: Saunders and Otley, 1839.

Rajan, Balachandra. *Under Western Eyes: India from Milton to Macaulay.* Durham, NC: Duke University Press, 1999.

Rajan, Rajeswari Sunder. *The Lie of the Land: English Literary Studies in India.* Delhi: Oxford University Press, 1992.

Rajchman, John, ed. *The Identity in Question.* New York: Routledge, 1995.

Ram, Subedar Sita. *From Sepoy to Subedar.* Ed. James Lunt, trans. Norgate. 1873. Reprint, Delhi: Vikus Publications, 1970.

Randolph, R. Sean. *The United States and Thailand: Alliance Dynamics, 1950–1985.* Berkeley: Institute of East Asian Studies, University of California, 1986.

Regnier, Philippe. *Singapore: City-State in South-East Asia.* Trans. Christopher Hurst. Honolulu: University of Hawai'i Press, 1991.

Renford, R. K. *The Non-Official British in India to 1920.* Delhi: Oxford University Press, 1987.

Reynolds, E. Bruce. "Opening the Wedge: The OSS in Thailand." In *The Secrets War: The Office of Strategic Services in World War II,* ed. George C. Chalou, 328–350. Washington, DC: National Archives and Records Administration, 1992.

Rhodes, Campbell. "The Anglo-Indians." In *Political India, 1832–1932: A Co-operative Survey of a Century,* ed. John Cumming, 147–152. London: Oxford University Press, 1932.

Robbins, Christopher. *Air America from World War II to Vietnam: The Explosive True Story of the CIA's Secret Airline.* Bangkok: Asia Books, 2001.

Roberts, Emma. *Notes of an Overland Journey through France and Egypt to Bombay.* London: William H. Allen, 1841.

Robinson, Jane. *Wayward Women: A Guide to Women Travellers.* New York: Oxford University Press, 1990.

Rodrigues, Dulcinea Correa. *Bombay Fort in the Eighteenth Century.* Bombay: Himilaya Publishing House, 1994.

Sandes, E. W. C. *The Indian Sappers and Miners.* Chatham: Institution of Royal Engineers, 1948.

Sardesai, D. R. *British Trade and Expansion in Southeast Asia, 1830–1914.* New Delhi: Allied Publishers, 1977.

Schweinitz, Karl de, Jr. *The Rise and Fall of British India: Imperialism as Inequality.* London: Methuen, 1983.

Scidmore, E. R. *Java, the Garden of the East.* 1899. Reprint, Singapore: Oxford University Press, 1984.

Scott, Nora. *An Indian Journal.* Ed. John Radford. New York: Radcliffe Press, 1994.

Scurry, James. *The Captivity, Sufferings, and Escape, of James Scurry, Who Was Detained a Prisoner during Ten Years, in the Dominions of Hyder Ali and Tippoo Saib.* London: Henry Fisher, 1824.

Semmel, Bernard. *The Methodist Revolution.* New York: Basic Books, 1973.

Shaw, J. C. *The Chiengmai Gymkhana Club.* Chiengmai, Thailand: Craftsman Press, 1997.

Sheppard, Tan Sri Dato' Mubin, ed. *Singapore 150 Years*. Singapore: Times Books International, 1982.

Sherwood, Mrs. (Mary Martha Butt). *Stories Explanatory of the Church Catechism*. Baltimore: Protestant Episcopal Female Tract Society of Baltimore, 1823.

Singh, Madan Paul. *Indian Army under the East India Company*. New Delhi: Sterling Publishers, 1976.

Smith, Malcolm. *A Physician at the Court of Siam*. 1946. Reprint, Singapore: Oxford University Press, 1982.

Smithies, Michael, ed. *Descriptions of Old Siam*. Kuala Lumpur: Oxford University Press, 1995.

Spear, Percival. *The Nabobs: A Study of the Social Life of the English in Eighteenth-Century India*. London: Oxford University Press, 1963.

Stark, H. A. *Hostages to India, or The Life Story of the Anglo-Indian Race*. Calcutta: Star Printing Works, 1936.

Stephens, Michael Dawson. *The Educating of Armies*. New York: St. Martin's Press, 1989.

Steuart, A. F. "Some Notes on the Position of Early Eurasians." *Asiatic Quarterly Review*, n.s., 2 (1913): 93–101.

Subramanian, Lakshmi. *Indigenous Capital and Imperial Expansion: Bombay, Surat and the West Coast*. Delhi: Oxford University Press, 1996.

Summerville, Helen. "Port Gregory." *Early Days: Journal and Proceedings of the Royal Western Australian Historical Society* 6, part 8 (1969): 74–88.

Sutton, Jean. *Lords of the East: The East India Company and Its Ships (1600–1874)*. London: Conway Maritime Press, 2000.

Symonds, Richard. "Eurasians under British Rule." *Oxford University Papers on India*, ed. N. Allen, 1:2, 28–42. Delhi: Oxford University Press, 1987.

Tan Poh Choo, Joceline. *History of Penang: A Selected and Annotated Bibliography*. Pulau Pinang: Universiti Sains Malaysia, 1991.

Tarling, Nicholas. *British Policy in the Malay Peninsula and Archipelago, 1824–71*. London: Oxford University Press, 1969.

Teltscher, Kate. *India Inscribed: European and British Writing on India, 1600–1800*. Delhi: Oxford University Press, 1995.

Thomas, Nicholas. *Colonialism's Culture: Anthropology, Travel and Government*. Cambridge: Polity Press, 1994.

Thomson, John. *The Straits of Malacca, Siam and Indo-China: Travels and Adventures of a Nineteenth-Century Photographer*. Singapore: Oxford University Press, 1993.

Thorbek, Susanne, and Bandana Pattanaik. *Transnational Prostitution: Changing Patterns in a Global Context*. London: Zed Books, 2002.

Treneman, H. R. "Port Gregory and Lynton." *Early Days: Journal and Proceedings of the Royal Western Australian Historical Society* 2, part 6 (1934): 1–5.

Trocki, Carl. *Opium and Empire: Chinese Society in Colonial Singapore, 1800–1910*. Ithaca, NY: Cornell University Press, 1990.

Trustram, Myna. *Women of the Regiment: Marriage and the Victorian Army.* Cambridge: Cambridge University Press, 1984.

Turnbull, C. Mary. *A History of Singapore 1819–1988.* 2nd ed. Singapore: Oxford University Press, 1989.

———. *A Short History of Malaysia, Singapore and Brunei.* 1980. Reprint, Singapore: Graham Brash, 1987.

———. *The Straits Settlements, 1826–67: Indian Presidency to Crown Colony.* London: Athlone Press, 1972.

Turner, John Munsey. *Conflict and Resolution: Studies in Methodism and Ecumenism in England, 1740–1982.* London: Epworth Press, 1985.

Tytler, Harriet. *An Englishwoman in India: The Memoirs of Harriet Tytler, 1828–1858.* Ed. Anthony Sattin. Oxford: Oxford University Press, 1986.

Urwick, W. *India 100 Years Ago: The Beauty of Old India Illustrated.* Delhi: Nanda Book Service, 1885.

Van Doren, A. *Christian High Schools in India.* Calcutta: Y.M.C.A. Publishing House, 1936.

Varma, Lal Bahadur. *Anglo Indians: A Historical Study of the Anglo-Indian Community in Nineteenth-Century India.* New Delhi: Reena Roy Prakashan, 1979.

Vibart, H. M. *Addiscombe: Its Heroes and Men of Note.* Westminster: Archibald Constable, 1894.

Vincent, Frank. *The Land of the White Elephant: Sights and Scenes in Burma, Siam, Cambodia, and Cochin-China (1871–2).* 1873. Reprint, Bangkok: White Lotus, 1988.

Viswanathan, Gauri. "The Naming of Yale College: British Imperialism and American Higher Education." In *Cultures of United States Imperialism,* ed. Amy Kaplan and Donald E. Pease, 85–108. Durham, NC: Duke University Press, 1993.

Wagner-Martin, Linda. *Telling Women's Lives: The New Biography.* New Brunswick, NJ: Rutgers University Press, 1994.

Wallace, R. G. *Fifteen Years in India, or, Sketches of a Soldier's Life: Being an Attempt to Describe Persons and Things in Various Parts of Hindustan.* London: Longman, 1822.

Walvin, James. *Fruits of Empire: Exotic Produce and British Taste, 1600–1800.* New York: New York University Press, 1997.

Warren, William. *The Truth about Anna and Other Stories.* Singapore: Archipelago Press, 2000.

Waterfield, Robert. *The Memoirs of Private Waterfield.* Ed. Arthur Swinson and Donald Scott. London: Cassell, 1968.

Watson, Francis. *A Concise History of India.* 1974. Reprint, New York: Thames & Hudson, 1987.

Welch, Edwin. *Spiritual Pilgrim: A Reassessment of the Life of the Countess of Huntingdon.* Cardiff: University of Wales Press, 1995.

Welsh, James. *Military Reminiscences; Extracted from a Journal of Nearly Forty Years Active Service in the East Indies,* vol. 1. 2nd ed. London: Smith, Elder, 1830.

Werner, Julia Stewart. *The Primitive Methodist Connexion: Its Background and Early History.* Green Bay: University of Wisconsin Press, 1984.

Western Australian Almanack, 1853–1857. Perth, Western Australia: Arthur Shenton.

White, A. C. T. *The Story of Army Education, 1643–1963.* London: George G. Harrap, 1963.

Wild, Anthony. *The East India Company: Trade and Conquest from 1600.* New York: Lyons Press, 1999.

Williamson, Thomas. *The East India Vade-Mecum, or Complete Guide to Gentlemen Intended for the Civil, Military, or Naval Service of the East India Company.* 2 vols. London: Black, Parry and Kingsbury, 1810.

———. *The General East India Guide and Vade Mecum: Being a Digest of the Late Captain Williamson, with . . . Improvements and Additions.* Ed. J. B. Gilchrist. London: Kingsbury, Parbury & Allen, 1825.

Winichakul, Thongchai. *Siam Mapped: A History of the Geo-Body of a Nation.* Honolulu: University of Hawai'i Press, 1994.

Wolpert, Stanley. *A New History of India.* 5th ed. Oxford: Oxford University Press, 1997.

Wood, R. W. *De Mortuis: The Story of the Chiang Mai Foreign Cemetary.* Bangkok: Craftsman Press, 1992.

Wood, W. A. R. *Consul in Paradise: Sixty-nine Years in Siam.* 1965. Reprint, Bangkok: Trasvin Publications, 1991.

Wyatt, David K. *The Politics of Reform in Thailand: Education in the Reign of King Chulalongkorn.* New Haven, CT: Yale University Press, 1982.

———. *Studies in Thai History.* Bangkok: Silkworm Books, 1994.

———. *Thailand: A Short History.* 2nd ed. New Haven, CT: Yale University Press, 2003.

Yeoh, Brenda S. A. "Municipal Sanitary Ideology and the Control of the Urban Environment in Colonial Singapore." In *Ideology and Landscape in Historical Perspective,* ed. Alan R. H. Baker and Gideon Biger, 148–172. Cambridge: Cambridge University Press, 1992.

Yorke, Lois K. "Edwards, Anna Harriette." In *Dictionary of Canadian Biography (DCB),* 232–234. Toronto: Toronto University Press, 1993.

Young, Douglas MacMurray. *The Colonial Office in the Early Nineteenth Century.* London: Longmans, 1961.

Young, Ernest. *The Kingdom of the Yellow Robe: A Description of Old Siam.* 1898. Reprint, Singapore: Oxford University Press, 1986.

Younger, Coralie. *Anglo-Indians: Neglected Children of the Raj.* Delhi: B. R. Publishing, 1987.

Yule, Henry, and A. C. Burnell. *Hobson-Jobson: Being a Glossary of Anglo-Indian Colloquial Words and Phrases and of Kindred Terms.* 1886. Reprint, London: Routledge, 1985.

INDEX

Elphinstone, Mountstuart, 48
Emancipation Proclamation, Lincoln's, 150–51
Emerson, Ralph, 84, 168
England: Anna's daughter, 6, 86–87, 104–8, 116, 136–40, 144, 153, 159–62; Anna's son, 161, 162, 198, 204; Anna's trips, 153, 160–63, 202–3. *See also* British; London
The English Governess at the Siamese Court (Anna), 107, 123, 168–71; Landon discovering, 212, 213; published and reviewed, 174–76; on royal harem, 128, 131–33, 151, 176; second edition, 177
Enniscorthy: Anna, 162–63, 213–14; Anna's daughter Avis, 106, 137, 160, 162; Anna's son Louis, 162, 172, 173–74, 182; King Mongkut's letter to, 171–72; Wilkinson family, 106, 137, 153, 160–62, 171–74, 182, 213–14
equality/inequality: Anna's beliefs, 85, 126–33, 151, 188, 195, 197, 199, 202, 204, 222–23; Anna's husband's beliefs, 77; Anna's identity inventions and, 79, 81; British and, 85, 194; in Buddhism, 151; Cobb's beliefs, 84–85; U.S., 85; women's suffrage, 202. *See also* imperialist attitudes; racism; slavery; social class; tolerance
Eurasians. *See* Anglo-Indian community

facts, 3, 6–7, 135. *See also* inventions
family: blended, 43. *See also* children; Donohoe family; Edwards family; fathers; Glascott family; grandparents; Leonowens, Thomas; marriages; mothers; Wilkinson family
fathers: Anna's (Thomas Edwards), 29–34; Patrick Donohoe (Anna's stepfather), 33–40, 49–50, 51, 59, 62, 144; William Glascott (Anna's grandfather), 11–33, 51, 56, 241, 243
Fay, Eliza, 18
Fa-ying, death, 141–42
feminism, 7, 202
Fenton, Bessie, 28, 240–41
Fields, Annie, 169*fig*, 180; Anna's introduction to, 168; Anna's lecture intro-

duced by, 178; Anna's letters to, 195, 197, 199, 204, 223; Stowe introduced to Anna by, 181
Fields, James T., 7, 168, 174–75, 178, 180, 190
film: Bollywood, 19. *See also* Hollywood movies
finance. *See* economics
Fineman, Daniel, 220
flogging, 132
Ford, Kathleen, 183
Fortune, "Our Stake in Thailand" (Donovan), 220
Foster, Jodi, 5, 101, 207
France: colonies near Siam, 95; liquor imports to Siam, 153–54; Siam consulate, 114, 142, 156–59; Siam's difficulties with, 155–58
Fryer, Dr., 21
Fyshe family, 186, 188, 192, 199, 214
Fyshe, Anna Harriett (Anna's granddaughter), 125, 204; "Anna and I," 199–200, 212–13; birth, 189; children, 205; education by Anna, 195; Germany, 53, 202, 203; marriages, 203, 205
Fyshe, Avis Annie Leonowens (Anna's daughter), 179*fig;* Anna's letters to, 29, 53, 81–82, 87, 104–5, 116, 186, 188–90, 195; birth, 6, 76, 77, 78, 79; brother Louis and, 104, 116, 137, 139, 140, 143, 160; Canada, 106, 184, 190–203; Cobb and, 87, 88, 116, 137, 144, 167–68; daughter Anna on, 199–200; death, 106, 203–4; education, 6, 86–87, 88, 99, 105–6, 136–39, 183, 184; England, 6, 86–87, 104–8, 116, 136–40, 144, 153, 159–62; first job, 174; Germany, 198; with Heritage family, 87, 104, 105, 106, 137, 139; honeymoon, 53, 81–82, 106, 186; letters from Siamese women and children, 145, 149; marriage, 106, 184, 188; Pratt contact, 79–81; Singapore, 86–87, 88; Thomas courting, 79, 183, 184; U.S., 79, 163–64, 167, 168, 173, 174, 179, 182–84; Wilkinsons and, 106, 137–39, 161–62, 167

22, 26; children's destitute condition, 29; drunkenness, 32, 37, 38; economics, 13–14, 23–29, 239, 242–43; marriages, 23–24, 235–42; moves, 36–37; officers, 14–15, 43, 49; topas, 20. *See also* Indian Army (EIC's private army)

Somawadi, Princess, 122, 145

Sonklin, 134, 146, 148–52, 161, 181, 195

South East Asia Treaty Organization (SEATO), 220

Special Logistics Agreement Thailand (SLAT), 221

Stacpoole, Henry de Vere, 162

Stacpoole, Rev. William Church, 162, 174

A Star Is Born, 8, 9

State Department, U.S., 218–21

Staten Island, 168, 173, 174, 182, 183, 193

stepfather, Anna's, Patrick Donohoe, 33–40, 49–50, 51, 59, 62, 144

Stowe, Harriet Beecher, 7, 149–51, 168, 177, 181; *Uncle Tom's Cabin,* 149–50, 217

Straits Times, Singapore, 149–50

Suez Canal, 11–12

Sunnyside, Canada, 193–94, 195, 199

Sutherland, Colonel Rutherford, 4

Swan River, Australia, 76–77

Taj Mahal, 228–29

Talap, Lady, 125–26, 134, 140

tea trade, 232

Telford, Rev. and Mrs. Robert, 113

Thailand: Anna's students, 147; Japanese, 218–19; Landons, 212, 217–19; military coup, 218; prostitution, 128; Singapore Agreement, 220; Special Logistics Agreement Thailand (SLAT), 221; U.S. relations (influences), 10, 178, 207–23; Vietnam war soldiers' R and R, 10, 221; World War II, 215, 218–19. *See also* Siam

"Thailand under the Japanese" (Margaret Landon), 219

Thiang, Lady, 134, 145, 146, 166

Thomas, Rosalina, 40

Thompson, Jim, 217, 220

Thouapp, Lady, 134, 140, 145

Ticknor and Fields, 168

Titanic, 163

tolerance: Anna's religious and social, 45, 125–26, 199; and mixed-race marriages, 241. *See also* equality/inequality

trading, international, 225–26; independent shipping firms and merchants in India, 22, 239–40; Indian "Mutiny" and truth of, 233; opium, 83, 113, 231, 232; tea, 232. *See also* East India Company (EIC)

Treaty of Nanking (1842), 231

Trott, Emilie, 40

Trubner & Co., London, 177

"The True Story of Anna Leonowens" (Bristowe), 6–7

Turnbull, Mary, 86

Twentieth-Century Fox, 216

Uncle Tom's Cabin (Stowe), 149–50, 217

United States, 5–6; Anna, 1–2, 3, 6, 7, 41, 81–82, 85, 107, 167–85, 205; Anna's daughter Avis, 79, 163–64, 167, 168, 173, 174, 179, 182–84; Anna's friendships, 168; Anna's identity, 166, 189; Anna's lecture tours, 177–84, 188, 190, 193, 195; Anna's physical appearance, 72; Anna's school, 173, 174, 178; Anna's son Louis, 174, 179, 182; Christian missionaries from, 3, 5, 90–91, 93, 110–13, 116, 126, 144, 165, 208–12; Civil War, 7, 84–85, 144, 150, 180, 205; Cobb, 84–85, 144, 164, 167–68, 183–85, 186, 190; era of Anna's time in, 7, 205; "Free Thai" forces, 219; imperialist attitudes, 93, 218–20; OCI/OSS/CIA, 214–15, 217, 219, 220, 222; postbellum idealism, 7, 180; Reconstruction, 180, 205; reviews of Anna's writings, 175–78; reviews of the movie *Anna and the King of Siam,* 216; Siam consulate, 93, 109, 114, 142, 155, 157, 158–59; Siam visitors from, 142; slavery, 7, 129, 150, 180, 217; social equality, 85; State Department, 218–21; Thai relations (influences), 10, 178, 207–23; World War II, 214–15, 216, 218–19. *See also* Boston; Hollywood movies; Landon, Margaret; New York

Text: 11/13.5 Adobe Garamond
Display: Adobe Garamond
Indexer: Barbara Roos
Compositor: Binghamton Valley Composition, LLC
Printer and binder: Thomson-Shore, Inc.